The Railroad

What It Is, What It Does

The Introduction to Railroading

4th Edition

by

John H. Armstrong

Simmons-Boardman Books, Inc.
1809 Capitol Avenue
Omaha, NE 68102
(402)346-4300 or 800-228-9670

The information presented in this book is in no way intended to supersede or negate any rules or regulations of government bodies, the AAR, or individual carriers. Further, it is not intended to conflict with any currently effective manufacturers operating, application, or maintenance instructions and/or specifications. The publisher is not responsible for any technical errors which might appear.

Printings

First Edition, First Printing, May 1978
Second Printing, January 1979
Second Edition, First Printing, March 1982
Second Edition, Second Printing, February 1984
Second Edition, Third Printing, January 1987
Second Edition, Fourth Printing, August 1988

Third Edition, First Printing, August 1990
Third Edition, Second Printing, March 1993
Third Edition, Third Printing, May 1994
Third Edition, Fourth Printing, December 1995
Third Edition, Fifth Printing, November 1996
Third Edition, Sixth Printing, July 1997
Fourth Edition, First Printing, June 1998

For more information on this book and other Simmons-Boardman Books, Inc. materials, call 1-800-228-9670 in the United States and Canada. For inquiries from other countries please fax to 402-346-1783.

Production staff: Jan Benson, Brian Brundige.
Additional illustration work: Starfire Engineering.

Library of Congress Cataloging-in-Publication Data

Armstrong, John H.

The Railroad, What It Is, What It Does

Includes index, glossary

1. Railroads – United States. 2. Railroads – Freight. 3. Railroad – Railroad Engineering. I. Title.

ISBN: 0-911382-04-6   CIP

Acknowledgement

We wish to thank the following people for their valuable technical assistance: J.A. Pinkepank, Burlington Northern Railroad Company; and W.J. Nail, Union Pacific Railroad; F.N. Wilner, author.

We are grateful to the following companies for their help in providing illustrations used in this text:

AAR (Association of American Railroads)
Amtrak
APTA (American Public Transit Association)
Betac Corp.
BNSF
Canadian National Railway
Canadian Pacific Railroad
CSX Transportation
DIFCO
FRA (Federal Railroad Administration)
GE Transportation
Greenbriar Intermodal Co.
Kratville, Bill, Photographer, Omaha, NE
Johnstown America
ORX
Railway Age Magazine
Starfire Engineering
Rescar Incorporated
Union Pacific Railroad
Union Switch and Signal
Wabco Railway Product, Co.
Wilson, Don, Photographer, Port of Seattle

Table of Contents

List of Illustrations

Preface to the Fourth Edition

As implied by its present-tense title, *The Railroad: What It Is, What It Does* is intended to present a basic but thorough overview of the railroad industry in North America as it currently exists and functions, with its primary perspective a description of railroad operations and their supporting technology interpreting the specialized terminology involved.

In the twenty years since publication of the first edition, and increasingly in the eight years since the third edition, organizational, and legislative matters have combined with technological factors – many the fruits of research – and a generally improving national economy to produce an advance in railroad traffic levels, efficiency and profitability of almost renaissance proportions.

Extensive revisions in this fourth edition reflect the administrative trends which, along with major technical advances, are largely responsible for this metamorphosis. These shifts have resulted in the replacement or virtual extinction of a host of such railroading perennials as the Interstate Commerce Commission, published tariffs, cabooses and order hoops. However, since today's technology and operations must be founded on and continue to fulfill the critical service and safety functions of their predecessors, historical reviews of the development and significance of obsolescent hardware and practices have been retained wherever they may be helpful in understanding how today's successors – the STB, end-of-train monitors and radio-transmitted track warrants – have evolved and must do their jobs...

John H. Armstrong

Railroad Technology –
The Tools of the Trade

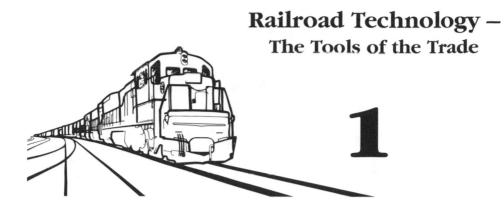

1

A railroad consists of two steel rails which are held a fixed distance apart upon a roadbed. Vehicles, guided and supported by flanged steel wheels, and connected into trains, are propelled as a means of transportation.

Key Inventions and Evolutions

Within that definition there is a host of variations in forms of propulsion, details of track structure, train make-up or "consist," dominant class of traffic, and so on, which fall within the meaning of the term "railroad." But those are the essential features, and there are good reasons why each is important.

Arguing whether the rail, the flanged wheel, or the train is the most basic invention is as futile as trying to decide which leg of a three-legged stool is most important. It is also unimportant whether the true ancestor of the railroad was grooved pavement on the island of Malta dating from the time of the Roman Empire, a medieval German mine tramway, or one of the cast-iron "plateways" operating in South Wales in the 18th century.

The *system* which evolved from these beginnings, however, was the first phase of the most important transportation advance in all history, the application of heat energy from a machine to transcend the limitations of animal power. Therefore, it's worth taking a minute or two to see what's distinctive about it, as an introduction to a closer look at its principal parts as they exist today.

The Cheap, Low-Friction Guideway

The railroad concept, in the first third of the 19th century, combined three critical factors:

1. It *reduced friction* to an extent that let the heavy steam engine not only move itself across the land but have enough power left over to move a good load at an unprecedented speed.
2. It *reduced the cost of a low-friction roadway*, making it possible for the railroad to penetrate any area of the country where raw materials were found or people lived and worked.

1

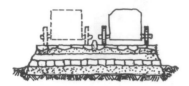

In Roman times, a major improvement in rolling resistance and a corresponding increase in load carried (particularly in bad weather) was achieved by building a stone-paved road on a deep foundation for hard-wheeled carts and chariots. The paving had to be more than twice the width of the vehicles and was very laborious and expensive to construct.

Some medieval miners had to push heavy loads through tunnels – extra width was costly, so carts guided by pulley-like wheels ran on a track of wood stringers nailed to crossmembers – thus "paving" only the essential strips of the roadway. Tracks later were extended outside the mines.

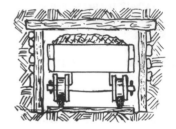

Eighteenth-century South Wales tramways used a single flange on the "plateway" – short segments of cast iron, usually mounted on stone blocks – to keep plain-wheeled carts on the track. Some of these plateways were 20 miles long; trackworkers in Britain are still called "plate-layers." A major problem was keeping the track clear of debris.

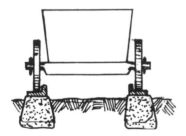

Single-flanged iron wheels running on the head of "I" or "T"-section iron rails held in gauge by wooden crossties rapidly proved to be a more satisfactory system – self-cleaning, readily crossed by roadways, relatively inexpensive, cushioned slightly by the wood's flexibility.

It was soon found that mounting the wheels rigidly on a rotating axle kept them in gauge better, made efficient bearings and lubrication possible.

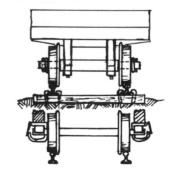

Fig. 1-1. Evolution of the Flanged Wheel and Railway

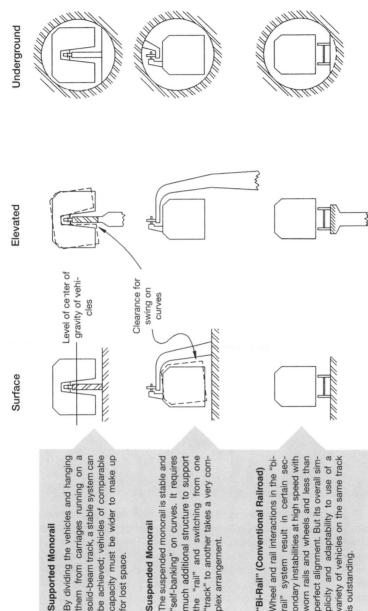

Saving half of the number of rails – and the job of keeping them level with each other and the right distance apart – has made the idea of the monorail a recurring dream. Its problem is that, like the bicycle, it is not a "statically stable" system – unless the "rail" is located *above* the vehicle's center of gravity.

Surface **Elevated** **Underground**

Level of center of gravity of vehicles

Clearance for swing on curves

Supported Monorail

By dividing the vehicles and hanging them from carriages running on a solid-beam track, a stable system can be achieved; vehicles of comparable capacity must be wider to make up for lost space.

Suspended Monorail

The suspended monorail is stable and "self-banking" on curves. It requires much additional structure to support the "rail" and switching from one "track" to another takes a very complex arrangement.

"Bi-Rail" (Conventional Railroad)

Wheel and rail interactions in the "bi-rail" system result in certain secondary instabilities at high speed with worn rails and wheels and less than perfect alignment. But its overall simplicity and adaptability to use of a variety of vehicles on the same track is outstanding.

Any general-purpose transit system must be adaptable to surface, elevated, and underground location without too serious a cost penalty. As compared to "bi-rail" only the supported monorail in the elevated mode is somewhat cost competitive.

Fig. 1-2. The Monorail Dream

3

3. It provided a *guideway*, removing the limitation of transporting every-
    thing in single vehicles. This spread the cost of motive power and
    crew over a practical number of loads.

Saving half of the number of rails – and the job of keeping them level with each
other and the right distance apart – has made the idea of the monorail a recurring
dream. Its problem is that, like the bicycle, it is not a statically stable system – unless the *rail* is located *above* the vehicle's center of gravity.

How Many Rails?

As in the development of any system depending on and combining several separate
inventions, there were many basic decisions to be made. There were many false starts,
misconceptions, and side issues that were resolved by time and experience. Even such
a fundamental question as the "right" number of rails re-emerges periodically, to the
extent that some recent studies of alternatives for urban transportation have used the
term "bi-rail" to disguise the fact that re-inventing the railroad turned out to be the best
technical answer to the requirements. Fig. 1-1 discusses the reasons why the monorail
remains a dream, useful only under extremely limited circumstances.

Fig. 1-3. Photo shows the remains of a turnout on an early 19th century predecessor of today's railroad – a 10-mile tramway transporting dressed granite from quarries on Dartmoor in Devon, England, down to a canal leading to the sea. Guiding surface on rows of separate granite blocks forming the "rails" allowed 12 four-wheel
wagons to be assembled into trains to roll their loads down to sea level by gravity.
Empty trains were hauled back up to the quarries by teams of up to 19 horses.
The gauge of the stone faces guiding the 3-inch-wide plain treads of the wagon
wheels was 4 ft 3 in. Turnouts, such as this with a single stone "switch point" piv-
oted on an iron pin, allowed trains to meet each other and to be guided into spurs
serving different quarries.

Where Does the Flange Belong?

Fig. 1-2 shows: (a) the way the *rail*road made reduced friction affordable, and (b) how the best way to keep the cars on the rails evolved. Almost from the first flanged metal wheels, one inch became the "standard" flange height, and no reason for any substantial change has ever been found.

Fig. 1-4 shows why the flange was found to belong on the inner edge of the wheel tread.

Why Trains?

Once there is a guideway, it becomes feasible to hook cars together into trains, with important savings in cost. One-car trains, as exemplified by the electric interurban railway and the streetcar, proved relatively short-lived variations of the theme, with the latter making its comeback (under the alias "LRV" or Light Rail Vehicle) in the form of articulated two-car units which can be combined into trains. Fig. 1-5 shows why combining the vehicles into trains is important in increasing the *capacity* of a narrow transportation corridor, particularly important in providing needed mobility without wasting vast areas of real estate.

In determining the practical traffic-handling capacity of a track, the efficiency of the signaling and control system in allowing vehicles to proceed with assurance at all times that there is no train closer than the stopping distance ahead must be considered. The actual vehicles-per-hour line capacities for the various consists and speeds will therefore always be lower than those shown in Fig. 1-5, but the ratios between them are representative.

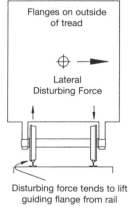

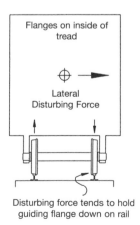

Fig. 1-4. Where Should the Flange Be?

Apart from cost savings from having one operator controlling a larger amount of transportation capacity, hooking vehicles together into trains greatly increases the capability of a single "lane" of space to handle, safely, large amounts of traffic at any required maximum speed.

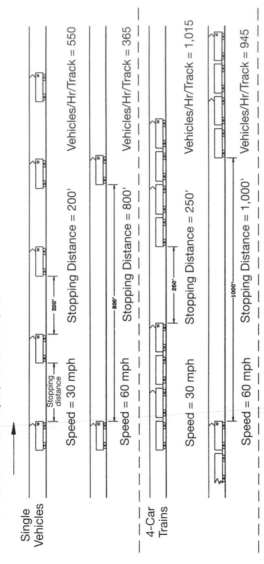

Single Vehicles

Speed = 30 mph   Stopping Distance = 200'   Vehicles/Hr/Track = 550

Speed = 60 mph   Stopping Distance = 800'   Vehicles/Hr/Track = 365

4-Car Trains

Speed = 30 mph   Stopping Distance = 250'   Vehicles/Hr/Track = 1,015

Speed = 60 mph   Stopping Distance = 1,000'   Vehicles/Hr/Track = 945

Stopping distance, which is the ultimate limit on how close together vehicles can safely travel, varies with the square of the speed; increasing the speed with vehicles traveling singly reduces the number of vehicles which one track can carry per hour. Even 4-car trains more than double the capacity of a single track to handle traffic at 60 mph, allowing for somewhat longer braking distance with a train (lower wind resistance, some delay in braking action).

For freight-length trains, capacity is much greater; even though the length of the train itself becomes the larger part of the "Track Occupancy Time." Trains of 7,000 ft length having 80 cars each, with 3,000 ft stopping distance, give a traffic capacity of 2,535 cars/hr at 60 mph.

Fig. 1-5. Why Trains?

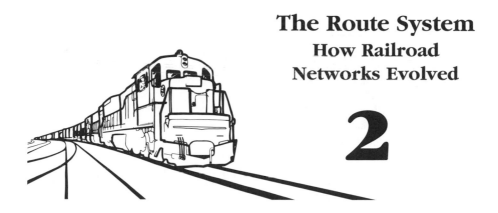

The Route System
How Railroad Networks Evolved

2

In the early part of the 19th century, the big question was whether or not the railroad idea would work. Cast iron rails sometimes broke under the first impact from the weight of the new steam locomotive. Boilers blew up, and huge costs were predicted for tunnels, in the belief that trains could climb only the gentlest of grades. However, within a few years, tough wrought iron rails became available. The timber crosstie proved not only cheaper than the massive stone blocks originally planned as "permanent" supports for the rails, but did a far better job of keeping the rails the right distance apart. Experience proved that useful loads could be hauled over mountain ranges on grades of more than 100 feet of rise per mile of track. The "pilot truck" guided the locomotive around sharp curves, and workable designs were developed for the many auxiliary devices. Track switches, headlights, and whistles were designed to make the railroad a complete commercial enterprise.

It became clear that a railroad could be built to go just about anywhere. With this wide-open choice, the real question became one of economics; railroads should be built where there was, or reasonably could be expected to be, enough demand for transportation to support the line and pay back the cost of building it. Prosperity and people usually *followed* rather than preceded the coming of the railroad, so faith and luck were important, too.

The North American Rail Network

In practice, developing a logical system of railroad trackage wasn't straightforward. Useful transportation is a matter of moving something from where it is produced, to where it is needed. Population affects both ends of the trip.

The first railroads had strictly limited objectives; they headed inland from established port cities to sources of raw materials and agricultural products. Unless there was water power or a good harbor to determine its location, a small village had little chance to grow. The Baltimore and Ohio Railroad changed this concept. They proposed to connect the ocean with the natural waterway of the Ohio River and offset New York's water-level Erie Canal. The B & O demonstrated that goods could now be carried across the mountains at a competitive price. And all year too!

7

The railroad network then began to grow on its own. Once a line was in operation, population grew more rapidly along it than elsewhere. Chicago became *the* metropolis of the Midwest because it was a major railroad junction. A new generation of cities such as Atlanta appeared, communities whose location was due solely to the fact that railroad lines crossed or terminated at that particular point. Other towns with equally good geographic locations withered on the vine or perhaps had to move a few miles, if main-line rail routes passed them by for some reason or other.

On the basis of purely technical reasons, locating a railroad line so that it can provide useful transportation at minimum cost is a complicated business, as we shall see. That's not the end of it, though. The technology of the time was a major influence; in opening up grain-growing regions in the late 19th century, branch lines were spaced so that all farms were within one day's horse-and-wagon range of the nearest railroad. Competitive, political, and even such emotional factors as civic pride, sheer optimism, and especially greed have often completely overwhelmed engineering considerations. Parallel lines were built which really were not needed. In other cases, the anticipated growth of the area served never materialized or the mineral wealth proved to be more limited than expected. Conversely, some lines that were shaky affairs at the start served to keep unpromising areas in business until new developments or discoveries let them blossom into prosperous, stable communities.

With all these historical factors and uncertainties, plus the effects of governmental regulation, the rail system of the North American continent evolved into and remains as a largely interconnected network which can move goods in quantity from anywhere to anywhere via a reasonably direct route or routes.

Fig. 2-1 summarizes the mid-1990s mileage of standard-gauge line and track in the United States, Canada, and Mexico over which freight is transported, together with a characterization by ownership of the organizations operating segments of this network. Because of the common standard (4 ft 8½ in.) gauge, numerous across-border connections and established agreements on such matters as equipment design and maintenance standards, rentals and customs administration, the railroads of the three countries are able to function as a single system. Ratification of the North American Free Trade Agreement (NAFTA) in 1994 can be expected to result in more extensive international trade; further privatization is also leading to increased cross-border railroad ownership.

Classification of Railroad Operating Companies in the U.S.

For regulatory purposes the Interstate Commerce Commission (since January 1, 1996, replaced by the Surface Transportation Board) has classified railroad companies solely on the basis of gross revenues, with the threshold for Class I status raised in steps from $1 million prior to 1956 to $50 million in 1978; this figure has been further adjusted annually on the basis of inflation and other factors. For 1994, the ICC classification was as follows:

The North American Standard-Gauge Rail Network 1996 Est.			
	Canada	Mexico	United States	Total
Miles of Line				
"First Track" of line-haul, common-carriers only, excluding rapid-transit, industrial, tourist lines. Track over which more than one company operates counted only once.	30,000	12,550	145,000	187,500
Miles of Track				
Including second, third and fourth tracks, switching and terminal companies, sidings and yard tracks operated by common-carrier railroad companies	38,000	15,000	238,000	291,000
Ownership – Miles of Line				
Private companies	28,000	12,500	142,000	182,500
National (government corporations)		—	700	700
Provincial, state, municipal	2,000	—	2,300	4,300
Number of Companies				
Ownership of the Consolidated Rail Corporation (Conrail) and the Alaska Railroad was transferred by the U. S. Government to private investors and the State of Alaska, respectively, in 1987. The Northern Alberta Railway is now part of the Canadian National Railways.	16	—	500	—

Fig. 2-1. The North American Standard-Gauge Rail Network

Class I: Annual revenues above $255.9 million.

Class II: Annual revenues $20.5 to $255.8 million.

Class III: Annual revenues less than $20.5 million.

In 1979, the ICC eliminated all financial reporting requirements for railroads in its Classes II and III. Subsequently, somewhat comparable data from these companies has been collected by the Association of American Railroads (AAR), which, on the basis of the emergence of a significant population of relatively large but smaller than Class I freight railroads, uses a modified classification: for the non-Class I's:

Regional Railroads: Line-haul railroads with revenues between $40 million and the Class I threshold or which operate more than 350 miles of line.

Local Railroads: Shortline railroads, including switching and terminal (non-line-haul) railroads with annual revenues of less than $40 million.

Some idea of the nature of railroads in these groups may be derived from the 1994 figures:

Railroad	Number	Miles Operated	Year-end Employees	Freight Revenue ($000)
Class I	12	123,000	189,200	$29,900,000
Regional	32	20,000	10,700	1,700,000
Local	487	26,000	13,100	1,400,000
Total	531	169,000	213,000	$33,000,000

(Included in local railroads are 160 non-road-haul switching and terminal companies.)

On the basis of gross revenues, the two major Canadian lines, the National Railways of Mexico, Amtrak (National Railroad Passenger Corp.), and three U.S. commuter railroads (over much of whose lines freight railroads have trackage rights) are of Class I size.

Mergers and Spin-offs

While there has been a continuing trend to merge large railroad companies into a few megasystems, some operating more than 20,000 miles of track, and Class I railroads operated 73 percent of the route mileage in the United States in 1994, in recent years these major companies have also spun off some 25,000 line-miles of secondary main-line, branch, and light-traffic trackage.

These lines, generally serving areas which, for one reason or another, cannot attract traffic which can earn a reasonable rate of return under the operating conditions to which the Class I railroads are committed and many of which otherwise would be subject to abandonment, are now owned, rented, or operated by a variety of investor, shipper, or (in a few cases, publicly) sponsored organizations; some of which in turn are the product of mergers. Several of the 32 regional companies are of a size which would have been Class I only a few years earlier.

Other groups of geographically separated lines of traditional shortline size are now owned or operated under contract by companies with a good track record in turning a profit by revitalizing and managing such properties; some of these have expanded their scope to include foreign or even overseas operations.

Thus, while the number of operating railroad companies in the United States is far smaller than it once was (there were 1,300 in 1910; in recent years the number has stabilized at about 500). Privatization of government-owner lines in Canada and Mexico is spawning additional small and mid-size operations.

Traffic Density and Network Consolidation

Railroad line mileage in the United States reached its peak in 1916. Since that time, although the remaining 168,000 miles are now carrying (on a ton-mile basis) more than three times the traffic, about half of that mileage has been abandoned. This has meant the elimination of many parallel and branch lines; much additional trackage has been downgraded from main-line to secondary status. Since the railroad works most efficiently as a "wholesale" generator of transportation, this concentration of traffic has played an essential role in keeping the whole system in business in the face of ever-growing competition. In 1994, the average mile of line in the United States carried approximately 17 million gross tons (lading, cars, and locomotives) of traffic, generating 8.5 million revenue ton-miles. The gross tonnage statistic, used as a good measure of the wear and tear on the track, of a particular line, may not be a precise measure of its relative importance since freight rates vary widely among the bulk, high-value, and time-sensitive commodities which make up its traffic mix, but remains the most widely available traffic density figure.

Today's Network

Fig. 2-2 shows all lines within the contiguous United States (excluding major track-crowded railroad-hub areas) which constitute the network over which rail freight could be routed in the mid-1990s time frame. Lines of the same width on this map represent anything from the busiest main line to the sleepiest of light-traffic branches, covering the territory over which this inter-connected mesh of lines can move goods from any productive source to wherever they are needed.

Fig. 2-3 includes only those main and secondary-main lines carrying at least 5 million gross tons (5 mgt) per year – roughly, 40,000 revenue carloads annually or 160 cars per business day.

The lighter-traffic lines not shown, which constitute more than one-quarter of the total mileage, generate less than one-twentieth of the ton-miles. Since the average carload travels some 800 miles, it is evident that these main and "core" lines carry-

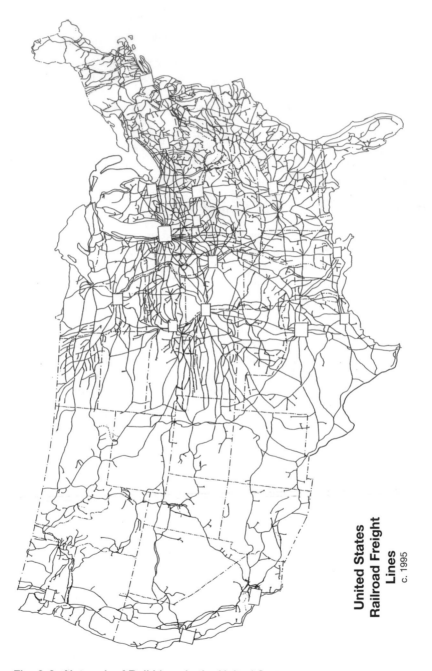

**United States
Railroad Freight
Lines**
c. 1995

Fig. 2-2. Network of Rail Lines in the United States

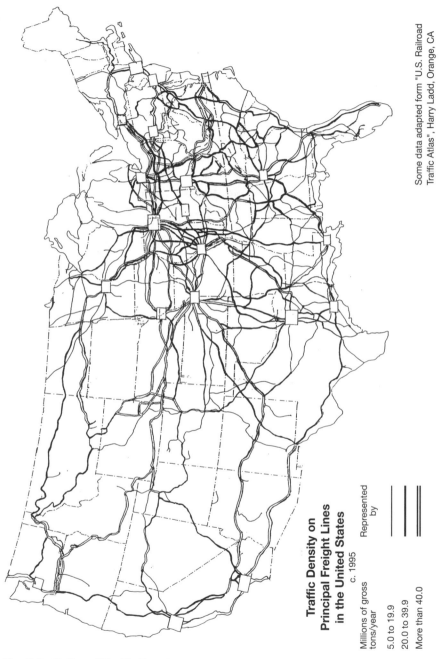

Traffic Density on Principal Freight Lines in the United States

c. 1995

Millions of gross tons/year

Represented by

5.0 to 19.9

20.0 to 39.9

More than 40.0

Some data adapted form "U.S. Railroad Traffic Atlas", Harry Ladd, Orange, CA

Fig. 2-3. Railroad Traffic Density

13

ing 20 to 40 and more than 40 mgt respectively are the arteries accounting for most of the system's revenues. This map also indicates the degree to which the main and core lines still provide for vigorous inter-railroad competition over heavy traffic lines for a high proportion of medium- and long-haul traffic.

Comparison between lines on the two maps also indicates how many areas are served directly only by *branch* (1 to 5 mgt) or *light-traffic* (less than 1 mgt) lines. Conversely, revenue from carloads originated or terminated on these lines represents a significant portion of the income of the Class I and larger regional railroads operating over their more lucratively loaded lines.

Route Rationalization

Communities served only by such low-density lines often have great importance to the industrial life of an area and a correspondingly high degree of public and political visibility; line abandonments, as well as the construction and ownership of new lines, remain within the purview of the federal regulatory system.

Determining the overall operational, competitive, and financial effect on a railroad of such line changes, particularly where severing a route by abandoning a segment directly serving no customers means that remaining traffic must move by a more circuitous route, is a matter for the most elaborate forms of computerized "operations research analysis," well beyond the scope of this text. Nevertheless, looking at one aspect of a selected geographical segment of this puzzle with real numbers can help to appreciate how the railroad system operates to use (and conserve) energy in moving the largest single-mode part (39 percent in 1994) of U.S. inter-city freight traffic.

A Look at a Single Railroad System

As an example, we will use the "East-West Railroad," a simplified, make-believe system typical of any fairly large line which has been formed by the gradual merger, lease, and purchase of dozens of smaller railroads over many decades. Like real railroads in both the eastern and western parts of the continent, it has at least one major mountain range to overcome, and the location of its lines is greatly influenced by the presence of river valleys and the irregularities of the coastline. The system map (Fig. 2-4) is not drawn to scale, but the distance from A to J along the East-West's main line is about a thousand miles.

Connections and Competitors

Other railroads in the same area as the E-W include the Northwest and Northeast (NW & NE) which taps territory generally north of the E-W and also reaches the ports at the metropolis of J and the industrial city of O; its main line goes to the port city of AA, which the E-W does not reach.

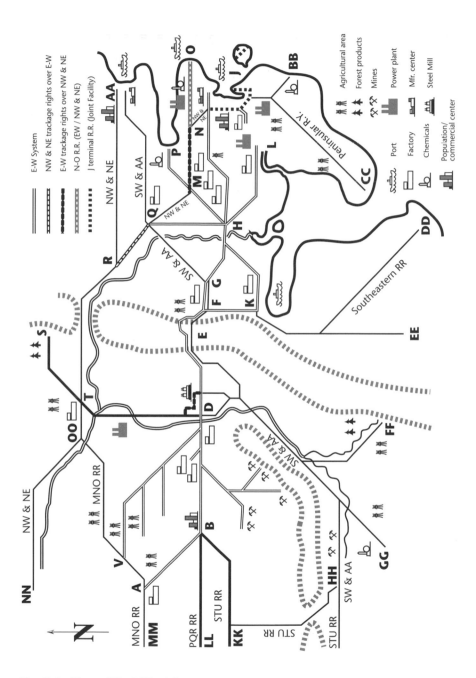

Fig. 2-4. Map of East-West System

The Southwest and AA (SW & AA) extends from an inland area south of the E-W's western terminals to AA, crossing the E-W at several points in the process.

The Southeastern Railroad and the Peninsular Railroad are shorter lines which serve areas south of F & J, respectively, which are separated by an arm of the ocean.

Coming in from the Far West are the so-called "transcontinental" railroads, not truly coast-to-coast, but extending two-thirds of the way and connecting at gateway cities such as B and HH with the Eastern roads. Even on this simplified map, two points are clear:

- There are many routes from almost any point to any other.

- The larger rail systems are connections with each other for traffic originating or terminating in their own territory and *competitors* for through traffic.

From point KK on the STU railroad, for example, shipment to AA could go south on the STU to the SW & AA connection and then directly to AA, involving only one interchange, or it could be routed STU to B, E-W to G, SW & AA to destination, a shorter route but with two interchanges.

The routing STU to B, E-W to T, NW & NE to destination is longer but does not take it up and over the mountain range between E and F.

Pulling the Map Together

For many commodities, the principal competition in recent decades is from other modes of transportation, common-carrier and unregulated contract trucks using the interstate highway system, barge traffic on open waterways and those made navigable by the Army Corps of Engineers, and pipelines. A more subtle form of competition is *decentralization*. Corporations manufacturing and distributing products have the choice, over a period of time, of arranging their plants and distribution centers so as to reduce the amount of transportation involved in the whole process. The extra cost of producing goods in smaller plants may be more than balanced by reduced transportation costs from being closer to more customers.

Whenever possible, therefore, the individual railroad companies will combine, coordinate, or connect their tracks and other facilities to hold down overall costs. Several examples of this, common throughout the country, are found here.

Paired Tracks. Both the E-W & AA built their single-track lines through the only practical pass through the mountain range. The two lines are now "paired" between E and F; eastbound trains of both railroads use the SW & AA track, while all westbound trains go via the E-W line. Thus each road gets the advantages of double track while maintaining only a single line.

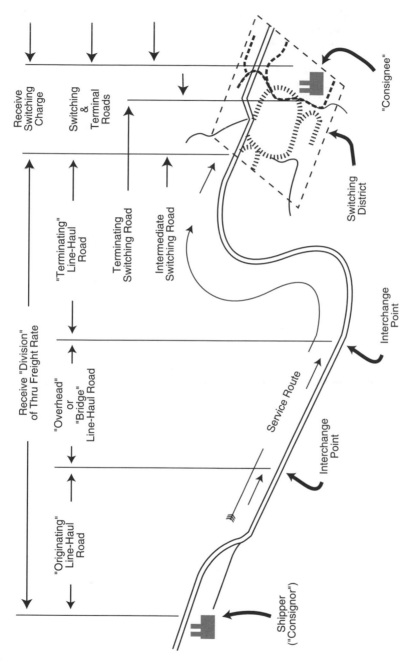

Fig. 2-5. Freight Movement Terms

Trackage Rights. From R to Q, the NW & NE run its trains over the E-W's track, using its own crews and motive power, by paying a specified toll, often referred to as a "wheelage" charge because of its being based on the number of cars involved.

From M to N, the arrangement is the reverse. Trackage rights arrangements vary with circumstances. Usually, the owning line does not grant rights to its tenant line to receive or deliver freight to on-line customers.

Joint Facilities. Between N and O, both E-W and NE & NW trains run over the N-O RR, a jointly owned company which is responsible for the operation of the line.

In the metropolitan area of J and its port, both lines connect with the Peninsular RR and reach many industries, terminals, and docks by way of the J Terminal RR, which is owned jointly by the line-haul railroads involved.

Detouring. All roads in the territory have standard detouring agreements with each other, so that in an emergency the trouble spot may be bypassed by the best available route.

Interline Terminology. In the United States, about 75 percent of all rail shipments involve at least two different railroads, so interchange of freight cars and the establishment of interline rates is an integral part of the business. Some of the terminology is illustrated in Fig. 2-5, and the side-effects will show up throughout further discussions of tracks and trains.

Haulage. In an arrangement that has become more common since the 1980s, the E-W pays the NW & NE to move its freight consists carrying traffic enroute via B to or from E-W points in the vicinity of V. These trains operate with NW & NE crews. In this "haulage" arrangement there is no interchange between the railroads and no division of the E-W's freight rate. Haulage is attractive to the E-W in this case, because it can offer better service and incurs less overall expense than it would in moving such traffic over its own more circuitous route via C, D, and U.

Which Way Is Best?

What is the "best" route for hauling coal between D and H (enroute from the mines in the W area to the huge power plant at L)? Assume that the route which takes the *least total energy* to do the job is best. (This is not the whole story by any means, but energy is a major influence when hauling freight.)

The Alternate Routes. Fig. 2-6 shows the routes available. The direct route D-E-F-G-H via the E-W's main line is the shortest, but it takes you up 4,000 feet and back down again. The alternate D-T-R-Q-H route, aside from using "foreign" trackage from T to R, is downhill all the way for the coal, but 250 miles longer. Which is more important?

Train Resistance. Train resistance may be divided into two main elements, *rolling resistance* (including the resistance to wheels rolling on the rail, friction in the journal [axle] bearings on the cars, and wind resistance) and *grade resistance*. The first is all friction, and once the energy is expended it is gone forever. Grade resistance results from the energy you must put into the train to lift it vertically. The energy is returned without loss when the train comes back down again.

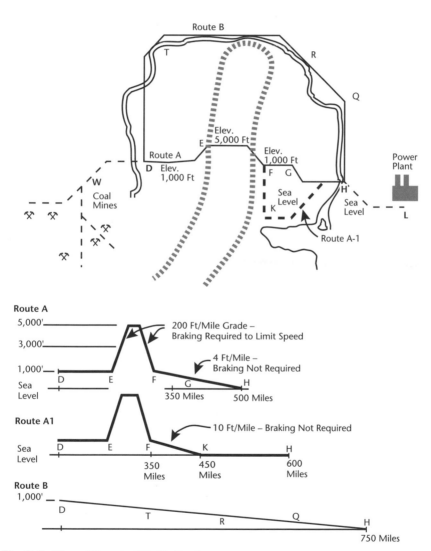

Fig. 2-6. Three Ways to H With Coal

On a gentle grade, one-third of one percent or less, all this energy can be recovered by letting the train roll along without applying the brakes; the locomotive has correspondingly less work to do in keeping the train moving at the desired speed. However, on a mountain grade (for example, two percent, or about 100 ft to the mile) almost all of this energy must be dissipated as heat using the brakes to keep the train from exceeding the speed limit. A great deal of the energy put into reaching the top of the mountain is lost.*

*Except in electric traction with "regenerative braking," not currently in use in U.S. freight operations.

Fig. 2-7 gives typical values for the rolling friction of cars of a type likely to be used to move trainloads of coal to a power plant, 100-ton capacity alloy-steel or aluminum-body gondolas weighing 25 tons empty. Rolling resistance varies with the weight of the car, being considerably more for a ton of empty than for a ton of load. It also increases gradually as the speed increases. We will use typical running speeds of 35 mph for the loaded train and 45 mph for returning the empties. The formulas usually used for estimating train resistance (Davis) gives 4.2 lbs *per ton* for the loaded car, and almost three times as much per ton for the empty. The following graph (Fig. 2-8) fully illustrates this principle.

Grade resistance per ton is 20 pounds for every percent (one foot rise in 100 ft of forward travel) of grade and doesn't vary with car weight or train speed. The energy it takes to lift a ton to the top of the mountain is entirely a matter of how high it is.

Adding Up the Horsepower-Hours

The mechanical energy or work we're concerned about here is the product of a *force* acting through a distance. The *rate* of applying energy to a job is *power*, pulling twice as hard at the same speed or moving twice as fast while pulling with the same force represents twice the power. James Watt chose "horsepower" as the unit for rating his 18th century steam pumping engines and defined it as 33,000 ft-lb of work (lifting pounds of water to a height in feet, for example) per minute; he chose a value somewhat above what any horse alive could keep on doing, presumably to avoid complaints. Today, power is often expressed in the unit named after James himself, the *watt*, and we pay electric bills on the basis of kilowatt-hours of energy. Since locomotives are still rated in horsepower, we'll stick with this unit; 746 watts (or three-quarters of a kilowatt) equals one horsepower.

Fig. 2-7 proceeds to calculate the energy in horsepower-hours it takes to roll an empty and a loaded car one mile on level track and to lift it 100 ft in elevation. The *energy* it takes to overcome a given difference in elevation is the same if you do it via a 0.05 percent grade or straight up in an elevator. As we'll see in studying locomotive performance later on, grade *does* make a huge difference in the tractive force needed. Now we're ready to see which route uses the least total energy in moving a 100-ton car of coal from D to H and bringing the empty back for another load.

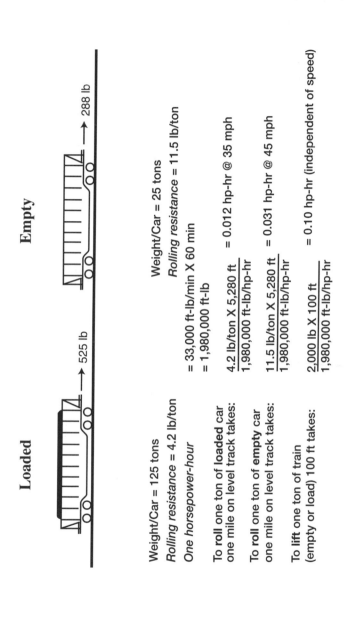

Fig. 2-7. How Much Energy It Takes to Move a Car

Route A. Fig. 2-9 adds up the two classes of resistance for loaded and empty trips by each route. Route A, over the mountains, uses 750 hp-hr to lift the car over a 4,000 ft summit. Practically all this energy is lost because the train must descend the steep eastern slope under careful control of the brakes, converting the energy into heat. From F to H (Fig. 2-10), no brakes are needed on the gentle grade, and we have a net *input* of 125 hp-hr to boost the car up 5,000 ft, none of which we can get back on this trip. Total = 1,638 hp-hr per car, or 16.38 hp-hr per net ton of coal hauled.

Route B. The entire 750 miles of descending water-grade can be run without using the brakes, so 125 hp-hr needed to overcome 750 miles of rolling friction is provided by the change in elevation. We have to put some of that energy back in returning the empties: the total for Route B works out to 1,605 hp-hr, about two percent less than for Route A, in exchange for an extra 500 miles of wear on wheels and roller bearings.

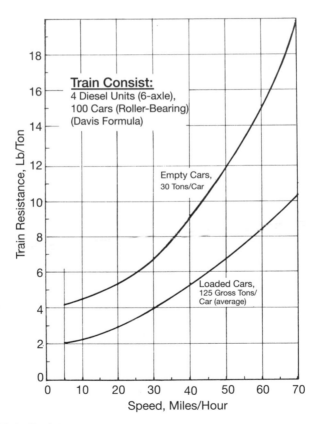

Fig. 2-8. Train Resistance

Route BA. We notice that while Route B was the overall winner, Route A used less energy in getting the empties back (513 to 605 hp-hr). This is because of the greater effect of rolling friction over the longer route on the relatively hard-pulling empties. This suggests looking at a circle route, with the loads going east along the river and the empties coming back over the mountain, Route BA. Sure enough, this does the job for 1,513 hp-hr, six percent less than Route B. This would be a very practical routing mechanically, since the same locomotives hauling the heavy loads east could probably get the empties over the mountain without a helper on the steep grade. From an overall operating basis, it might be more costly because such one-way movement over long distances results in a lot of "deadhead" costs in getting the train crews back for their next trip.

Route A-1. The idea of hauling those cars all the way back empty suggests another look at Fig. 2-6. Suppose there is important iron ore which could come into the port at K and be hauled to the mills at D – this would mean an extra 100 miles in a side-trip from H to F via K, but it's physically practical since the dense iron ore can be hauled as a partial load in the big coal cars (the reverse, of course, won't work). It turns out that the total energy *charged to the coal movement* is only 1,241 hp-hr. Energy used to lift the weight of the cars back up from K to the summit of the pass is part of the cost of the ore movement, which still has a favorable situation because the coal movement is now taking 23 percent less energy than via Route B. Again, whether this is the best arrangement depends on other factors. The car utilization may not be nearly as good if, for example, ore-ship arrival is irregular. And extra car-days cost money, as does diesel fuel.

Route BA-1. Finally the lowest energy routing turns out to be the "circle route" via the river eastbound with return through K to pick up the ore. A total of 1,116 hp-hr, or 32 percent less energy is expended than on Route A at a cost of a 35 percent increase in mileage, and with loaded car-miles 81 percent instead of 50. Quite an incentive to the railroad to do whatever it can to develop the K-D ore traffic!

Overall Train Performance

This single-factor analysis omits many refinements and details which would have to be included in any real-life assessment, including the effects of track curvature, the relative energy, and other costs associated with various train speeds, comparative energy costs with local vs. through-train haulage, and the equipment-ownership, fuel, crew, and competitiveness costs of line congestion.

General Performance Factors

To give a little better feel for the ways speed, grade, curvature, and "stop and go" affect railroading, Fig. 2-10 puts these difference factors on one chart, based on cars loaded to 80 tons each (a typical average for the mix of loads and empties likely to be found in service). By looking at this graph, we can get some idea of just how eas-

Horsepower – Hours Per Car
(100 Tons of Coal)

Route		Eastbound (Loaded)	Westbound (Empty)	Total Energy (HP-HR)	Round-Trip Distance (Miles)
Route A: (Over the mountain)	Rolling Lifting	125 x .012 x 500 = 750 + 125 x .10 x 40 = 500 - 125 x .10 x 10 = -125 1,125	25 x .031 x 500 = 388 25 x .10 x 50 = 125 513	1,638	1,000
Route B: (Along the river)	Rolling Lifting	125 x .012 x 750 = 1,125 - 125 x .10 x 10 = -125 1,000	25 x .031 x 750 = 580 25 x .10 x 10 = 25 605	1,605	1,500
Route BA: (Circle route)		Eastbound Route B (Along the river) 1,000	Westbound Route A (Over the mountain) 513	1,513	1,250
Route A-1: (Side trip to pick up ore load)	Rolling Lifting	125 x .012 x 500 = 750 + 125 x .10 x 40 = 500 - 125 x .10 x 10 = -125 1,125	25 x .031 x 150 = 116 (H to K only-K to D with ore load) 116	1,241	1,100
Route BA-1: (Circle route with ore load on return)		Eastbound Route B (Along the river) 1,000	Westbound Route A-1 (Via K, to pick up ore load) 116	1,116	1,350

Fig. 2-9. Comparing the Energy It Takes to Deliver the Goods

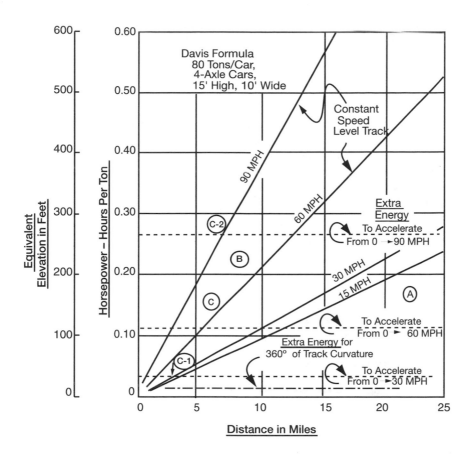

Fig. 2-10. How Easily the Trains Roll

ily the cars roll; later on, these matters will show up in the way tracks are laid out and locomotives are designed.

Grades and Power vs. Distance. Considering the curve on the chart for 15 mph, for example, we see that the extra energy it takes to lift the train upgrade to an elevation of 200 ft would move it about *21 miles* at that speed if it were on level track (Point A). No wonder that trains can move the goods with little energy input and need good brakes on even the gentlest grades. The second set of figures on the vertical axis puts the same thing in terms of horsepower-hours per ton. Two-tenths of a horsepower-hour (running your lawnmower for four minutes) would move that ton of train the 21 miles!

Power vs. Speed. That same 0.20 hp-hr that moved the ton 21 miles at 15 mph would only take it about 9.5 miles at 60 mph (Point B), but at 30 mph it would make 18 miles. This shows that there is little to be gained by running a freight train on level at less than 30 to 35 mph, but that at 60 mph the extra resistance (primarily wind resistance) has begun to require significantly more energy.

Track Curvature. Some extra friction occurs in hauling trains around curves, but the extra energy involved may not necessarily be large. As the line near the bottom of the graph shows, it adds about 0.014 hp-hr per ton (the equivalent of lifting the weight 14 ft) to go around curves which are equivalent to a full 360° circle. Since a railroad following a river in hilly country may have the equivalent of several complete circles, curves can show up in the fuel bill. Wear on wheels and rails is a more expensive result.

Stop and Go. Point C shows that the energy it takes to get a train up to 60 mph from a stop is equal to what it would take to roll it about 5.5 miles on the level at the same speed. The energy equivalent at 30 mph is about three miles (C-1) and seven miles at 90 mph (C-2). This shows that stops and slowdowns take significant energy; a 60 mph train stopping every 10 miles will use about as much energy in accelerating as it will in covering the distance. Since it takes only one-third as much energy to go from 0 to 30 as it does from 30 to 60, a series of 30 mph speed restrictions is almost as much of a handicap.

Train Performance Analysis

Figures in Fig. 2-10 are based on the "Davis Formulas," a set of equations assembled by W. A. Davis in 1927 to summarize the best available data on factors (journal bearing friction, rolling resistance, losses from impact and vibration, air resistance and curvature) affecting the resistance of train consists and trackage typical of the era. With modifications to their coefficients on the basis of changes in roadway, equipment, and operating practices, and the availability of new test data and analytical procedures over the years, they still provide the framework for continuously more refined *train simulation models* now used for highly accurate computer predictions of in-train dynamic forces, schedule performance, and energy consumption for any train consist running over any specific route.

As of 1989, the Train Operation and Energy Simulator (TOES) and related Train Energy Model (TEM) programs, refined on a continuing basis by the Association of American Railroads to reflect analytical, laboratory, test track and field data measured in cooperation with the FRA, railroads in the United States and Canada (and now with inputs from railroad organizations worldwide as well) have been released in modules compatible with hardware of personal-computer capability. This enables railroad operating personnel to use them in such day-to-day matters as comparing the energy efficiency of alternate train-braking practices on a given run, as well as for longer-range planning and costing operations.

System Operations Analyses

Along with these refined computations for the movement of individual trains, computerized *system* operational analyses seeking to optimize plant and scheduling by studying the interactions among trains in moving traffic over a network of routes under various systems of train control have become a major factor in railroad planning. The usefulness of such optimizations depends upon the applicability of such items as the mathematical model relating individual axle loads to the degradation of track ballast particles, a factor included by AAR researchers in its evolving TM (Track Maintenance) Cost program; accordingly, a fundamental goal in numerous ongoing industry research programs on everything from the detection of bearing fatigue to the effect of rail lubrication on wear and resistance is to validate increasingly sophisticated descriptive models based on comparative field and laboratory test data. In particular, the AAR/FRA Heavy Axle Load Test program (p. 52) has provided critically important inputs.

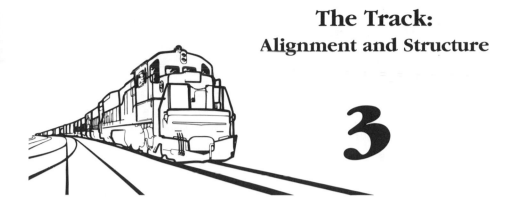

The Track:
Alignment and Structure

3

A four-unit, 12,000-hp diesel locomotive consist weighing 750 tons roaring around a curve at 70 mph is being guided and supported by 260 ft of track which is made up of:

- 11.5 tons of steel rail, held in place by
- 600 lb of spikes, and resting on
- 3.1 tons of steel tie plates, resting on
- 16.7 tons of treated wood crossties, resting in
- 130 tons of crushed rock ballast, which in turn is supported by the subgrade and the right-of-way.

With those tremendous weights and forces at work, it's easy to see that every item in the track has to be designated and maintained to do its part through rain, cold, heat, vandalism, and the encroachment of weeds and brush. While railroad track seems massive in terms of weight, in comparison to the loads it must sustain, it is a relatively delicate, precisely balanced system.

Track Alignment

Although there are stretches of tangent (without curves) track in the United States as long as 78.66 miles, most trains are required to make numerous changes of direction, both vertical and horizontal. The effects of grade show up primarily in the locomotives it takes to overcome them (they will be considered in the next section). In hilly or mountainous territory, a reasonable grade and a practical cost of construction requires curving the line to follow the shape of the land.

Tangent and Curves

Railroad civil engineers refer to straight track as "tangent," and use as much of it as possible because it is much easier to build and maintain. In the United States the sharpness of curved track is not measured by radius (it would take an awfully long string to lay out the typical main-line curve), but by "degrees," as illustrated in Fig. 3-1. Typical maximum speeds for some curves are also indicated. Wherever practical, main lines will get where they're going with curves of one or two degrees. But

29

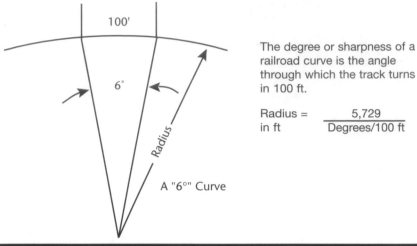

The degree or sharpness of a railroad curve is the angle through which the track turns in 100 ft.

$$\text{Radius in ft} = \frac{5,729}{\text{Degrees}/100 \text{ ft}}$$

Degree of Curve	Radius Feet	Typical Max. Speed	Extra Curve Resistance, lb/ton	Equivalent Increase in Grade, %
1°	5,729	100 mph	0.8	0.04
5°	1,146	50 mph	4.0	0.20
10°	573	30 mph	8.0	0.40
15°	383	25 mph	12.0	0.60

Fig. 3-1. Track Curvature

in mountain crossings it is often necessary to have at least a few curves in the 5 to 10 degree or sharper range to minimize grades. These curves add significant drag to the train, which helps the brakes going downhill, but must be overcome going uphill. Where curves and grades occur together, a common practice is to *compensate* for curvature by reducing the grade on the curved track so that the combined resistance is the same for both tangent and curved segments of the grade.

Superelevation. To compensate for the effect of centrifugal force, the outer rail on a curve may be raised (superelevated) to tip the cars inward. The maximum superelevation or "banking" ordinarily used on a standard-gauge line carrying general traffic (the difference in elevation between the two rails, also referred to as "cross-level") is six inches.

Six inches of superelevation fully compensates for centrifugal force (Fig. 3-2) at 95 mph on a one-degree curve or at about 45 mph on a five-degree curve. By long experience embodied in current Federal Railroad Administration (FRA) regulations, operation at speeds resulting in an outward force beyond that compensated for

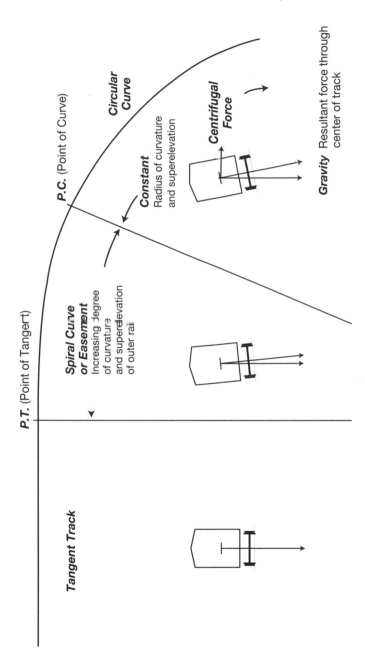

Fig. 3-2. From Tangent to Curve – Smoothly

31

by the "cant" (tilt or superelevation) equivalent to three inches may be allowed; this is the maximum "cant deficiency" that is permitted in setting speed limits without a waiver covering a specific situation. Under most freight-traffic situations railroads will limit cant deficiency to a lower figure.

If heavy trains run curves regularly at much less than the speed for which they are superelevated, the wheel flanges will ride the inner rail and wear it rapidly. Therefore, the maximum and minimum speeds on a given track cannot be too far apart on lines where there are many curves.

Spiraling. To attain the superelevation gradually so that the car suspensions can adjust to the change in "cross-level" of the track, a "spiral" or "easement" of gradually increasing curvature is used between each tangent and curved section of mainline trackage, as shown in Fig. 3-2. The length of the spiral depends on the allowable speed and the amount of superelevation, and may be more than 600 ft in high-speed territory.

Track Gauge

The most basic characteristic of track forming the North American rail network is its common "standard gauge" of 4 ft 8½ in., which allows freight cars to freely roll from the Arctic to Central America and from coast to coast. Fig. 3-3 shows how gauge is measured.

The actual measurement between railheads on a standard gauge railroad varies intentionally from this nominal dimension, and, of course, it changes somewhat with wear in service. There is a nominal clearance between the wheel flanges and the railheads of about ¾ inch. On some systems, such as rapid-transit lines where it is possible to maintain track to higher than normal standards of accuracy, a nominal gauge of 4 ft 8¼ in. can be used with the same wheel gauge. This tends to result in smoother running by reducing side-play.

Why Such an Odd Gauge?

The peculiar "standard" of about 4 ft 9 in. was common on English tramways before the invention of the steam locomotive. Additionally, there is some basis for tracing this back from cartwheel spacing to the five-foot width of Roman stone gateways. George Stephenson and his son Robert, who were prominent promoters and engineers of railroad *systems* on an international basis, adopted 4 ft 8½ in. as their standard. It is used throughout Europe (except in Spain, Portugal, Ireland, Finland, and the U.S.S.R.); it was adopted as recently as 1955 by Japan in starting construction of its new high-speed passenger rail system.

Initially in North America there were many different gauges. It was not until 1863, when President Lincoln designated 4 ft 8½ in. as the gauge for the railroad to be built to the Pacific Coast, that it became clear that all the railroads of the United

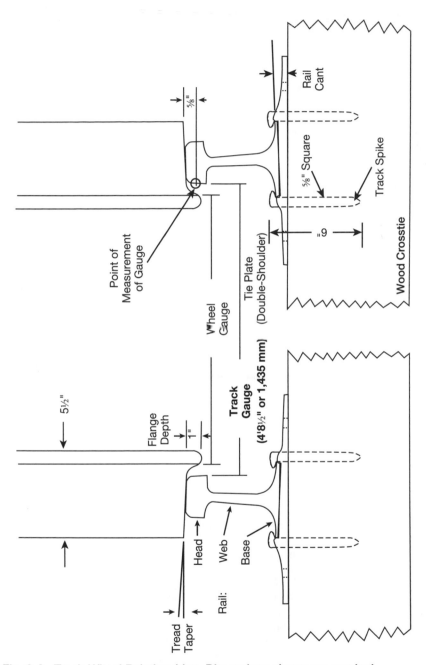

Fig. 3-3. Track-Wheel Relationships. Dimensions shown are nominal.

States would eventually be of this width. Railroads south of the Potomac and Ohio Rivers were mostly of 5 ft gauge until 1887, when several thousand miles of track were changed to standard over a single weekend. It then became possible to do away with transferring loads or switching car trucks at "break-of-gauge" points.

Is It the Right Width?

The uniformity of gauge is more important than the exact width chosen as a standard. "Wide Gauge" systems such as those in India (5 ft 6 in.) and the Soviet Union (5 ft) use rolling stock of about the same size as that in North America, while heavy-duty railroading is carried on in South Africa, parts of Australia, East Africa, Japan, and Brazil on tracks of 3 ft 6 in. and meter (3 ft 3⅜ in.) gauge. Though there are situations in which a wider gauge could be advantageous, it appears that for general service, taking all cost factors into consideration, the present gauge is not far from optimum.

The Track Structure

The track structure's function is to transform the intense load of the wheel on the head of the rail to a moderate, distributed pressure which the earth underneath can sustain under all weather conditions without settling. Figs. 3-3 and 3-4 show the main elements of typical present-day track structure on a heavy-duty main line.

All of the major track components have undergone continual change and upgrading on the basis of research and experience. Improvements affecting the way they work together also continue; an example within recent decades is the now-common use of roadbed stabilization fabrics at locations such as turnouts and highway grade crossings where impact loads and unfavorable drainage conditions affect track geometry, and maintenance is particularly difficult and expensive. Tough and reasonably inexpensive synthetic fabrics of controlled porosity have some effect in distributing rail loads while acting as a barrier in preventing subgrade particles from infiltrating the ballast and reducing its stability and drainage effectiveness.

Exploratory efforts continue to develop a radically different track structure (such as a continuous concrete-slab foundation) which will remain smoother, cost less, and require less attention while withstanding heavier loads traveling at higher speeds. However, the same basic rail-tie-ballast system has continued to be used to date, as it represents the most practical compromise among the conflicting requirements for high performance, minimal maintenance, and overall low cost.

Many minor aspects of track design have come about only through long experience. For example, it is standard practice to put the head end of the bolts of a rail joint alternately on the inside and outside of the rail. This prevents a derailed wheel from knocking off *all* the bolts in a joint and allowing it to separate completely under the rest of the train, a one in a million possibility, but one that's considered worth avoiding. Now, let's look briefly at the main parts of the track structure to see

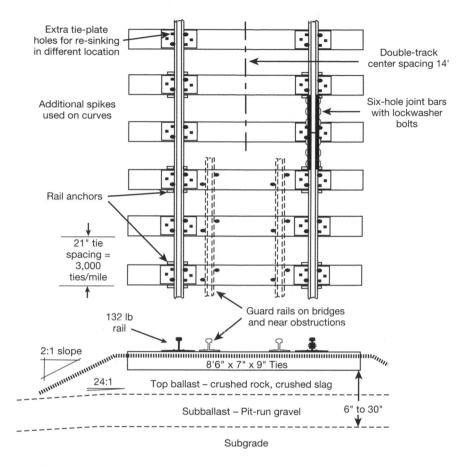

Fig. 3-4. The Track Structure – Typical Main-Line Track

how each has developed to pull its own weight in the total job of guiding and supporting the trains.

Rail

Iron alloys represent the only metals abundant and cheap enough to serve as the basic material for a *rail*road, and it's indeed fortunate that steel also has the most suitable combination of hardness, strength, and stiffness of any engineering material. Early rails were made of either high-carbon cast iron (hard but too brittle) or wrought iron (tough but too soft). The mid-19th century inventions of the Bessemer and open-hearth processes for economically converting iron to steel reduced steel's cost by about 80 percent and were an indispensable factor in continuing development of railroads.

Rail Sections. Rail is rolled from high quality steel containing 0.7 to 0.8 percent carbon and very limited amounts of the impurities sulfur and phosphorous. In cross-section, rail is an inverted "T," and every dimension and radius is in accordance with designs (usually A.R.E.A., American Railway Engineering Association, standards) developed over many years, to get the best fit with new and worn wheels and the best combination of stiffness and freedom from points of high stress under all types of top and side loading.

Rail currently being produced weighs from 112 to 145 lbs per yard (56 to 72 kilograms per 1 meter), stands from 6 to 8 inches high, and has a uniform base width of 5½ inches for compatibility with tie plates or other rail/tie fastening systems. Most new rail is of 115-, 132-, or 136-lb sections; extra head metal in the 136-lb section prolongs its "first-service" (main line) life under conditions (typically, on curvy routes) where gauge-face wear governs. Less than 10% of the rail in main track is lighter than 100 lbs.

Rail Life. The service life of rail is measured in terms of the gross tonnage it has carried; a track carrying a 10,000-ton train every hour would accumulate 600 million gross tons in about seven years, a figure which in recent years would be considered excellent for tangent track. New rail is removed from main-line service on the basis of either head wear or the development of defects at a rate indicating metal fatigue under today's heavy axle loads.

Such "relay" rail which has served its time on the main line is commonly relaid on secondary, branch, and yard tracks. For reasons discussed below, the first-service life being obtained with today's mix of considerably improved (harder) "standard" and premium (alloy or head-hardened) rail continues to increase, to the extent that in the 1990s fully maintaining track to carry almost twice the tonnage total of the 1950s requires less than half the mileage of new rail laid annually in the earlier period.

On sharp curves, rail wear– generally, gauge-face wear on the "high" (outside) rail, metal flow on the low rail – is much more severe. It is common practice to maximize use of the steel by *transposing* rail from one side or location to another.

Despite the rapidity with which the running surface rusts between trains in wet weather, loss of cross-section from corrosion is rarely significant. Total rail life before scrapping may be as long as 70 years.

Rail Defects and Developments. Over the decades it was found that a certain small percentage of rails would develop "transverse fissures," fatigue cracks starting inside the railhead and growing gradually until the rail broke under a train. For a long time, the principal defense against these failures was keeping a record of the location of all rails rolled from each "heat" (or batch) of steel and removing them from the track if any of the heat developed such defects.

In 1926 the Sperry detector car was developed; it uses a magnetic (now supplemented with ultrasonic) nondestructive test process to detect and pin-point flaws as it passes over the rails. In the 1930s, it was established that a controlled-cooling process following rolling of the rails could virtually eliminate the "shatter cracks" in the rail steel which lead to transverse fissures, and all rail rolled since then has been so produced. Because of the extremely long life of rail, however, not all of the earlier steel is out of service.

With the increase in railhead stress from the introduction of 100-ton freight cars in the 1960s, metal fatigue and its associated increase in the number and rate of growth of defects, as well as head wear, may determine rail's first-service life. Since the mid-1980s, adoption of newer technologies such as inert-gas stirring and continuous- or vacuum-casting to produce "cleaner" rail that contains fewer inclusions to act as fatigue-crack starting-points has become a must for rail-mill survival in a competitive market.

In use for many years, the automatic *wayside rail lubricator* reduces head wear by applying a thin film of grease to each wheel flange in approach to sharp curves. Improved wear resistance may be achieved in *premium rail* either by alloy metallurgy or by post-rolling heat treatment of the head; cost/life relationships are such that such rail is now also generally specified for curved territory, accepting some restrictions on welding practices.

Railhead grinding, typically by a contractor-owned rail-grinding train using a large number of grinding stones to measure and, under computer control, to correct the railhead contour (usually in a single pass), is now likely to be a routine procedure. Grinding serves not only to remove corrugations which may have developed in service (for reasons still not completely understood) but also to contour the wearing surface of the railhead to a shape calculated, in combination with the characteristics of the wheels passing over it, to minimize wear and the development of gauge-corner fatigue defects. On curves, properly mating contact surfaces help guide car trucks so as to reduce sliding-contact wear significantly. With properly timed grinding, it is expected that the first-service life of much of the rail now being laid will exceed one billion tons.

Bolted and Continuous-Welded Rail

After some 65 years working to a 39 ft standard length (compatible with shipping in 40 ft cars), mills have been re-equipped to produce double-length rails, thus halving the number of welds in the strings of continuous-welded rail (CWR) now in primary demand.

In bolted-rail track, joint bars (Fig. 3-4), arranged to allow some length-wise motion of the rails, connect the rail lengths. A gap, regulated to suit the temperature when the rail is laid so that it will just close on the hottest day, causes the rhythmic clickety-clack as a train moves along the track. Despite a great deal of design research, the joint is always less rigid than the rest of the rail and deflects enough to allow gradual wear and battering of the rail ends. This can be corrected by building up the rail surface with weld metal and grinding it to its original contour.

The reduced stiffness at the joint also causes greater load on the ballast and sub-ballast, resulting in "low joints" and resonant "rock and roll" of certain freight cars as well as rough riding unless overcome by frequent bolt tightening and tamping of the ballast.

The perfection of techniques for welding rail into continuous strings, transporting them to the site, and fastening them in place so as to overcome the effects of expansion and contraction (Fig. 3-5) has resulted in the present standard practice of minimizing joints in main-line track. Using an electric flash-butt welding process which can be precisely controlled and monitored to ensure the quality of each weld, lengths of rail, either new or relay, are welded into lengths (usually about 1,500 ft) in a central facility. Loaded on racks on a permanently coupled "rail-train," they bend easily around curves as they are hauled to the point of installation. There, the train is pulled out from under each pair of rails, which descend to the roadbed, ready to be substituted for the old rail. The remaining joints can be eliminated by in-place welding with portable equipment.

The laying of continuous-welded rail is restricted to a narrow range of temperatures near the upper limit of those expected at the particular location (heating the rail if necessary to lay it in cooler periods) so that it will always be relatively unstressed or in tension. Care must be taken not to reduce the lateral stability of the track by disturbing ties or ballast at times when high longitudinal stresses – particularly in compression – may be present.

Remaining joints may be eliminated by in-place welding, usually by a Thermit process in which one-man kits of expendable molds and the essential exothermic mix pre-heat the rail ends and then generate and guide molten metal forming the weld. While quality and quality control of these "field" welds has improved greatly in recent years, most "pull-aparts" in cold weather – a less serious problem than hot-weather "sun kink" (track buckling) since they do not usually result in a derailment – occur at these points. Where a large number of field welds are to be made, a less flexible alternative now available is the use of a large but transportable rig capable of making electric flash-butt welds in the field.

Track circuits require insulated joints. To approach the stiffness and endurance of the rail itself, these are now commonly made with special permanently bolted angle bars encased and sealed with epoxy under controlled shop conditions within short "plugs" of rail. These are then field-welded into place.

As of 1980, over 80,000 miles of track in the United States was laid with continuous-welded rail.

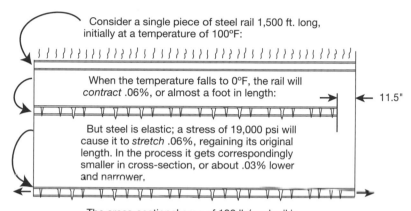

Consider a single piece of steel rail 1,500 ft. long, initially at a temperature of 100°F:

When the temperature falls to 0°F, the rail will *contract* .06%, or almost a foot in length: ← 11.5"

But steel is elastic; a stress of 19,000 psi will cause it to *stretch* .06%, regaining its original length. In the process it gets correspondingly smaller in cross-section, or about .03% lower and narrower,

The cross-sectional area of 132 lb/yard rail is 13 sq. inches, so if the rail is restrained so as to develop lengthwise tension of about 250,000 lb (13 x 19,000), it will *remain the same length* despite the 100° temperature change. In effect, the shrinkage is forced to occur in the cross-section rather than in the length; it amounts to about .002" in a rail 6" wide.

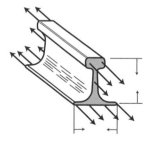

Since rail steel can withstand at least 75,000 psi without permanent deformation, all normal temperature variations can be accommodated within its elastic range. If laid at a temperature near the upper end of the range in the area, the rails will be in tension (tending to straighten rather than buckle the track) at all times when the temperature is lower.

Fig. 3-5. How Can Continuous-Welded Rail Be Practical?

Crossties

In an effort to create a truly "permanent way," some of the earlier railroads mounted their rails on stone blocks bedded firmly in the ground. This construction was impressively expensive in comparison to the practice of spiking rails to wooden cross-members or "ties" laid on the surface, but it turned out to be a lot less satisfactory. The lack of any cushioning between rail and stone resulted in a jarring ride that damaged both rail and vehicle, and shifting of the blocks threw the track out of gauge.

On the other hand, the wooden tie turned out to have a combination of near-ideal properties. Hardwood is strong in tension (to hold the rails in gauge), in bending (to distribute the load to the ballast uniformly), and in compression (to support the rail) while providing enough flexibility to cushion impacts of wheels on rail. And, it is "nailable," so that the very simplest method of fastening rail to tie can be used.

Two major modifications have been made over the years to extend tie life. Steel *tie plates*, as long as 18 in. for the heaviest traffic, spread the load of the rail over a large enough area to prevent local crushing and cutting of the wood.

Pressure impregnation in which as much as 25 lbs of preservative is forced into a 200 lb tie prevents decay. With these and other refinements, such as pre-drilled spike holes (which reduce fiber damage and improve the grip of tie on spike), the service life of first-quality ties has been extended to the range of 25 to 30 or more years.

Wood Substitutes

Reinforced concrete ties of many different designs are in widespread use throughout the world in areas where timber is in short supply. As of 1990, approximately 2,500 miles of track in the United States and Canada is now or will soon be (on the basis of tie-purchase contracts) laid on concrete ties. Most of this trackage is on the Northeast (Washington-Boston) Corridor or on severely curved segments of heavy-traffic freight lines in mountain territory.

Concrete ties are highly uniform but necessarily used in a considerably different overall track system; deficiencies of concrete in tensile and bending strength and in resilience are offset by pre-tensioned steel reinforcement and cushioning pads between rail and ties, with spring clips mating with cast-in-place metal inserts to clamp the rails in place. Under traffic, dynamic action is primarily between tie and ballast, rather than between rail and tie plate as in wood-tie track. Concrete-tie track tends to be more stable, primarily because of the greater weight of the ties (about 700 lbs vs. 225 lbs each) although they are usually spaced about 25% farther apart to take advantage of their uniformity.

The overall relative economy of the two types of track will depend mostly on how long ties actually remain serviceable in practice.

Steel ties save ballast (they're hollow) and have a long service history leaving little uncertainty with respect to lifetime cost, but find use primarily on nonsignaled secondary trackage where assuring long-term electrical insulation between rail and tie is not a factor.

Rail Fasteners

Track stays together primarily because of its geometry. The rail remains upright and in place not because the spike heads prevent it from overturning, but because the wheel forces acting on it (even on curves) are mostly downward rather than sideward and actually tend to keep the rail from turning over. Tightly spiked rail does avoid some of the wear associated with movement between parts as passing wheels slam rail and tie plate down against the tie, but the principal job of any fastening system is to keep the rail from shifting sideways; a standard practice for strengthening track on curves against heavy traffic is the use of additional spikes (in the tie-plate holes provided) to hold the plate more firmly in place. Its shoulders then hold the rail from sliding.

The many proprietary elastic spring-clip rail-tie fastening systems developed for nonwood ties are also adaptable, via a special tie plate spiked in place, to wood-ties track, forming a system of intermediate characteristics usually requiring no separate rail anchors. Also avoided is spike-killing, the damage from multiple re-spiking that may govern wood-tie life on curves where rail must be changed out repeatedly.

Creep

Rail also tries to move lengthwise or "creep," forcing ties and switches out of line and developing stresses tending to make the track buckle sideways. Therefore, all heavy-duty track is equipped with *rail anchors* or *anticreepers*. These are spring clips (Fig. 3-4) which snap onto the base of the rail and come up against the tie to restrain motion. As many as four per tie may be required in places where temperature changes, heavy grades, and train braking, particularly with loaded traffic in one direction, conspire to make the rail "run."

Ballast and Substructure

As you can see by watching wheels closely as they roll along the rail, even the heaviest, best-maintained track is not absolutely rigid; there is a "wave of deflection" moving along under each axle. The amount of this deflection is quantified by the track modulus, defined as the force required to depress the rail one inch for each inch of track length along which the load is considered to be applied. Track modulus values range from less than 2,000 lb/in. for the softest usable track to about 8,000 lb/in. for the heaviest main-line track on the best subgrade; corresponding deflections under the range of axle loads may range from 0.025 to 0.50 inch. As long as this deflection is uniform along the track, the ride can still be perfectly smooth. While this deflection provides some cushioning effect on the unsprung wheels and

41

axles of rolling stock and the upper parts of the track structure itself, track modulus in general tends to be too low rather than too high; the smaller the deflection the less movement and wear there is between the rails, fastenings, and ties.

The major job of the ballast is to hold the ties in place, prevent lateral deflections and spread out the load, which averages about 100 psi underneath the tie, to a pressure lower than the "endurance limit" of the subgrade. This accounts for the modern ballast section standards which cover the tie ends with a shoulder, sometimes 12 to 18 inches from the end of tie. The endurance limit is the pressure which a soil can withstand repeatedly without further settling; it may be as high as 50 psi for some sand-gravel soils, or it may be much lower. In problem areas such as swampy ground, it may be necessary to drive wood piles or even use concrete slabs to spread the load and provide a stable enough foundation to support the ballast and subballast (Fig. 3-4).

Ballast Materials

More than 80 percent of the weight of the track (above the subgrade) consists of ballast, so a primary requirement for ballast material is availability within a reasonable hauling distance. Crushed rock (granite, trap rock, or certain hard sandstones), hard crushed furnace slags, and some forms of dense lava make the best ballast; washed gravel with enough crushed particles to make it interlock into a rigid mass may be almost as good. For lighter duty, limestone, pit-run gravel, cinders, oyster shell, and even coarse sand have been used; today's prevalence of 100-ton freight cars on even secondary trackage is resulting in a shift toward higher-grade ballasting on all lines.

In service, the ability of the ballast to resist degradation from the effects of tie motion (generating "fines" which may "cement" into an impervious mass) and continue to perform its most important function of draining rainwater freely is vital in achieving a low-maintenance, stable track structure. Soggy ballast also freezes in winter, causing higher stresses in the rail and tie system from rough-riding equipment and track heaving when it thaws in the spring.

Overall, good track drainage is of paramount importance. In level country, track is usually laid on a low embankment with side ditches. Where subsoil conditions are good, ballast may be laid directly on the subgrade; in less favorable situations, a subballast of pit-run gravel may be essential. At such high-stress locations as turnouts and grade crossings, addition of a carefully chosen "geotextile" fabric to further spread the load and maintain clean ballast by blocking the migration of subgrade dirt has become virtually standard practice. *Average* traffic "life" of good ballast (to replacement or, more typically, "demotion" to the subballast by burial under new stone) works out to about 250 million gross tons.

Turnouts, Crossings, and Trackwork

Another key "invention" in railroad technology is the "turnout," which diverts the train from one track to another. This relatively simple arrangement (Fig. 3-6), only two moving parts, is built in various lengths to suit the speed required in operating through the diverging (curved) route. Turnout sharpness is designated by the angle of its "frog," the assembly which lets the flanged wheels cross over the opposite rail. The longest turnout in common use is the No. 20 (some railroads go up to a No. 24) which is 152 ft long from point to frog and will allow a train to enter a passing track or branch line at speeds as high as 50 mph. "Equilateral" turnout arrangements which "split the difference" and divide the curvature between the two tracks allow speeds in excess of 50 mph at important junctions or in entering and leaving a section of double track.

To the operating department of the railroad, a turnout is always a "switch," presumably because the only moving parts are the point which divert the wheels from one set of rails to the other. Fig. 3-6 also defines some of the other parts of the turnout assembly.

Crossovers and Crossings

Other important items of "trackwork" are the crossing, crossover, double slip or "puzzle" switch and ladder, illustrated in Fig. 3-7. The most severe impacts on wheels and track elements occur at the frogs in turnouts and crossings. Designing items to accommodate both new and worn wheels as smoothly as possible has been a major challenge. Special features, such as high-manganese, work-hardening steel inserts in turnout and crossing frogs (now usually pre-hardened by detonating a sheet of explosive on the wearing surfaces), and stout rail braces to withstand the side thrust at switch points, are necessary to reduce wear and keep the rails in line without continual adjustment.

Because of effects on track geometry of the forces and impacts involved and the closer tolerances required for safe tracking, maintenance expenditures on such trackwork are high; in heavy-traffic territory, some 40 to 60 percent of the total cost of track maintenance is associated with turnouts.

Nevertheless, it is this simple and versatile system which can be designed to direct trains and cars through any pattern of trackage that made what we call "conventional" railroads so much more flexible and practical than their predecessors.

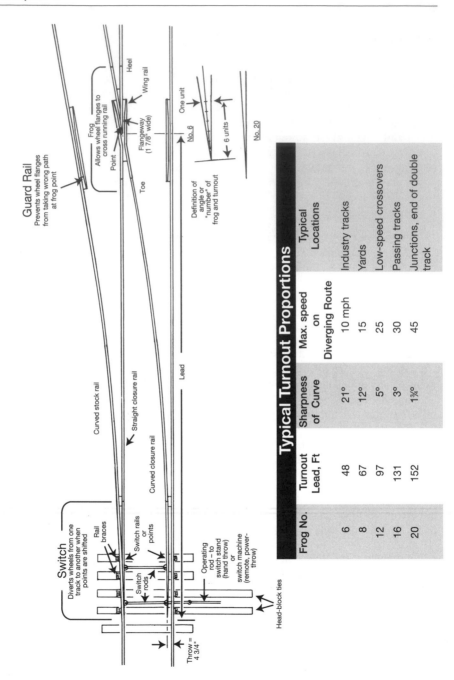

Typical Turnout Proportions

Frog No.	Turnout Lead, Ft	Sharpness of Curve	Max. speed on Diverging Route	Typical Locations
6	48	21°	10 mph	Industry tracks
8	67	12°	15	Yards
12	97	5°	25	Low-speed crossovers
16	131	3°	30	Passing tracks
20	152	1¾°	45	Junctions, end of double track

Fig. 3-6. The Turnout (Left-Handed No. 6 Shown)

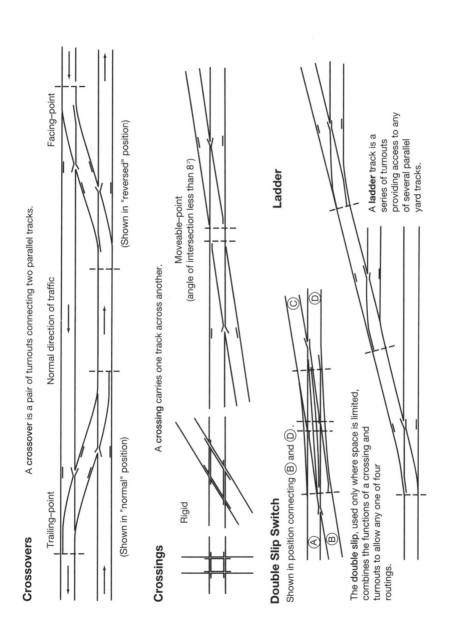

Crossovers

A crossover is a pair of turnouts connecting two parallel tracks.

Trailing-point

Normal direction of traffic

Facing-point

(Shown in "normal" position)

(Shown in "reversed" position)

Crossings

A crossing carries one track across another.

Rigid

Moveable-point
(angle of intersection less than 8°)

Double Slip Switch

Shown in position connecting Ⓑ and Ⓓ.

The **double slip**, used only where space is limited, combines the functions of a crossing and turnouts to allow any one of four routings.

Ladder

A **ladder** track is a series of turnouts providing access to any of several parallel yard tracks.

Fig. 3-7. Trackwork

Track Maintenance and Standards

One of the important characteristics of track in its present form is that all of its components – except for the subgrade itself, which tends to improve with age as it becomes thoroughly settled – wear out and can be replaced on an individual basis without much interruption to traffic. The renewal process does not vary in principle from that of a hundred years ago – worn rail is taken up and replaced; bad ties are singled out, removed, and new ones are slid into place; new ballast is added. After a period of time the entire track consists of new material, but at no time has it been out of service for more than the interval between trains. On branch lines and short-line railroads, the entire process can be handled by a small, well-trained track crew, equipped with relatively simple tools.

The process by which virtually all main-line track maintenance is accomplished, however, has changed completely because of the need to keep costs within reason by mechanizing all possible aspects of the process. Typically, special gangs equipped with major groups of specialized on-rail machines work on a system-wide basis to accomplish two major programs:

- **Tie and Surface Gangs:** Individual crossties (several hundred per mile) are re-placed as required; a "lift" of new ballast is added, the track is realigned and smoothed as directed by laser-sight-controlled machines, and the ballast tamped, compacted, and dressed to contour.

- **Rail Gangs:** Strings of continuous-welded rail (CWR) are installed (or trans-posed) in place of the existing rail (CWR or jointed), and de-stressed as required; strings are re-joined with field welds and insulated-joint plugs.

When track conditions make it appropriate, the two operations may be combined. A line being upgraded or which has reached a seriously deteriorated condition may have to be renovated by a "sledding" or ballast-undercutting procedure in which the entire track is raised, old ballast is removed or cleaned and replaced, and the track returned, realigned, tamped, and compacted and stabilized, reducing subsequent maintenance costs dramatically.

In addition to a spectrum of machines which perform virtually all operations, from spike-driving and anchor-placing to shifting the track superstructure to putting the rails into the desired alignment horizontally and vertically and tamping the ballast to keep it there, an overall measurement of track condition is provided by the *track geometry car*, a relatively recent development now in almost universal use by individual railroads and as part of the FRA inspection responsibility discussed below. Auxiliary wheels and sensors measure the position, curvature, and smoothness of the two rails and the cross-level, gauge, and alignment of the track as the car, a self-propelled or locomotive-hauled unit about as complex (and expensive) as a locomotive, travels rapidly over the line. Instrumentation aboard generates an analog plot which can be used directly in evaluating and correcting deviations from standard and also digital data which can be used in statistical analyses as a basis for longer-term, system-wide scheduling and planning of track maintenance.

Bridges

On many rail routes bridges represent an investment second in size only to the track structure itself; there are approximately 100,000 such structures on railroads in the United States, with an estimated replacement cost of $70 billion in current dollars. The status of one major bridge with respect to today's axle loads may determine the fate of an entire line.

From a track standpoint, bridges may be categorized as open deck or ballast deck (Fig. 3-8). For other than light-traffic, moderate-speed routes, ballast deck is preferred. From a ride-quality standpoint it avoids the jolt from the sudden change in track stiffness entering and leaving the structure; from a maintenance standpoint, it allows continuing normal surfacing and lining procedures across the structure while minimizing the problem of matching railhead elevations between approaches and bridge as periodic reballasting raises the track.

Wood, Concrete, and Steel. Although many miles of them have been replaced with reinforced concrete structures over the years, timber trestles – many with ballast decks – represent some 28% of today's rail bridges vs. 18% for their masonry counterparts, and continue (often with concrete caps between vertical piles and longitudinal stringers) to accommodate main-line loads and speeds.

Steel bridges, accounting for 54% of today's bridges, progress in complexity through simple beam or girder, simple truss, continuous truss, arch and cantilever designs as span lengths increase, with a mixture of types typical in multi-span structures. Any span may be of deck or through design (Fig. 3-8), depending on whether the strength members are beneath or beside the track. In general, the more complex and costly through spans are used only where required to provide the minimum required clearance above a roadway, rail line, waterway, or watercourse.

Bridge Load Ratings. Apart from those solid stone arch structures of the 19th century which, often without reinforcement, will continue to carry loads of 21st century proportions, thanks to the compressive strength of masonry, the load carrying capacity of railroad bridges must be assessed and assured in determining the routing of and preparing for today's heavier and faster trains.

Steel bridge load ratings are still commonly expressed in terms of the Cooper E-system established early in the 20th century. Ranging from about 30 to 80, this rating expresses the calculated ability of the structure to carry a live load represented by double-headed steam locomotives hauling a train of uniformly loaded cars. An E-60 rating assumes that the locomotive driving-axle load is 60,000 lbs and the cars weigh 6,000 lbs per foot of length. To account for the effects of speed and "ham-

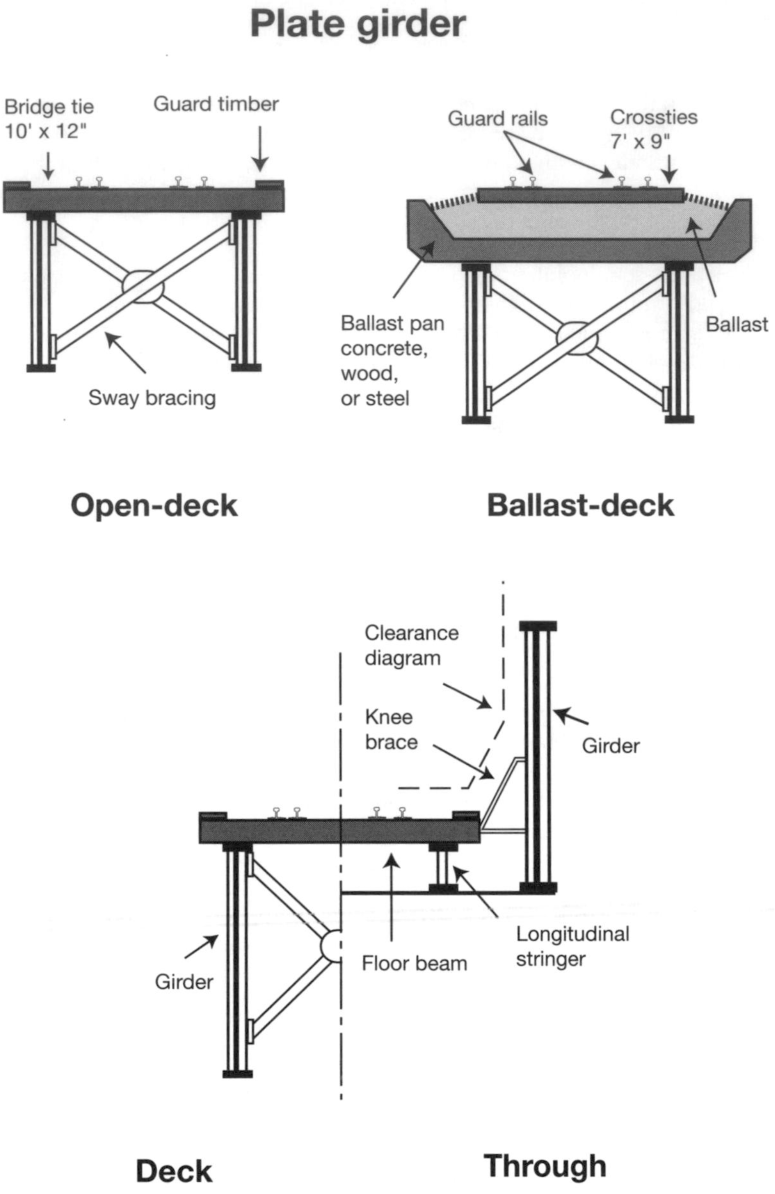

Plate girder

Bridge tie
10' x 12"

Guard timber

Sway bracing

Open-deck

Guard rails

Crossties
7' x 9"

Ballast pan
concrete,
wood,
or steel

Ballast

Ballast-deck

Clearance
diagram

Knee
brace

Girder

Girder

Floor beam

Longitudinal
stringer

Deck

Through

Fig. 3-8. Some Classification of Bridges

merblow" from the unbalanced reciprocating parts of the steam locomotive the static load is multiplied by a generous "impact" factor.

Typical standards to which main-line bridges were designed progressed from E-50 in the World War I era to as high as E-75 by the 1930s. While axle loads have increased greatly since then, locomotives and cars have also grown longer so that the increase in load per foot is considerably smaller; with due regard for the absence of pounding side-rods on diesel-electric locomotives, bridges on many routes have continued to sustain 1990s loadings.

Another concern in bridge survival is fatigue, the development and growth of cracks in steel members related to the number and depth of stress cycles to which a structure has been subjected. The main structural members in a long span experience only one load cycle as a train crosses, whereas elements nearer to the rail such as floor-beam reinforcements may "feel" the passage of each truck or axle and thus accumulate cycles at a rate hundreds of times greater. Warding off possible fatigue collapse under heavier traffic is therefore seen as a matter of stepped-up inspection of such elements to detect early signs of distress.

FRA Standards

The Railroad Safety Act of 1970 for the first time gave the federal government (through the Federal Railroad Administration) jurisdiction over track quality. This has resulted in the establishment of "minimum" safety standards for inspections, roadbed and track structure, geometry, and corresponding speed limits. Six classes of track are defined, ranging from Class 1 (10 mph freight, 15 mph passenger) to Class 6 (110 mph), with "Class 7" geometry and inspection standards certifying 125 mph operation on specific Northeast Corridor segments. State and federal inspectors are empowered to suspend operation over substandard track. Civil monetary penalties are assessed for failure to correct reported deficiencies.

It has been recognized that FRA standards, developed to provide a practical framework relating objective measurements to the minimum track conditions necessary for the safe passage of trains, within the limits of available methods of measurement and decades-old understanding of vehicle/track dynamics, do not necessarily cover all aspects of track structure that can affect safety and also may be more restrictive than necessary in other respects.

From a railroad operating standpoint, the safety standards generally do represent a minimum, since most railroads find that track built and maintained to higher standards results in lower long-term maintenance-of-way and operating expenses.

Since the early 1980s, such research and development funding as the FRA itself has been allocated has been directed solely toward *safety* aspects of railroad operations and maintenance. Continuing technological developments in the power and sophistication of data collection and analysis have improved the understanding of

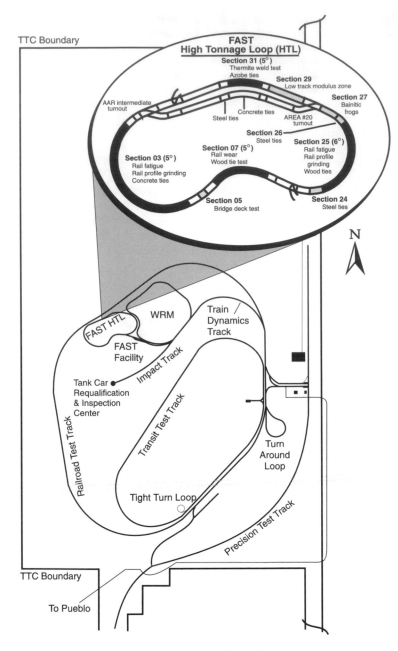

Fig. 3-9. Transportation Technology Center Track Layout

track-train dynamics. Relating the cumulative effects of a series of track irregularities ("low joints") – in rocking a car toward a wheel-lift derailment, for example, rather than that of individual deviations from cross-level – is leading toward a goal of greater precision in revised standards. Making use of such newly available equipment as a split-axle track-loading vehicle that can nondestructively measure track's yard-by-yard resistance to gauge-widening promises to make possible more realistic performance-based standards.

High-Tech and Accelerated Track Testing

One of the main obstacles to the development and widespread adoption of any "better," i.e., more durable and economical as well as safe, track (as well as vehicle) technology is the time it takes in normal service to wear out various components and thus get reliable "whole life cycle" cost comparisons. Since 1976, operations at the Facility for Accelerated Service Testing have been addressing just this problem.

The 52-square-mile Transportation Technology Center (TTC) (Fig. 3-9) is located northeast of Pueblo, Colorado. TTC, established by the federal government as the High-Speed Ground Test Center in the 1960s and still FRA property, has operated in recent years primarily to advance "conventional" railroad and rail transit technology; since 1984, it has been managed and staffed by the Association of American Railroads to carry out tests in support of association, government, individual railroad, and industry supplier research and development programs. Beginning January 1998, AAR's Board of Directors approved a "spin off" of RT operations to form a wholly owned subsidiary of the AAR, now doing business as Transportation Technology Center, Inc.

In addition to the FAST, high-speed (electrified) railroad and transit track loops, major TTC facilities include the Rail Dynamics Laboratory with massive, vehicle dynamics ("roller rig") and fatigue-life test machines, impact tracks, a brake/wheel dynamometer and a variety of test cars including a Track Loading Vehicle capable of safely applying vertical and horizontal forces to evaluate lateral ("gauge-holding") track-strength on a tie-by-tie basis and determining the effect of L/V ratios and rail contours on derailment probabilities.

On the FAST "High-Tonnage Loop," every day's operation of a test train of 11,000 tons or so can subject the track to as much as 15 times the daily gross mainline tonnage. While not all the aspects of "real world" railroad speeds, consists, and climatic variations – as well as those deterioration effects associated with time itself – can be represented in FAST experiments, crucial and otherwise unobtainable quantitative insights in many matters have been obtained:

- Effects of track lubrication on wheel and rail wear.
- Comparative curve wear of standard and premium (heat-treated and alloy steel) rail.

51

- Effects of track structure and alignment on the development of rail corrugation (periodic shallow depressions in the wearing surface of the railhead from heavy traffic, which must be treated by removing metal with a rail-grinding train).
- Life and stability of various materials, sizes, cross-sections and treatments of ballast.
- Benefits of operating improved suspension of freight car trucks.

A somewhat unexpected revelation from FAST testing in the late 1980's was that railhead lubrication significantly reduced drag (and therefore wheel wear and fuel consumption) on tangent track as well as on curves. Confirmed by subsequent over-the-road testing, this finding led to widespread, routine extension of flange lubrication to straight track (primarily by the addition of flange lubricators to about 8,500 locomotives within four years) for calculated net annual before tax fuel (immediate) and maintenance (long-term) savings or more than $250 million.

Among the most significant experiments have been the Heavy Axle Load tests conducted to determine the variable-cost comparisons and safety implications associated with general operation of "125-ton" (39-ton axle load) cars vs. the 33-ton axle load of the current 100-ton vehicles. Maintenance costs will go up, but how much – enough to negate the cost savings associated with moving the tonnage with fewer cars? Instrumentation measuring forces and wear at numerous points throughout the track structure has also pinpointed unanticipated types of degradation indicating specific areas in which research and redesign or changes in maintenance standards and practices should pay off.

Researchers continued to assess the benefits of increasing axle loads in Phase III of the Heavy Axle Load (HAL) program, which surpassed 300 million gross tons of testing in 1997. The HAL program is jointly sponsored by the Association of American Railroads and the Federal Railroad Administration.

The industry is pushing toward implementing heavier axle loads to offset decreasing track-time availability and higher operating costs. However the benefits of hauling more cargo in fewer cars must be weighed against increased wear of equipment and track structure.

Phase III of the HAL program at the Facility for Accelerated Service Testing (FAST) focuses on controlled-environment research to demonstrate the benefits of using improved-suspension trucks to reduce applied forces of heavy axle loads.

Analysis shows that the higher equipment costs associated with improved-suspension trucks are more than offset by reductions in expenditures for track capital and maintenance, equipment maintenance, and fuel.

In tests at FAST, improved-suspension trucks doubled the wear life of premium rail and standard rail on medium curves.

Other studies at FAST have shown that the use of improved-suspension trucks under heavy axle loads reduces wear on other components, including wheels and wood ties. This is due to the lower lateral forces imparted to the track.

In addition, fuel consumption at FAST was reduced by 23 percent in 1997 due to reduced curving forces offered by the improved suspensions.

AAR researchers in 1997 also continued ongoing analysis of revenue-service studies on the effects of heavy-haul traffic on turnout components. This long-term study of a Union Pacific coal line through Lusk, Wyoming, compared the effects of heavy axle loads on frog life of standard and high-integrity rail bound manganese (RBM) frogs and spring-rail frogs.

The No. 20 high-integrity RBM frogs are lasting more than three times longer than the No. 20 standard RBM frogs, allowing the railroad to move an average of 495 million gross tons of traffic before replacement. In addition, these high-integrity frogs permitted an increase of tonnage between repairs. The No. 10 spring-rail frogs have given average life of more than 10 times longer than standard No. 10 frogs.

Some Current Track Developments

Swing-nose frogs in which the frog point is also movable to provide continuous support for wheels crossing the opposing rail are beginning to find application in North America in two situations: reducing maintenance in extremely heavy-tonnage situations where the life of explosive-hardened manganese-steel frog inserts may be measured in months rather than years and accommodating No. 30 or shallower crossing angles compatible with speeds through the diverging route of 70 mph and above where passenger train schedules may benefit.

For sidings where most of the traffic is via the main route, the century-old spring-frog turnout, with recent improvements, is back in favor on many roads. The wing rail is spring-loaded against the frog point but pushed aside by wheel flanges on the secondary route, eliminating impact at the frog by providing continuous support to wheels on the main track.

High-speed scanning and data collection technology, much of it laser-based, is making possible such feats as real-time railhead wear and dynamic gauge-widening (a measure of track strength) data collection. Track geometry, including pin-pointing the location of a defect within a matter of feet, is now routinely carried out at 125 mph.

Continuous-action track machines, which maintain steady forward motion while their active components (tamping heads, for example) do their thing in stop-and-go fashion, are significantly increasing productivity in such major maintenance functions as track surfacing and rail renewal.

Compactor/stabilizers apply vibratory forces directly to the rails, effectively simulating the effect of thousands of gross tons of traffic in settling track after maintenance. This eliminates or greatly reduces the need for or duration of traditional post-track-work slow orders.

The Locomotive

4

It was the development of a practical steam locomotive that revolutionized land transportation, and it is still the locomotive, diesel-electric or straight electric, that makes the railroad go. Though the locomotive is a complicated machine, there are just two factors, *horsepower* and *tractive force (or tractive effort)* which determine its ability to move trains. The particular combinations of horsepower and tractive effort needed for any particular job determine the type of locomotive that is needed. The range of assignments the motive power department of a railroad must handle will determine the make-up of its fleet of engines.

Tractive Force

Developing the tractive force to move a train involves several variables. Fig. 4-1 indicates the *tractive force* needed at the driving wheel rims to start and move tonnage up various grades. The locomotive generates this pull by gripping the rails with its driving wheels. To keep the wheels from slipping, the weight they carry (usually the entire weight of the locomotive, since all wheels are drivers on most of today's diesels) must be several times the tractive force to be developed: Tractive force = weight on drivers x coefficient of adhesion. The *coefficient of adhesion* of wheel on rail does not vary much with the size of the wheel or with the weight it is carrying, but it varies all over the lot with rail condition and it has recently been established that it also varies with the amount of *creep* (relative motion) between wheel and rail, being significantly higher when the tread is slipping slightly on the rail than when there is no slippage. Once *rapid* slippage occurs, the coefficient of friction drops far below the static value and power must be reduced to regain traction.

The static coefficient of adhesion may be less than 0.1 (10 percent) on slimy, wet rail or as high as 0.4 on dry, clean, sanded rail. With the adhesion-control systems used during most of the diesel era many railroads have settled on a dispatchable adhesion factor of about 0.18. In assigning motive power, this is a level expected to provide good assurance that the train will, under normal weather and other conditions, successfully surmount the ruling grades on its run. This assumes the benefit of the sanders (a byproduct of the steam era which blew dry sand on the railhead in front of each wheel) with which all locomotives are equipped. Recent advances (discussed later) make 25% adhesion an attainable figure, in which case the weight on drivers must be four times the tractive force needed to start the train and keep it moving. This is the figure assumed in Fig. 4-1. As is pointed out in the performance summary of Fig. 4-11, making full use of the *horsepower* of road locomotives requires high adhesion ratios only at the lower speeds.

The right side of Fig. 4-1 shows the total locomotive weight needed for various amounts of tonnage and grade. Since most modern diesels for main-line service carry about 60,000 to 70,000 lbs on each axle, there is another scale on the extreme right side of Fig. 4-1 that shows about how many powered locomotive axles it will take. The graph stops at 250,000 lbs because that is the point at which the possibility of coupler knuckle failure (minimum strength 350,000 lbs) begins to appear. If more force is needed, some of it should be supplied by a second locomotive, "pusher" locomotive, or "helper." Other factors affecting the load a locomotive can pull are ruling grade and slack. On level track a locomotive can start a lot of tonnage. On practically any section of railroad, though, the track is not all level, and the *ruling grade* determines what can be hauled. This is the particular point on the run at which the combination of grade and curve resistance makes the train pull hardest and, therefore, "rules" how heavy a load can be given to the locomotive. It may not be the steepest grade on the route, since a short grade may not affect all the train at the same time. And it may not occur at the same point for all trains. Also on a long train of lighter cars, the rear end may be coming downhill and helping push the front end over the top. Fig. 2-10 additionally shows that energy in a train going 60 mph is enough to lift its weight 115 ft, so a short incline may be run as a "momentum grade," if conditions are such that trains can get a good run for the hill.

The pull required to *start* moving a single freight car may be as much as 15 or 20 lbs per ton. The *rolling* friction of 4 to 6 lbs is used in calculation because the slack in the couplers and draft gear between cars allows the locomotive to start the train one car at a time, with the cars already moving helping start the ones to the rear. With the very large tractive force available with most diesel combinations, "taking slack" to start isn't usually necessary. Virtually slackless trains such as consists of RoadRailer or articulated multi-platform double-stack equipment, may warrant a higher friction figure, although the horsepower assigned to keep these trains on schedule usually results in low adhesion requirements.

Horsepower

As discussed previously in connection with the amount of energy required to move trains by various routes (Fig. 2-10), horsepower is a measure of the *rate* of doing work. At zero speed, horsepower is by definition also zero, but to move the train at any desired speed above that takes horsepower. Fig. 4-2 shows how much it takes to move one gross ton (locomotive, cars, and lading) at any speed, on level track and various grades. The curves on the graph are for straight track and cars averaging 50 tons weight, so the exact figure representing the best estimate for a par-

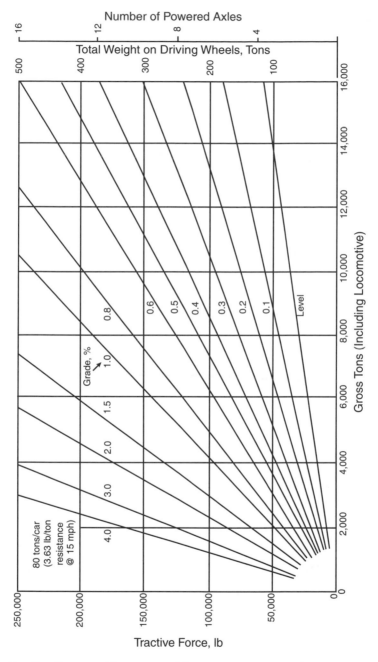

Fig. 4-1. Tractive Force vs. Tonnage and Grade

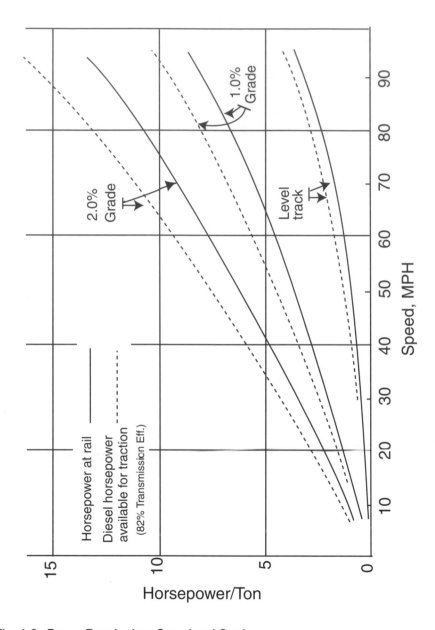

Fig. 4-2. Power Required vs. Speed and Grade

ticular situation will vary with factors such as wind, roadbed quality, uncompensated curves, heavier or lighter cars, etc. Some generalities from these curves will give a feel for motive power requirements:

- Power requirements for overcoming rolling friction are moderate; a 3,000-hp locomotive can move more than 5,000 tons at 30 mph on level track.

- Grade is highly significant for a heavy train; a train powered at 1.5 hp per ton, which could make 60 mph on level track, will slow to about 22 mph on a grade of one percent and to 10 mph on two percent. A train powered at 4 hp per ton (for example, having an 8-hp engine in your automobile) has a "balancing speed" (at which power available just balances train resistance) of more than 90 mph; it can make 55 mph up the one percent grade or 33 mph up two percent.

Compared to the effects of grade, the increase in train resistance with speed is moderate. Below 30 mph or so, horsepower increases only slightly more than directly with speed – twice the power to do the same amount of work in half the time if speed is doubled. Even at 70 mph with a train of empty cars where most of the power goes to overcoming air drag, resistance is less than that from a one percent grade (Fig. 2-8). Because it is a long, narrow thing which has had to knock only a small hole in the atmosphere for its total weight, a freight train's energy consumption rises much less rapidly with speed than that of a highway vehicle.

Diesel Horsepower and Electric Horsepower

Fig. 4-2 shows two sets of curves; the upper curves are for the nominal "diesel horsepower available for traction" which is usually given as the locomotive's rating. Fig. 4-3 shows what happens to this power within the locomotive as it is converted to electricity and then back to tractive force by the traction motors. The lower curves on Fig. 4-2 represent the horsepower which is actually developed at the rims of the driving wheels. This is typically about 82 percent of the diesel horsepower available for traction.

Drawbar Horsepower

After some of the horsepower at the rail is used to move the locomotive itself, we have the useful horsepower at the rear coupler which moves the train. There is no "typical" percentage which goes into moving the locomotive because it varies due to relative weight of engine and trains. If a 400-ton locomotive is hauling 8,000 tons, over 95 percent of the rail power is being used to haul the cars, but if it has only 400 tons in tow it is using half its power to move itself, good reason for using, as closely as possible, the lightest locomotive that will do the job.

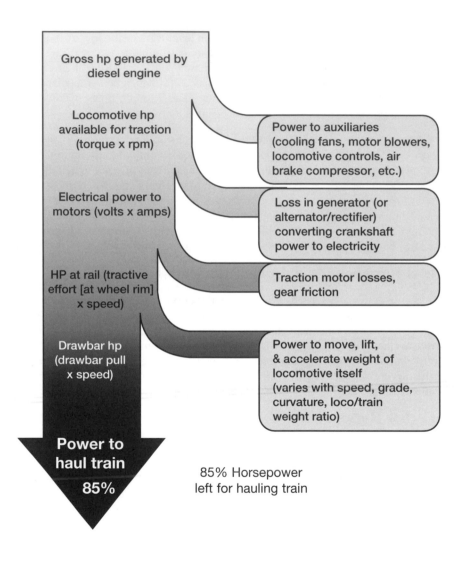

Fig. 4-3. Different Horsepower Ratings

Acceleration

The rate at which a train can gain speed is determined by the amount of tractive force remaining after overcoming train resistance. To provide the same tractive force at *twice* the speed takes *twice* the horsepower, so gaining speed takes more and more locomotive power as speed increases. Fig. 4-4 shows a few of the innumerable combinations of acceleration rates and grade in terms of the horsepower per ton required at different speeds. At low speed, acceleration may be fairly rapid – up to 1.5 mph per second for a commuter train and up to 0.3 mph per second for a fast freight. As the speed increases, horsepower doesn't mean too much; our hotshot freight with 4.0 hp per ton can accelerate at only about 0.1 mph per second at 70 mph.

The Diesel-Electric Locomotive

The key invention that made the steam locomotive powerful enough to haul itself briskly and still have enough left over to haul a useful load was discovered by Richard Trevithick in 1803; he took the steam which was exhausted from the locomotive cylinders after it had pushed the pistons and directed it up the smokestack through a nozzle. The intermittent puffing action not only made the machine into a "choo choo" but sucked air so vigorously through the firebox that the boiler could generate steam at a rate many times greater than had been possible in a stationary engine of the same size and weight. The scheme was also self-regulating; the harder the locomotive worked, the more steam went out the stack, the faster the fuel burned, and the more steam was available.

Many other inventions, from equalizers (to keep the proper amount of weight on each wheel while going over rough track) to a headlight (to allow running trains at night on unfenced American routes), were needed to make the basic "iron horse" suitable for its work. However, for 125 years the reciprocating steam locomotive with its exhaust-stimulated white-hot fire represented the most effective way to get the necessary horsepower out of a machine no more than 11 feet wide, 16 feet high, short enough to swing around railroad curves at speed, and simple enough to be operated by two men. Numerous attempts to adapt more sophisticated and theoretically efficient steam generating systems to locomotive requirements were made; none had any lasting success.

Those involved in locomotive engineering and design eventually turned to another energy generating source, diesel power. The diesel engine was invented in 1901, at a time when the principles of electric railroad traction were fairly well understood. From the start it was apparent that the diesel could be several times more efficient in converting the energy in fuel to mechanical power. But it was not until the 1930s that the weight and bulk of the diesel began to be reduced to the point where it could compete with steam in other than low-speed switching service. The key developments leading to the eventual shift to diesel power for all railroad ser-

61

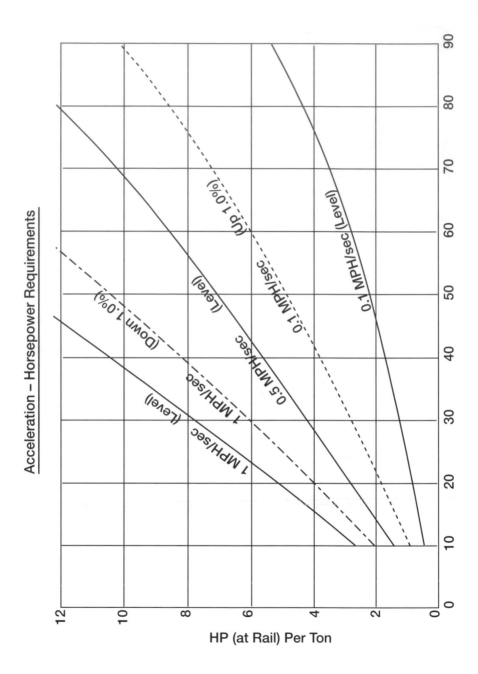

Fig. 4-4. Acceleration-Horsepower Requirements

vices (completed in the mid-1950s) were made in the 1920s. These were primarily in the area of reliable controls to match the load of the electrical generating and propulsion systems to the fuel input and power output of the diesel engine.

Diesel Locomotive Configurations

The American diesel-electric locomotive is now in its third generation of development, being a significant part of the motive power fleet for somewhat over 45 years and demonstrating a typical lifetime in heavy main-line service of 15 to 20 years. For the most part there have been only two or three companies manufacturing main-line locomotives during the diesel era. Despite standardization efforts, as Fig. 4-5 indicates, the number of locomotive configurations has been considerable. Many are now virtually extinct or live on only in the form of components in "remanufactured" units; only Types 7, 9, 10, 12, and 13 are currently represented in the builders' order books. The vast majority of freight locomotives are of just two types (four- and six-axle "road switchers"), able to handle all main-line assignments by being assembled into appropriate multiple-unit (MU) combinations under the control of a single engineer.

After remaining at a relatively constant 28,000 from the completion of dieselization in 1958 until 1982, Class I railroad diesel-unit ownership (including Amtrak) declined steadily to slightly fewer than 20,000 by 1988 and has remained relatively constant since. While most new units are now of 4,000 to 6,000 hp (as permitted by advanced adhesion-control systems) vs. 2,000 to 3,000 hp for those being retired, and average horsepower has thus risen slightly, most of the overall increase in traffic in the later years of this period has been moved only by virtue of the improved availability typical of new and rebuilt units and much more intensive utilization, including extensive use of such time-honored practices as power-sharing on run-through engine assignments and seasonal, short- or long-term leases – from other railroads or the more recently numerous manufacturer, rebuilder, and private-owner leasing fleets.

In addition to the locomotives operated by the Class I railroads there are an estimated 2,500 to 3,000 units, mostly switching and general-purpose road locomotives of 600 to 2,000 hp, on regional, local, and switching and terminal railroads.

Anatomy of One Unit

Fig. 4-6 shows the arrangement of principal components in a typical high-horsepower (3,000 hp) "road switcher" unit as built in the 1980s. The term road switcher does not necessarily indicate a locomotive's function but refers to its body configuration, with a narrow hood (the "long end") enclosing the engine and other machinery and a short hood at the opposite end of the cab, a vestige of the enclosure providing space for a steam generator in the first such multi-purpose units (Type 7 on Fig. 4-5). With reasonable visibility from the cab in either direction, running gear

	Diagram	Type of Locomotive Unit	AAR-Std. Axle-Truck Designation (See Note)	Typical Horsepower (Per Unit) (Dates Built)
	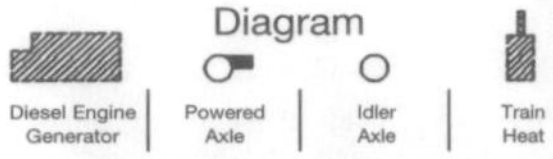 Diesel Engine Generator / Powered Axle / Idler Axle / Train Heat			
1		Road Freight Cab (A- Unit)	B-B	1,350-1,750
				1941-1950
2		Road Freight Booster (B-Unit, Hostler Controls Only)	B-B	1,350-1,750
				1941-1950
3		Passenger Cab Unit (B-Units also built)	A1A-A1A	1,800-2,400
				1937-1950
4		Light-Duty/ Industrial Switchers "Commercial" Diesel Engines often radio controlled	B-B	300-350/1,000
				1926-Date
5		Medium/Heavy- Duty Switchers (100 & 125 ton units)	B-B	600/1,000- 1,000-1,500
				1936-1980
6		Loco + "Slug" Combination ("Powered Trailer" Semi-permanently coupled)	Various– B-B & B-B Illustrated	1,500-3,600
				Usually Rebuilds
7		General-Purpose Road Switcher (Hood-type Car body; Steam Boiler optional)	B-B	1,000-2,300
				1940-Date
8		Low-Axle-Load Road Switcher	A1A-A1A	1,000-1,800
				1946-1950
9		"Special-Duty" Six-Axle Road Switcher (Later models low nose)	C-C	2,400-4,000
				1955-Date
10		High-Horsepower Road Switcher (Low nose)	B-B	2,500-4,000
				1961-1994
11		Dual-Engine "Unit Roduction" Locomotive (Wide-cab hood car body)	D-D (Also built as B-B + B-B)	5,000-6,600
				1964-1969
12		Cowl-Car Body Passenger 3ø 480V "Head-end power" For electric train heat/AC	B-B	3,000-4,000
				1974-Date
13		Wide-("Safety") Cab Freight (May also have cowl car body)	B-B and C-C	3,300-6,000
				1984-Date

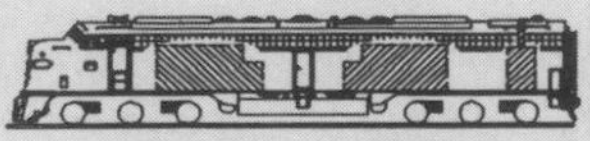

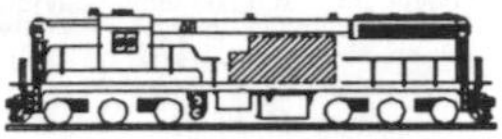

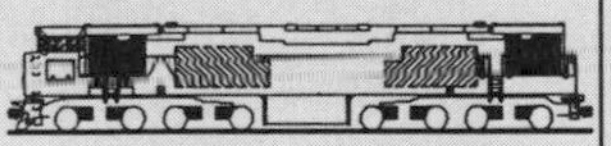

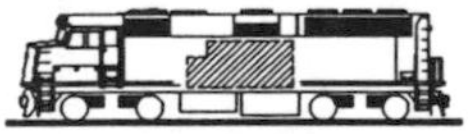

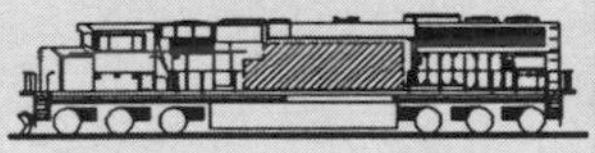

Note: "Bo-Bo" and "Co-Co" in European designation, where "B" and "C" are used to designate connected drive between axles of two- or three-axle trucks. 1,2,3 = idler (non-powered) axles, in both systems.

Fig. 4-5. Representative Diesel-Electric Locomotive Types

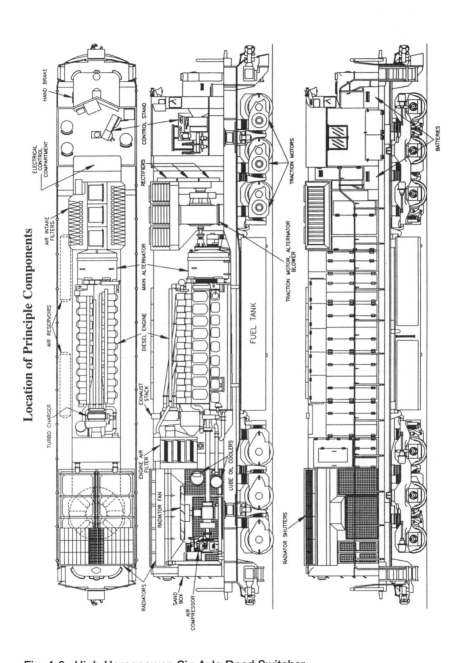

Location of Principle Components

HAND BRAKE

ELECTRICAL CONTROL COMPARTMENT

CONTROL STAND

RECTIFIERS

AIR INTAKE FILTERS

MAIN ALTERNATOR

AIR RESERVOIRS

DIESEL ENGINE

TRACTION MOTORS

TURBO CHARGER

EXHAUST STACK

TRACTION MOTOR, ALTERNATOR BLOWER

ENGINE AIR FILTER

FUEL TANK

LUBE OIL COOLERS

RADIATOR FAN

BATTERIES

RADIATOR SHUTTERS

RADIATORS

SAND BOX

AIR COMPRESSOR

Fig. 4-6. High-Horsepower, Six-Axle Road Switcher

and gearing suitable for road speeds, and adaptability to supplying heat for passenger train use, these units could literally do anything and ushered in the second generation of diesel power in the early 1950s.

Cab Configurations

With the short hood chopped to a low-nose configuration, the road switcher (Fig. 4-7) with a full-width windshield (but still some degree of grade crossing collision protection for the crew when running short-end forward) has become a more single-ended machine. Diesel locomotives *operate* equally well in either direction, so to avoid having to be concerned about the matter some railroads now locate the engineer's control stand on the left side (looking out over the low nose). When operating long-end forward, this places the engineer on the right where he can see signals, and the unit again becomes a bi-directional machine.

Starting in the late 1980s, high-horsepower freight locomotives built for service in the United States joined their Canadian counterparts (configured earlier on in connection with car bodies better matched to the winter climate) in sporting enclosed full-width cabs. Also better accommodating the conductor and his paperwork in cabooseless consists, the sound-insulated, air-conditioned "comfort" cab is entered from the ground via the front platform, nose door, and a passage way through a heavily reinforced nose structure rather than via a ladder and side door.

Inside, the standard "AAR Control Stand" located beside the engineer's seat is superseded by a forward-facing control console behind the full-width front windows which, in accordance with FRA standards for anti-vandal vehicle glazing, must be capable of protecting occupants from specified-caliber bullets and cornerwise impact of a concrete block at 35 mph.

To organize and coordinate an ever-increasing number and variety of revisions and sophistication of cab displays, an AAR configuration standard is in effect. Traditional dials and gauges – speedometer, air pressure, motor current, train radio controls, and cab signal indications – are merged with the recently added EOT (end-of-train) and slave-unit monitors on console-mounted displays directly in front of the engineer, with provision for the orderly addition of more complex locomotive diagnostic read-outs and such other anticipated items as the Positive Train Separation location, authority, and supervisory link and, perhaps, such train-handling aids as onboard computer-generated displays of train vs. trackprofile travel, acceleration/deceleration and calculated coupler forces throughout the consist.

By 1995, FRA rule "ditch lights" of the type found effective in Canada in improving the crew's view of the right-of-way have been phased in. With the headlight (kept lighted by day since 1948), they form a distinctive triangular pattern to augment motorist train-awareness at highway crossings.

Fig. 4-7. Road Switcher – EMD SD40-2

Units intended only for yard switching duties (Fig. 4-8) have less horsepower, simpler trucks not suitable for road speeds, a lower long hood for 360° visibility, no short hood, and, usually, no provision for multiple-unit (MU) operations. Nevertheless, many of their components, from traction motors to cylinder assemblies, are interchangeable with those of road power – an important saving in everything from parts inventory to the training of machinists. The general principles of locomotive design and operation in present-day Type 5 units are similar to those in the Type 9 and 10 units.

The Diesel Engine

The prime mover itself is a single V-type diesel with 8 to 20 cylinders rated at about 125 hp per cylinder if "normally aspirated" or up to 250 hp per cylinder if turbocharged. General Electric-built locomotives use four-cycle engines (one power stroke per two revolutions); General Motors units (prior to 1997) have always used the two-cycle principle.

In accordance with North American practice, the diesel is a relatively low-speed machine, idling at about 400 rpm and developing full power at about 1,000 rpm, because it is designed for long life and low maintenance cost rather than for light weight. Even so, the diesel engine and its attached main generator represent less than 15 percent of the total locomotive weight. Many locomotives are "ballasted" (usually by making the underframe of thicker steel plate than necessary) to provide more tractive force.

The other part of the power plant is the generator or (on recently built high-horse-power units) alternator which converts crankshaft motion into electrical energy (600 volt DC) for traction. In the same scheme as now used in automobile electrical systems, AC produced by the alternator is immediately converted to DC by solid-state rectifiers. The alternator, with slip rings on its rotor instead of a multi-segment commutator and brushes, is somewhat simpler and, most important, smaller in diameter, so that up to 4,000 hp can be developed in the space available.

Numerous auxiliary systems in a locomotive provide: compressed air for the brakes; power for blowers for traction motors; cooling for lube oil, and dynamic brakes; and 78 volt DC for battery charging, fuel pump motors, and locomotive controls. Typical capacities for a 3,000 hp unit are: engine cooling water, 300 gal.; engine lube oil, 250 gal.; fuel, 3,000 gal.; and sand, 2 tons.

The Turbocharger

High-horsepower units use a turbocharger driven by the diesel exhaust gases to ram extra air into the cylinders each power stroke. Since the amount of fuel that can be burned is determined by how much air is available, this increases the power of the engine by up to about 50 percent without increasing its size or operating speed. The turbocharger is a compact but high-speed device requiring considerable main-

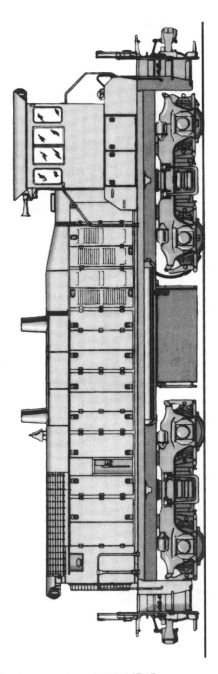

Fig. 4-8. Switching Locomotive – EMD MP15

tenance, so many two-cycle locomotives used in switching or local services where horsepower is less important are built without turbocharging.

Running Gear

The following discussion relates to the series DC traction motor, universal in North American locomotive service until 1985 and which will remain in the majority of units for some time to come. Technology, characteristics, and acceptance of the AC traction motor and its power supply are discussed later.

Standard design uses two swiveling trucks per unit, each with two or three axles and traction motors. The traction motor is rated at 600 volts DC. Its magnetic field windings are connected in series with its armature to provide high starting torque. To adapt a common motor to all classes of service with the standard 40-inch diameter driving wheels, different gear ratios are used. Typical ratios range from a 15-tooth pinion on the motor shaft engaging a 62-tooth gear on the axle which provides a maximum speed of 71 mph to a 57:20 ratio for 102 mph. The traction motor speed is thus kept at a maximum of about 2,400 rpm.

The motors are arranged in the "nose-suspended" configuration illustrated in Fig. 4-9, exactly the same principle used in streetcars since 1890. This is the simplest way to allow the wheels to move up and down over track irregularities while transmitting the motor torque to the spring-supported truck frame. About half of the nose-suspended motor's weight is supported by the axle and is, therefore, "unsprung," subject to impact loads and, in turn, subjecting the track to similar forces.

The wheels, axles, gears, gear case, and traction motor in the nose-suspended system constitute a single unit or "combo" which can be changed out for rebuilding with a minimum of out-of-service time. But the engineer is kept aware of the impact problem with this arrangement because of the requirement that power be shut off while the locomotive is passing over crossings with another railroad track. Otherwise, the bouncing of the motor brushes can cause big voltage transients and motor arc-overs. Traction motors are cooled by a torrent of air supplied via flexible ducts from body-mounted blowers. Improvements in motor insulation and design have allowed continuous power ratings to approach 1,000 hp per motor in a unit that will fit between the wheels and clear the roadbed. At starting and low speed the current required to generate full tractive force creates more heat than the blowers can take away.

At any current level above the continuous rating the motors will be burned out if the overload lasts too long.

If the combination of tonnage and grade is appropriate for the locomotive power and gear ratio, the train will reach the summit of the hill or attain a speed where blower cooling can keep up with the heat being generated before the motor windings reach a dangerous temperature. If it doesn't, the engineer must stop and allow

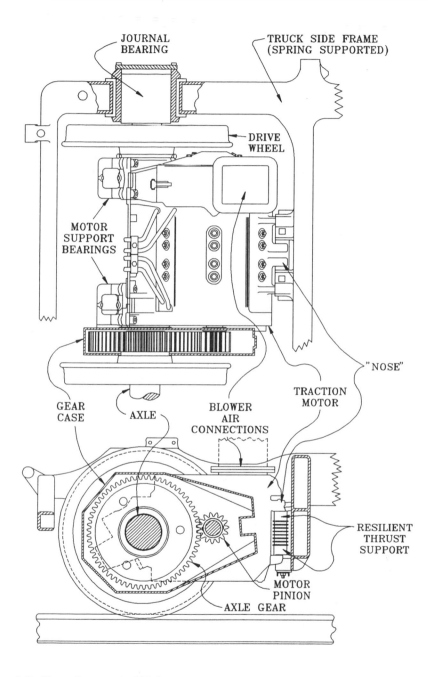

Fig. 4-9. Nose-Suspended Motor

ings reach a dangerous temperature. If it doesn't, the engineer must stop and allow the motors to cool.

Radial Trucks

To accommodate three traction motors and transmit tractive force from the wheel treads to the locomotive frame with a minimum of weight shift among its axles, the six-wheel truck designed for maximum adhesion has a relatively long wheelbase. This can generate extra flange wear and severe lateral rail forces on curved track, to the extent that only four-axle units may be allowed on some routes. As discussed in Chapter 5 in connection with car-truck design, allowing the axles to "steer" themselves into a radial attitude can be expected to improve curving performance significantly. Although the fore-and-aft motion in adjusting to an eight-degree curve (about the maximum through which full steering is practical) is small – one-half inch or so at the journal box – rather precise stiffness and damping relationships between the frame and wheelsets must be maintained if both radial action and freedom from hunting on tangent track are to be achieved. There already being no shortage of gear cases, blower ducts, and the like to fill up the interior of a power truck, accommodating the steering arms and diagonal linkage required in a radial truck in a maintainable configuration has been challenging, to say the least. Nevertheless, such a production six-wheel truck that entered service in 1994 has demonstrated significant reduction in wheel wear and lateral curving forces no higher than that of a standard four-wheel counterpart.

Fig. 4-10. Radial Truck

Fig. 4-11. General Electric Desk Top Console With Two PC Screens

Locomotive Controls

Controls to utilize the locomotive's full capabilities in responding to the engine-man and to allow several units to be coupled into multiple-unit consists controlled from one cab are among the most complex parts of the machine. The control stand itself now has a minimum of levers, but each works through elaborate circuitry (now mostly solid-state) to keep the diesel fuel supply and the electrical load on the generator in step so that properly graduated power levels are applied to moving the train.

Primary controls are the *reverse/selector handle* which determines the direction of travel and selects power or braking action (if the locomotive is equipped for dynamic braking) and the *throttle* handle with which it is interlocked so that improper combinations are impossible. The throttle has eight positions or run zones above "idle," each representing a higher horsepower output.

The primary throttle control adjusts the fuel injection control system of the diesel to maintain a specific rpm for each notch. This determines how much power it can develop, since it takes in a specific amount of air for each revolution and can thus effectively burn fuel and convert it into energy at a corresponding rate.

At the same time, the magnetic field of the generator is regulated so that the electrical power it is producing (and, therefore, the resistance it offers to the turning of

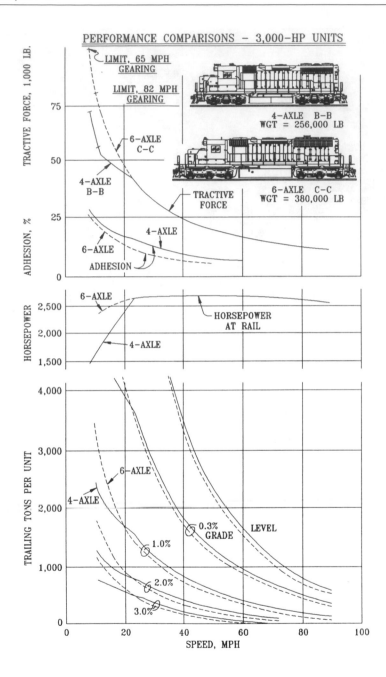

Fig. 4-12. Performance Comparisons – 3,000 HP Units

the crankshaft) just matches the horsepower the diesel can develop, and the system is stable at the governed speed.

As the train speed increases, the traction motors generate more and more voltage ("back EMF") opposing the voltage they are receiving from the generator; at a certain speed, net available generator voltage will become insufficient to develop full traction motor power. At this *"transition"* point, the motors, which have typically been connected in series to keep the low-speed motor current draw within limits, must be reconnected in parallel to put full generator voltage across them and let train speed continue to increase. In early-model diesels, transition (like shifting gears in an automobile) had to be made by the engineer; if required, it is now automatic.

The engineman's principal guide to locomotive performance is the *ammeter,* which shows the current actually going through the motors and, therefore, the rate at which they are heating up. It is marked to indicate the maximum continuous current draw allowable and the time limits which must not be exceeded at several values above this.

Locomotive Performance

Fig. 4-12 shows what can be expected from a 3,000 hp diesel-electric unit and compares the two versions available – the four-axle locomotive with its short-wheelbase trucks and the six-axle unit, weighing about 50 percent more, with its six traction motors but carrying the same diesel engine/alternator combination. Either can be equipped with different gear ratios for the desired maximum and minimum speed limits.

Why Six Axles Instead of Four?

The six-axle locomotive has two extra traction motors and gear sets to maintain, and its long-wheelbase trucks can be a problem on track with sharp curves. Over most of the speed range, tractive force is limited by engine horsepower, and the curve is the same for both types of units. The four-axle unit will actually haul a little more tonnage because it has some 55 tons less of its own weight to pull along.

The difference shows up below about 23 mph, where the adhesion required by the lighter unit to develop the tractive force corresponding to its horsepower begins to reach the limit for *reliable* traction – 16 to 18 percent. To keep the engine from being "slippery," its control circuitry is arranged to cut back its power at lower speeds. The six-axle unit thereby moves out in front in hauling capacity. With 50 percent more traction motor thermal capacity, the C-C unit can "lug" that much more tonnage up a grade where low-speed horsepower is needed.

As one would expect, six-axle units are prevalent on divisions where heavy trains must be hauled up long or steep grades, but scarce on lines whose loads are lighter and grades are such that all trains can get over them without dipping below 25 mph for more than brief periods.

Adhesion Control

To increase the spectrum of services in which the less costly four-axle unit can do the job, recent design refinements emphasize achieving adhesion ratios higher than the traditional 18 percent which can be counted on to get the train over the ruling grade in any weather without tying up the main line.

In locomotives with electric drive, the axle with the poorest rail condition (usually the lead axle) governs the performance of the entire consist. One improvement results from connecting all motors in parallel, since this will tend to automatically reduce the power to an individual motor if it starts to run faster than its mates; advances in alternator and motor current and voltage ratings allowing the unit to develop full power over its operating range in permanent-parallel connection have been introduced. Previous methods of detecting incipient wheel slip by comparing the speed differential between axles have been supplemented with more sophisticated electronic computation of the acceleration of individual axles or of differences between wheel-rim and locomotive ground speed (as measured by a radar unit) in current automatic *adhesion-control* systems. These control instantaneous power levels to make full use of the wheel slip/adhesion relationship and replace manual control of the sanders in the case of more serious loss of traction. Under certain circumstances these improvements may increase the tonnage rating of an engine of a given weight by as much as one-third.

Since there is little indication in the cab when wheel slip is occurring somewhere in the locomotive consists, a "wheel slip" light in the control stand is provided in all road units to warn of persistent loss of adhesion requiring the engineer to reduce the throttle setting until conditions improve.

Multiple-Unit Arrangements

On level track a 3,000 hp unit will move the 4,760 gross tons of the "average" freight train at about 34 mph. Most lines, however, have at least some grades in the 0.3 percent range or greater where more than "drag" speeds must be maintained for practical schedules. Tonnage is likely to be assigned, in accordance with computer train performance analysis, on a *horsepower per ton* basis for the particular class of service, which results in more than one unit per train in most cases.

Units to be placed in multiple-unit consists are provided with four or five air hose connections controlling braking and the sanders on all units and a standard 27-pin electrical connector controlling all other functions. It is possible to interconnect units of different makes, horsepower, number of motors, gear ratios, and brake-control equipment and still have the resulting lash-up function as one locomotive. If the units are not matched, there is usually some loss of performance of the more capable units. Maximum speed will be limited to that of the unit with the lowest gearing, for example. But the flexibility of being able to use everything in the roundhouse while providing total power matched to the requirements of each train is a very important factor in achieving good locomotive utilization.

Remote-Control Units

Where heavy trains must be moved up steep grades, additional tractive force must come from somewhere back in the train, if the total required is beyond coupler strength limits. On fairly short grades, helper locomotives run by another engineman are used – usually on the rear end to minimize time lost switching them in and out of the consist. Where there are several major grades scattered throughout a run, it is more economical to use *remote-control units* located at a point in the train where their tractive force will result in the smoothest handling (usually about two-thirds of the way back). These "slave" units are controlled by the engineman in the lead unit by radio control signals somewhat similar to those transmitted by jumper cable to MU'ed trailing units.

The receiver-decoder for these signals is located in one of the slave units (which in turn controls the units MU'ed with it), or in a separate car which can be used with any locomotives. A digital code is used to ensure that the slave listens only to its master's voice, and the slave units automatically go to "idle" if radio communication is not verified every few seconds.

Push-Pull

For commuter train service with its numerous short trips, a great deal of terminal switching is saved by providing a control cab in the rear passenger car, connected to the locomotive by train-line control wires, from which the engineman can run the train on the return runs.

Dynamic Braking

Since a motor can act as a generator if its shaft is turned by an external source of power, the traction motors on most locomotives for over-the-road service are used to provide braking, particularly on descending grades. The current generated is fed to resistance grids where the energy developed from retarding the train is dissipated as heat. The controls are arranged so that the engineman can use the same throttle positions and ammeter readings to control braking and to guard against overheating the motors and sliding the wheels. The saving in wear and tear on brake shoes and rigging throughout the train is sizeable.

Slugs and Mates

Sometimes, the traditional locomotive set-up isn't capable of performing certain tasks. When it comes to pushing cars over the crest in a hump yard at a steady 2 to

4 mph, a single unit has plenty of horsepower but not enough tractive force or traction motor cooling capacity. To remedy this situation, excess power is fed from the diesel unit's generator to a "slug" unit. The slug is a ballasted four- or six-axle unit having traction motors but no engine or generator. This usually home-made combination provides multi-unit, low-speed tractive force with single-unit fuel consumption and engine maintenance. For some over-the-road services where particularly heavy loads must be handled at moderate speeds, "road slug" or "mate" units married to standard road locomotives also furnish that needed tractive force.

Head-End Power

Passenger trains require "hotel" power for heating, lighting, and air conditioning, traditionally obtained from axle-driven generators on the cars and steam piped from a steam-generating boiler on the locomotive. The HEP (Head-End Power) system now in practically universal use in the United States uses 480 volt, three-phase power trainlined from the locomotive unit to provide all such power. In most cases, an alternator coupled directly to the propulsion diesel engine generates the power, with the engine controls programmed to "idle" it at high enough speed to develop full HEP output when no traction power is being produced. Typical HEP output is 500 kW or about 675 hp, which is subtracted from the diesel horsepower available for traction.

Fuel Efficiency

A fundamental shift in locomotive design and operating goals occurred with the many-fold "oil shock" price increases of 1974 and 1979; in the latter year, fuel costs for the first time exceeded locomotive maintenance expenses and became (after labor) the second largest operating cost item. Responses include:

- Multi-microprocessor control systems in post-1986 (and to varying degrees, in upgraded older) locomotives enhance efficiency of the prime mover over the range of operating conditions and tailor the output of power-consuming auxiliaries such as cooling fans more closely to demand.
- Trade-offs in basic engine, turbo, transmission, and auxiliaries design between fuel efficiency and mechanical, electrical, and aerodynamic refinement, first-cost, and complexity have been re-examined.
- Engines and controls are adapted to lower idling speeds (e.g., 250 rpm); units are shut down rather than idled between runs, with stand-by heating and other provisions to facilitate safe shut-down (railroad diesel engines are not adapted to the use of antifreeze) and re-starting in low ambient temperatures.
- Some railroads report fuel savings from MU controls that allow individual units in a consist to be idled during portions of a run where their power is not required to maintain schedule.

Microprocessor Applications

In what is probably the biggest single contribution to diesel efficiency (and low-ered exhaust emissions, a factor of increasing importance as environmental re-quirements are phased in), microprocessor-controlled electronic fuel injection has been widely adopted. Combustion efficiency is improved because the timing as well as the amount of fuel injected can be optimized for each load and speed condition throughout the engine's operating range.

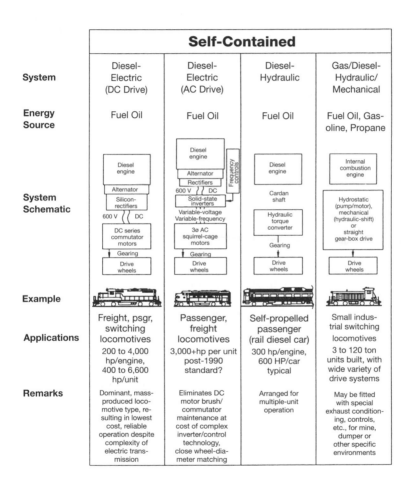

	Self-Contained			
System	Diesel-Electric (DC Drive)	Diesel-Electric (AC Drive)	Diesel-Hydraulic	Gas/Diesel-Hydraulic/ Mechanical
Energy Source	Fuel Oil	Fuel Oil	Fuel Oil	Fuel Oil, Gas-oline, Propane
System Schematic	Diesel engine → Alternator → Silicon-rectifiers 600 V DC → DC series commutator motors → Gearing → Drive wheels	Diesel engine → Alternator → Rectifiers 600 V DC → Solid-state inverters Variable-voltage Variable-frequency → 3ø AC squirrel-cage motors → Gearing → Drive wheels (Frequency controls)	Diesel engine → Cardan shaft → Hydraulic torque converter → Gearing → Drive wheels	Internal combustion engine → Hydrostatic (pump/motor), mechanical (hydraulic-shift) or straight gear-box drive → Drive wheels
Example				
Applications	Freight, psgr, switching locomotives 200 to 4,000 hp/engine, 400 to 6,600 hp/unit	Passenger, freight locomotives 3,000+hp per unit post-1990 standard?	Self-propelled passenger (rail diesel car) 300 hp/engine, 600 HP/car typical	Small indus-trial switching locomotives 3 to 120 ton units built, with wide variety of drive systems
Remarks	Dominant, mass-produced loco-motive type, re-sulting in lowest cost, reliable operation despite complexity of electric trans-mission	Eliminates DC motor brush/commutator maintenance at cost of complex inverter/control technology, close wheel-dia-meter matching	Arranged for multiple-unit operation	May be fitted with special exhaust condition-ing, controls, etc., for mine, dumper or other specific environments

Fig. 4-13. Rail Propulsion Systems (Self-Contained)

The locomotive electronic air brake control (not to be confused with the hoped-for electro-pneumatic train brake discussed elsewhere) substitutes a microprocessor and electrically operated valves to replace the plumber's nightmare of piping within the control stand in quietly handling the complex functions of the modern air brake control logic.

Other Locomotive Types

Although 99 percent of all locomotive horsepower in the United States is diesel-electric, a number of basically different types of motive power are also in use. Multiple-unit, self-propelled commuter and rapid-transit train operations, which are discussed later, amount to several million horsepower. The other important form of locomotive is the straight electric, usable, of course, only where overhead catenary or third rail power supply is available. Fig. 4-13 and 4-14 summarizes the various types of motive power in use, including some hybrids developed to allow running across power-supply boundaries.

The Electric Locomotive

The straight electric locomotive draws its power from an overhead conductor via a sliding shoe held against the wire by a pantograph. The important difference between the electric and diesel-electric is in the electric's ability to draw almost unlimited power from the wire while accelerating its train. The traction motors have a continuous rating, the same as that on their diesel counterparts. But the electrics have a short-time rating (five-minute, for example) which may be almost double that rating. At low speed, the tractive force is adhesion-limited, just as on the diesel, but as the speed increases, the extra horsepower can be used to keep the tractive force at a high value. As Fig. 4-4 shows, the result is much better. A six-axle electric with a continuous-duty rating of 6,000 diesel-equivalent horsepower (about 5,000 hp at the rail) loaded to 4 hp per ton could still be accelerating at 0.2 mph per second at 70 mph on level track and reach that speed well before the five-minute rating period had been used up. Over an entire run involving many stops or speed restrictions, the time difference is considerable; an electric can be loaded considerably more heavily than an equivalent diesel and still make the same schedule.

The electric locomotive cannot be considered apart from *electrification,* the process of providing the power distribution system. Recently built electric locomotives and MU cars (Fig. 4-14) are adaptable to high-voltage (25 or 50 kV) 60 Hz ("commercial frequency") power, which can be provided by public utilities rather than railroad-sponsored power plants and picked up from relatively light weight catenary. Some commuter districts in New Jersey and in the Northeast Corridor have been so converted and some recently built spur lines serving mines or power plants operate at 25 or 50 kV; however, despite numerous economic studies and re-studies, no main-line freight electrifications remain in service in the United States or Canada.

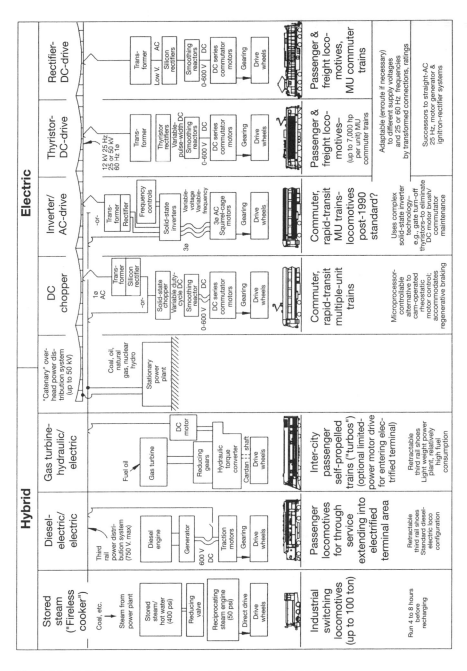

Fig. 4-14. Rail Propulsion Systems (Hybrid and Electric)

Locomotive Maintenance

The principal emphasis in recent locomotive design changes has been on improving reliability and reducing maintenance rather than simply increasing power. For example, internal locomotive compartments, particularly the high-and-low voltage electrical control cabinets, in current models, are fed filtered air, maintaining them at a pressure a little above atmospheric so that dirt is blown out of these sensitive areas instead of leaking in.

There is also a continuing battle to simplify the design of basic components and help compensate for the increased complexity that creeps in with each improvement in performance. The pressure-retaining 26L air brake control stand allows trains to descend grades without having to stop to set up brake retainers on the freight cars. But the added features do make air brake equipment more complicated, especially since it must be compatible with older units not so equipped; in partial compensation for this, composition brake shoes with their higher coefficient of friction have made it possible to reduce the number of brake shoes per wheel on the locomotive from two to one, getting rid of considerable brake rigging in the process.

AC Traction Motors

Availability of solid-state inverters capable of converting direct current (or rectified AC) to three-phase VVVF (variable-voltage variable-frequency) power–particularly those based on GTO (gate turn-off) technology in which a relatively small control current can stop as well as start conduction in hockey-puck-size transistors capable of carrying locomotive-size currents–led in the late 1980s to the selection of AC traction motors for significant numbers of new or rebuilt rapid-transit and commuter cars. Under microprocessor control, an extremely complex inversion/smoothing process generates three-phase power providing acceptable traction characteristics (including dynamic or regenerative braking down to a standstill) with relatively light weight "squirrel cage" traction motors and thus eliminate brush and commutator maintenance.

Characteristics of DC and AC traction-motor counterparts affecting railroad use are presented in Fig. 4-15. Estimates place overall first- and maintenance/failure-savings for AC traction motors themselves at as much as 40 percent, which must, of course, be balanced against the extra cost of the power conditioning equipment (inverters) they require. The inherent speed-torque characteristics of the three-phase motor in combination with microprocessor control of the supplied frequency in relation to the driver rotation raises "dispatchable" adhesion levels toward a new plateau, with numbers as high as 40 percent being reported.

Motors fed from a single inverter tend to move in "lock step," improving adhesion because an individual axle encountering poor rail conditions will automatically lose torque as it starts to slip – provided that all wheels are of very closely (¼inch)

Rail Traction Motor Types – Characteristics

DC Series

Commutator/brush length subtracts from volume available for field and rotor copper and iron. Field and armature structures are complex.

Torque-speed characteristics match rail traction requirements – with maximum torque at starting. Feed-back or separate field-current control required for full use of available adhesion.

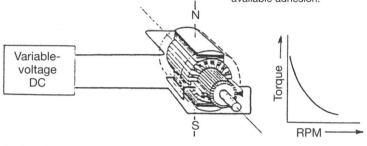

AC Induction

(Asynchronous, "squirrel cage") No mechanical commutation required—entire length available for torque generation. Motor speed not limited by commutator/brush performance, flash-over voltage: totally-enclosed, self-ventilated design feasible (with some weight penalty).

Supply frequency must be regulated with respect to vehicle speed to keep slip within high torque region. Torque drop toward synchronous speed provides degree of adhesion control. Motors fed from common frequency source are electrically locked together, will share load only if wheel diameters are closely matched.

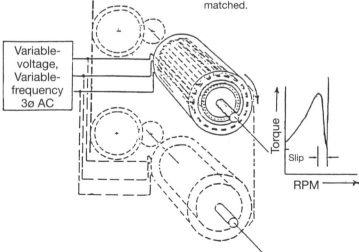

Fig. 4-15. Traction Motor Types, Characteristics

matched diameter. If each motor is fed by its own inverter, wheel diameters need not be so closely matched but maximizing adhesion requires corresponding individual control of the frequency supplied. At this time competing designs of the two major locomotive builders take opposite approaches.

Despite rather limited in-service experience, quantity production and introduction of AC-drive freight locomotives in North America began in the early 1990s, fostered by large-scale commitments to the new technology on the part of some major railroads. By late 1994, AC drive was present in the majority of new locomotives produced by both builders, while the compactness of the motors and the adhesion levels being demonstrated resulted in commitments to provide units of 6,000 horsepower by 1997.

Inspection and Running Repairs

One of the most obvious hazards of early railroading was the boiler explosion. The design, construction, inspection, and maintenance of steam locomotive boilers have been regulated by the federal government since 1911. By extension from the boiler inspection, power brake, and safety appliance acts and the Railroad Safety Act of 1970, diesels and other types of locomotives, and MU cars are subject to mandatory daily, 92-day, annual and biennial inspections, and tests of all components and adjustments that are considered to affect safety; compliance is subject to verification by FRA inspectors and enforcement by civil monetary penalties. The 92-day inspection requires such items as calibration of air gauges and putting the locomotive over a pit where the underside can be thoroughly examined.

Safety inspections are accompanied, as a matter of good maintenance practice, by increasingly refined diagnostic tests such as spectrographic analysis of the lube oil to detect early indications of unusual engine wear or internal leaks. A major recent advance in efficiently checking out the ability of a unit to pull its weight as it leaves the shop is a built-in capability to test the diesel and electrical systems under load by running them with the full generated power being dissipated in the locomotive's own dynamic brake resistors.

Major Repairs

Most of the repairs and adjustments found necessary at periodic inspections can be taken care of with little time out of service; modern diesel design is such that even major casualties to prime mover, auxiliary, or electrical components can be handled by quick exchange with spares in running-repair shops. Components removed are then remanufactured on a production-line basis in railroad, contractor, or manufacturer shop facilities. Nevertheless, after four years (possibly 250,000 miles) or so, depending, of course, on the severity of the service to which it has been assigned, a unit will be ready for a major overhaul. This could entail rebuilding trucks, replacing a "power assembly" or other major work.

After about 8 or 10 years, complete rebuilding may be in order, with new engine crankshaft bearings, trucks whose frames have been built up by welding to as-new tolerances, and a new paint job.

End of the Line?

The nominal life of a diesel-electric in its original form is typically about 20 to 25 years, but at the end of this time there are several options. Some components, such as traction motors and truck frames, may still be useful as parts for remanufacturing to updated specs. For this reason, the units may be "traded-in" on new locomotives, not necessarily to the original manufacturer, since there is considerable interchangeability of components between makes and considerable mortality among manufacturers. The new locomotives may not contain any parts of the trade-in's, but there is a substantial credit on the purchase price.

The units may be rebuilt or remanufactured – by contract rebuilders or railroad shops (some of which do such work on a contract basis) into essentially new locomotives of a type currently in demand. An elderly high-nose road switcher may be stretched into a wide-cab commuter locomotive with head-end power, for example,

Fig. 4-16. General Electric Model 7FDL-16 4,500 GHP Diesel Engine

with the original prime mover remanufactured to updated specification but with new electrical controls of a later generation.

Remanufactured units of low or moderate horsepower (1,200 to 2,300) are likely to be the choice of local and regional railroads which can make good use of locomotives that are at home on spindly branch line assignments but which can then be MU'd to haul a combined consist to its Class I connection.

The units may be "remodeled" (by the railroad's own shops, by a contract rebuilder, or even by another railroad's shop which does such work on a contract basis) into essentially new locomotives of the type the railroad now needs, changed from streamlined road freight engines into chopped-nose road switchers, perhaps, with new engines of a later, higher horsepower series. Since locomotive underframes are fabricated by welding them up from heavy steel plate, even this most basic component may be redesigned in the process.

Sporadic successful prototyping but no large-scale production of units re-engined with larger versions of the commercially available "antifreeze compatible" diesels, long used in small industrial locomotives, has occurred in recent decades. Readily re-started after shut-down at low temperatures, served by worldwide spare-part networks and now matched to sophisticated microprocessor controls but operating at rpm's (1,800-2,100) that have had some problems in earlier rail adaptations, they promise major fuel savings in cold-climate, low-utilization service where off-shift cold-weather idling is traditional. As a third alternative, the units may be cannibalized for parts to keep sister engines in service and finally cut up for scrap.

The Railroad Car

5

R
ailroad cars, primarily, are designed to conveniently carry and protect their contents and to stay on the track as individual vehicles, but they also must serve as links in a very strong chain. Within the first few years of railroading in the United States, the basic durable car configuration evolved: a long car body built around a strong center sill and supported on two swiveling four-wheel trucks.

The Basic Eight-Wheel Car

The basic eight-wheel car may not be the perfect design for railroad cars, but it has proven to be a solid performer. All of the hundreds of major and minor deviations from the basic design – four-wheel cars, guided trucks, six-wheel trucks, articulated (hinged) cars – seem to be less satisfactory and efficient on an overall system cost basis. This has been borne out in all types of services, from high tonnage ore hauling to high-speed passenger trains and in car lengths from 24 to 95 feet.

It was also quickly found best by early railroaders to have the wheels attached rigidly to an axle which in turn revolved in stationary metal bearings, in contrast to the previous horse-drawn carriage practice (in which the wheels revolved on a stationary axle). These bearings could readily be provided with a continual source of lubrication by enclosing them in a "journal box" packed with oil-saturated wool fibers (waste).

It was found that, once in motion, the bearing actually carries its load on a film of oil, floating with a friction load equal to only about two pounds of pull to move a ton of weight. The total friction, including that of the wheel rolling on the rail, is about twice that.

Early cars, primarily of wood construction, weighed about as much as their loads. As freight cars grew bigger and changed from wood to steel, the loaded-to-empty-weight ratio improved and is currently almost four to one, even though every item of the car has been strengthened to withstand service at higher speeds and the increased longitudinal forces from longer, heavier trains.

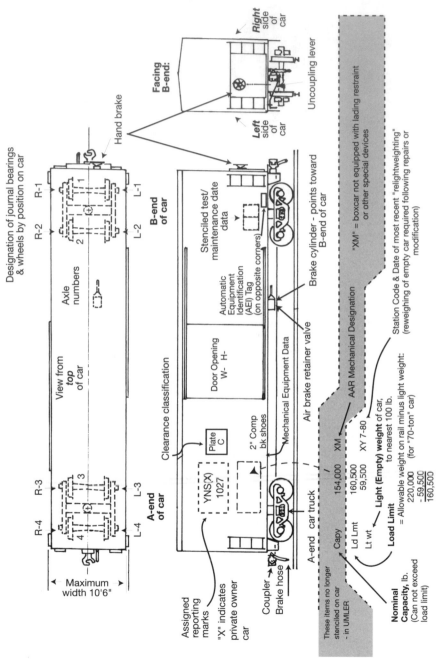

Fig. 5-1. The Freight Car

Standardization and Interchange

Car design is a compromise between two conflicting goals – diversity to achieve the most efficient loading, transport, and unloading of a particular lading vs. standardization on a minimum variety of general-purpose cars likely to cost less and achieve better utilization. Specific car types and designs for the principal classes of freight are illustrated in a later section on railroad operations.

Most freight cars, specialized or general purpose, are interchanged between railroads and may be traveling in a train coupled to any of the other nearly 1.5 million cars making up the North American car fleet. In a continuation of the process started with the formation of the association of Master Car Builders in 1873 and now administered by the Mechanical Division of the Association of American Railroads (AAR), the basic dimensions, design criteria, construction, and maintenance standards for the operating parts of a car making it suitable for interchange are rigidly specified.

Interchangeability and Evolution

The parts of a car subject to wear or damage in service must be as few in number and as interchangeable as possible, since they may need repair or replacement at repair ("rip") tracks or car shops anywhere. Even cars in "captive" service on a single railroad enroute are for the most part built to interchange requirements, since the cost of developing and building nonstandard designs usually outweighs other possible advantages.

Who Pays for Repairs?

Interchangeability of parts allows the nearly 1.5 million cars in existence to go just about anywhere, and be repaired just about anywhere. Interline repair billings of hundreds of millions of dollars are run up every year by cars operating in interchange service. These are charges for work done by a railroad on another company's car which was due for preventive maintenance or developed problems on line. To avoid confusion and litigation, standards must be set to determine who pays for which repairs. These standards are contained in the "bible" of the railroad industry, the "Field Manual of A.A.R. Interchange Rules," a pocket-size book of inspection standards, comparability of parts, repair and paperwork procedures, and responsibility rules. Pricing of all parts and repairs is determined by the A.A.R. "Office Manual."

Who Pays How Much for What?

In general, repairs are divided into those of a normal wear and tear nature, such as worn out wheels, and those associated with damage from treatment received (from railroad, freight shipper or receiver, act of God, or vandalism) on the handling line after it received and accepted the car at the interchange point. Wear and tear is "owner's responsibility." The handling line pays for damage. Over the years, solutions to most of the thousands of common ("Who pays for the grease?") and questionable ("Who flattened the wheels?") problems have been determined: an arbitration board continues to decide new issues as they arise.

Car Capacity

The basis for much of the rather remarkable degree of standardization in car repair parts that has been achieved is nominal car capacity. Wheels, axles, journal bearings, truck side frames, and many other components whose size and strength is affected by the load they must carry come in 30-, 40-, 50-, 70-, 100- and 125-ton sizes. The smallest capacities are rarely found except for cabooses, since practically all cars remaining in service are larger; 125-ton cars are restricted to use by special interline agreement on roads and routes with track rated to support their 79,000-lb axle load. Thus, just three car capacities encompass most of the fleet, and most cars now being built are either 70- or 100-tonners.

Not all "70-ton" cars can carry exactly 140,000 lbs, however. Total load on the rail is the governing force.

Nominal Car Capacity		Total Load on Rail (4-axle car)	Journals (diam. & length)
30-ton	60,000 lbs	103,000 lbs	4¼x8 in.
40-ton	80,000	142,000	5x9
50-ton	110,000	177,000	5½x10
70-ton	154,000	220,000	6x11
100-ton	200,000	263,000	6½x12
125-ton	250,000	315,000	7x12

Note: On the basis of economic studies in the late 1990's, many new freight cars with 6½" x 12" journals have been built with truck and other components designed for a total load on rail of 286,000 lb. and an increasing mileage of line cleared for this loading

Load Limit

The "load limit" for a particular car then becomes the difference between its empty (light) weight and the above total load on the rail. Some 100-ton cars, such as hopper cars intended for a dense commodity like rock which requires only a small cubic capacity, may weigh only 55,000 lbs empty and be able to carry 208,000 lbs. A 100-ton tank car built to carry relatively light liquefied petroleum gas and which must be built to take 350 psi pressure, on the other hand, may weigh over 100,000 lbs and thus have a load limit equal to only about 80 tons. Both cars will use the same size wheels, roller bearings, axles, and other weight-related parts.

Car Clearances

Overall car size is also standardized by AAR interchange regulations. A car fitting within the diagram "Plate B" (10 ft 8 in. wide by 15 ft 1 in. high, maximum, with further restrictions on width for extra-long cars so they will clear structures near sharp curves) can go anywhere. A 15 ft 6 in. high "Plate C" car, although listed, in common with higher cars, as acceptable for limited interchange, was restricted on less than five percent of all routes by 1963. Routes over which higher cars, such as the 17 ft 1 in. high-cube auto parts cars fitting within the dimensions of "Plate F" (1974) or the double-stack equipment built to carry 9 ft 6 in. high containers fitting beneath the 20 ft 2 in. limit of "Plate H" (1991) standards, can travel are called out in "Railway Line Clearances," an annual publication detailing allowable axle loads and the critical "top-corner" restriction (allowable width at each height in three-inch increments) for each line segment of the railroad network.

For tracking quality reasons, overall car body length is limited to 89 ft (about 95 ft over the couplers). When the center of gravity of a loaded car exceeds 98 in. above the rail, "high-wide" handling is required.

Safety Appliances

The Federal Safety Appliance Act of 1893, which required automatic couplers and power brakes on railroad cars, also included standardization of the steps, ladders, grab irons, and running boards necessary for a brakeman to climb from car to car atop the train. A brakeman's original function was to control train speed with the hand brakes and, in the air brake era, to pass hand or lantern signals to the engine crew. Radio communication has made it unnecessary for trainmen to traipse up and down the train; employees are now expressly forbidden to go atop cars in motion, and the ladders and running boards are being eliminated except where needed in connection with loading or unloading operations. The hand brake (now primarily a "parking" brake to keep stationary cars where they belong) has been relocated to a lower, safer position. For many years it has been of a geared design which can be set without using a "brakeman's club" to twist the wheel. Grab irons and steps for riding the cars during switching movements continue to be required, in standardized locations, so that an employee can count on a foot or handhold where expected, regardless of car age or ownership.

The Railroad Safety Act of 1970 extended FRA authority to all aspects of car design and maintenance, not just brakes, couplers, and safety appliances. The principal effect of this has been to give many requirements originally established for interchange purposes the force of law. After a period in the 1970s when what proved to be a very expensive program of periodic safety inspections and certifications of all freight cars was mandated, safety regulations were changed in 1980 to eliminate subsequent periodic inspection requirements. Inspection for defects judged critical for safe operation is required at the location where cars are placed in trains for road movement and penalties ($500 to $2,500 per offense) may be assessed for any car subsequently found in service with such a defect. Cars developing defects must be tagged and moved for repair under restrictions determined by a qualified person.

Outlawed Designs and Components

Over the years a great many design improvements have become mandatory, and outmoded designs, whether single components or major aspects of design such as wooden underframes, outlawed. Passenger car structural design requirements are descended, for example, from Railway Main Service specifications developed in the process of requiring that all railway post office cars be the equivalent of "all steel" construction.

Critical Car Components

With all these constraints, the job of the car designer in coming up with a vehicle that will make money is made possible only by the fact that there is considerable flexibility in using standard parts for the items where compatibility and interchangeability are required and then conceiving a car body and its specialty items that will best meet the demands of traffic. From about 1962 on, there has been an increase of as much as 1.5 tons a year in the *average* freight car capacity, as new cars averaging over 80 tons capacity have replaced retired 40-, 50- and even 70-ton cars. Wheel rail stress levels are such that there is considerable question (studied quantitatively in a major 1988-1990 research program) as to the net benefits in raising car weight limits to the 125-ton level for general service over even the best of conventional trackage. To the extent that handling much more than 100 tons as a single unit is desirable, it is likely to be accomplished by grouping individual "platforms" of about the present size into permanently connected multi-unit "cars" by articulation (one four-wheel truck supporting each intermediate "joint") or with slackness drawbars.

The freight cars being built new today are bigger, lighter, stronger, require less maintenance and are a great deal more expensive (about four times the cost vs. 30 years ago) than the ones they replace. Taking a closer look at the critical components that determine how the freight car does its job as a vehicle and a container will show how the freight car has become larger, better, and costlier.

Car Truck Design

Fig. 5-2 shows the standard freight car design now in use, giving the established names for its parts. The individual pieces undergo constant improvement and change, but the basic arrangement which allows quick disassembly and assembly in changing out worn parts is of long standing. The whole 9,000-lb truck is held together only by gravity and the interlocking surfaces on the principal parts. In the roller-bearing truck, wheel and axle assemblies are changed out simply by lifting the truck. Jacking up the bolster allows the spring group to be lifted off its seat in the side frame and taken out sidewise; the bolster can then be lowered, disengaging

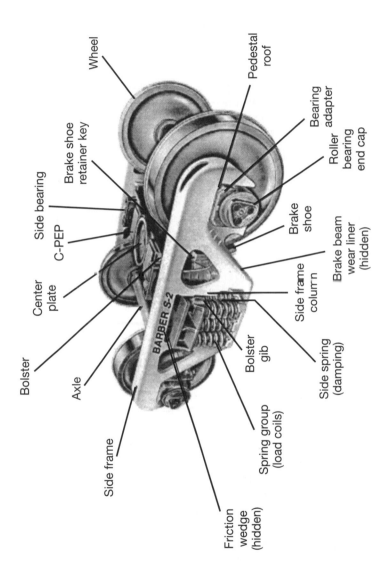

Fig. 5-2. Freight Car Truck – Component Nomenclature

the side frame and taken out sidewise; the bolster can then be lowered, disengaging its gibs from the side frame. The entire truck is disassembled as simply as that.

Car Suspensions

Almost from the beginning it was apparent that some kind of system to isolate the car and its contents from the impacts of the unyielding metal wheels on the hard rails was needed. Also, since the wheel flanges are only an inch high, the vehicle must have enough flexibility to ensure that all its wheels are on the rails at all times. Although the theory underlying a "good ride" was not at all well understood at that time, the rough track typical of American railroading was a powerful incentive to develop effective suspension systems. Both passenger and freight car suspensions of a basic type which has proven hard to beat (steel coil or leaf springs) were in existence by the 1870s.

Unsprung Weight and Spring Deflection

It is now known that the ability of the suspension to reduce shocks and vibrations at the wheel depends primarily upon two factors. The smaller the portion of the car's weight that is "unsprung," that is, supported directly on the rail without intermediate cushioning by something flexible, and the greater the deflection of the suspension under the weight of the car (the softer the springing), the better the ride can be. Obtaining a lasting and satisfactory ride in a simple, affordable system is certainly a great challenge.

Freight Suspensions

The freight truck has a single-stage suspension, one set of springs isolating the bolster (upon which the car body rests) from the side frames which are supported directly from the wheels. The inventory of car springs is greatly reduced by the fact that anything from a 30- to a 125-ton truck is supported on the same springs, nesting inner and outer coils in different numbers and combinations to produce the total load capacity.

The softness of the suspension depends on the spring travel, the difference between the "free height" of the spring and its length when compressed by the weight of the car loaded to the limit. This travel ranges from 1⅝ inches in the D-1 spring (now rarely used) to 4¼ inches in the new D-7s. Most cars have D-3, D-4 or D-5 springs with 2½ to 3¹¹⁄₁₆ inches of travel. The suspension cannot be softer than this in freight service because the difference in coupler height with a car empty and loaded would be too great and lead to breaks in the train. Longer-travel springs not only provide a better ride but have greater reserve margin against "going solid" under severe track conditions and subjecting the car and its load to very high loads.

Locomotive, Passenger Car, Premium Freight Car Suspensions

The bolster and side frames of the ubiquitous "three-piece" freight car truck necessarily interlock somewhat loosely. The resulting assembly has limited resistance to going "out of square," which may allow development of severe lateral flange forces on curves and the onset of "hunting" (discussed later) at moderate speeds on tangent track. Passenger-train car and locomotive trucks, on the other hand, have relatively rigid, one-piece frames to keep wheelsets parallel and in line.

Passenger-train and rapid-transit cars and road locomotives also have two-stage suspensions with one set of resilient elements between wheels and truck frame and a second set between truck frame and bolster (or its equivalent) on which the car body rests. This reduces unsprung weight, improving the ride and reducing track loads at high speeds. They also include *swing hangers* (Fig. 5-3) or equivalent elements which isolate the car body from lateral impacts and tend to keep it upright. Spring travel can total up to about seven inches since there isn't much difference between empty and loaded weight. On rapid-transit and some passenger-train cars, "air bag" suspensions which use train air to adjust car-floor height with varying loads are in use.

Premium freight car truck designs to provide some of these features at an acceptable cost (maintenance included) have long been an elusive goal for the inventor and builder as discussed in connection with radial ("steering") trucks.

Rock and Roll

Any single-stage suspension has a *resonant frequency*. Repeated jolts at or near this frequency, such as from "low joints" on bolted rail, will build up motion until something drastic happens unless there is *damping* to sop up energy. This was automatically provided in passenger cars by the use of leaf springs, which absorbed energy in friction between their leaves. Freight car suspensions now include one or another of various proprietary "snubber" arrangements which reliably generate an appropriate amount of friction between the bolster and side frame, preventing excessive vertical bounce of the car body at the resonant speed.

Certain cars have a high center of gravity and truck spacing about the same as the 39-ft lengths of rail in jointed track. These cars can build up a resonant *rocking* motion to a point where wheels on one side lift off the rail. They can easily derail if on curved track at the time they go through the 15 to 25 mph speed range at which the resonance occurs. This rocking mode is harder to control because it happens at lower speed, and much more damping is required. The problem is being attacked by the combination of welded rail, additional snubbing arrangements, and (in the interim) operating restrictions in the attempt to keep trains out of the forbidden speed range on curved track.

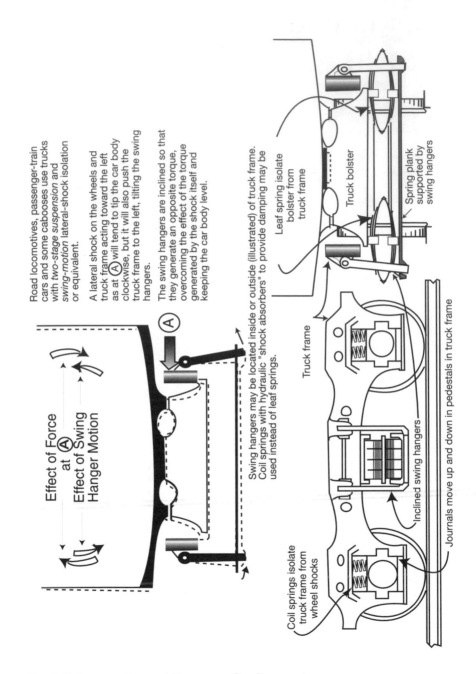

Road locomotives, passenger-train cars and some cabooses use trucks with *two-stage suspension* and *swing-motion* lateral-shock isolation or equivalent.

A lateral shock on the wheels and truck frame acting toward the left as at Ⓐ will tend to tip the car body clockwise, but it will also push the truck frame to the left, tilting the swing hangers.

The swing hangers are inclined so that they generate an opposite torque, overcoming the effect of the torque generated by the shock itself and keeping the car body level.

Swing hangers may be located inside or outside (illustrated) of truck frame. Coil springs with hydraulic "shock absorbers" to provide damping may be used instead of leaf springs.

Effect of Force at Ⓐ
Effect of Swing Hanger Motion

Leaf spring isolate bolster from truck frame

Truck bolster

Spring plank supported by swing hangers

Truck frame

Coil springs isolate truck frame from wheel shocks

Inclined swing hangers

Journals move up and down in pedestals in truck frame

Fig. 5-3. Locomotive and Passenger Car Suspensions

Journal Bearings

A most critical element in car design is the journal bearing. From an efficiency standpoint, the babbit-faced brass bearing resting atop the axle and lubricated by oil-saturated wool waste enclosed in a hinged-lid journal box, the plain bearing assembly, is still unbeatable. One man using only a jack can replace a bearing in three minutes. Also, the lateral motion between bearing and axle tends to reduce wheel wear in comparison to that of roller-bearing trucks. However, the journal bearing has barely enough heat dissipating capacity under adverse conditions for 70-ton cars and requires frequent attention if "hot boxes" are to be avoided.

Hot Boxes

The overheated journal bearing or hot box is one of the most hazardous aspects of railroad operation. If undetected, bearing malfunction rapidly results in friction heating of the end of the axle to a point where the steel is so weakened that the weight of the car breaks it off. This drops the truck frame to the roadbed, resulting in a potentially major derailment.

Following World War II increased loads and speeds led to an intolerable number of delays in setting out cars with hot boxes. This rate was reduced by better than 90 percent within the space of a few years in the early 1960s by a mandatory replacement of the loose waste packing with spring-loaded, wick-fed lubricator pads. These keep loose strands from getting into the bearing (waste grabs) and are less sensitive to packing methods. At the same time, improvements and cost reduction in roller bearings (which had long before become standard for passenger cars) made their use in freight cars more practical. All cars built since 1963 have been required to have roller bearings; by 1980, about 80% of all freight car mileage in the United States was on cars so equipped.

The principal cost benefit from roller bearing application is reduction in maintenance; plain bearings must be inspected by opening the journal box lid to verify the condition of bearing assembly, lubricator and oil supply, whereas carefully monitored service measurements of grease consumption in latest-design roller bearings have allowed them to be certified to run the full 10 years before disassembly and refurbishing on an "NFL" (No Field Lubrication) basis. However, a roller bearing assembly which does fail can progress to disaster more quickly and with less warning than a plain bearing, so the detection of incipient trouble is even more important, as will be discussed in the section on signaling devices.

Axles

The rotating axle which solved the problem of keeping the wheels in gauge also produces a bending stress which changes from compression to tension at any point in the axle every time the wheel revolves. This condition can result in *metal fatigue*, in which a crack develops progressively at a stress level below that which would cause

97

any effect on a single steady application of load. Study of axle failures as far back as the 1850s was the first situation in which this condition was recognized. The most recent change to design a more durable axle was the development of the *raised wheelseat* axle. This design lowers the concentrated stress in the axle at the inner face of the wheel which comes from the heavy force-fit used to keep the wheel in place.

Today, axles are forged from medium carbon steel, machined all over to reduce surface fatigue possibilities, weigh as much as 1,200 lbs, and have a very low failure rate.

Wheels

Freight car wheels for cars of up to 70-ton capacity have been standardized at 33 in. diameter for many years. Larger wheels (36 in. for 100-ton and 38 in. for 125-ton cars) are used in high-capacity service to help spread out the concentrated load at the point of contact between wheel and railhead. A special 28 in. wheel is used on some piggyback flatcars to lower the deck three inches and help accommodate high truck trailers on routes where clearances are tight.

Cast and Wrought Wheels

When iron is cast into a metal mold, the sudden cooling produces a white "chilled iron" structure extending a half-inch or so from the surface and then blending into the soft "grey iron" of the rest of the casting. The chilled iron is extremely hard – so hard that it can't be machined. Until the 1930s most freight car wheels were made of iron, cast into a "chill ring" surrounding a sand mold so that the tread and flange were hard but the center was soft and reasonably tough. The axle hole could then be bored concentric with the rim and pressed onto the axle. These economical, long-wearing wheels were not adequate for the heavier loads of the postwar years; all freight car wheels are now made of steel, either cast or forged.

Thermal Loads

In addition to its functions of carrying the load and serving as the guiding element, the wheel tread must also survive the heat shock of serving as the brake drum and dissipating much of the heat energy resulting from descending grades and emergency stops. The locomotive dynamic brake is a big help, but wheel tread temperature of 800 degrees F. from a single high-speed emergency stop on a passenger car wheel is typical. The most severe stresses inside the wheel rim occur when the train has descended a long grade, raising it to a dull red heat; when these hot wheels are hit by the icy blasts of a blizzard, it takes a tough material to stand up to such torture.

Wheel material selection is a compromise between wear and thermal shock properties. Class A, B, and C heat-treated wheels are of increasingly higher carbon content, hardness and wear-resistance but of decreasing resistance to developing thermal cracks in service where extreme braking loads are frequent. Thus, a passenger train making frequent stops might require the use of the softer Class A wheels, while

EMD Locomotive set

New 100-ton
freight car set

Light rail
vehicle set

Plain bearing set

Heavy rail
vehicle set

Reprofiled freight
car set

Fig. 5-4. Wheelsets

a heavily loaded unit-train car would get high wheel mileage from Class C wheels if its route did not involve long grades.

Wheels may also be overheated from a stuck or unreleased brake. Modern stress-analysis procedures led in the early 1970s to the development of designs with a curved ("deep dish") contour between rim and hub that allows the tread to accommodate severe temperatures without generating dangerous stress levels in directions tending to cause catastrophic crack propagation. Under current rules, however, wheels with no detectable cracks but discolored to a depth of more than four inches from the rim must be scrapped, at a cost in the vicinity of $100 million a year by 1988.

Extensive destructive testing has established that thermal discoloration of heat-treated versions of low-stress wheels has no correlation with susceptibility to crack propagation; under an extensive FRA-approved service-test program, effective in 1989 and expected eventually to confirm this conclusion in the field, wheels of this class found discolored may remain in service, subject to certain route and service restrictions.

Wheel Wear

The exact contour of the tread and flange of the wheel as it has been refined over the years is also a compromise. It's designed to ride well over its life and to last as long as possible before it begins to wear to a hazardous shape, either by developing a high flange with a vertical face which can climb the rail or a hollow tread with a "second flange" on the outside which can take the wrong route at a track switch. Wheel contour is one of the most closely gauged items in freight car inspection. On the basis of extensive analytical and field-test research, the "AARIB" contour was adopted in 1989 as standard for new wheels. Visibly almost indistinguishable from the long-standard "AAR 1:20 taper" tread, subtle contour modifications reduce rolling resistance (and hence rail and wheel wear) by as much as 20% over the range of curvature and railhead shapes typical of main-line track while raising hunting-speed and wheel-climb thresholds throughout the wheel's service life.

In heavy service, the point at which 50 percent of a given lot of wheels have been changed should range from 200,000 to 350,000 miles. "Two-wear" wheels – popular for cars in "captive" service where the benefits of lower whole-life cost will be reaped by the owner who paid the initial-cost premium – are made with a thicker tread so that they may be turned (as guided by a computer program that minimizes metal-removal in restoring tread and flange to a contour good for a second life) once before becoming scrap. With some 1.6 million wheels to be replaced or turned per year, the process of handling them (they weigh from 700 to 1,000 lbs each) has been highly automated.

Car Body Structure

The car body structure for the most part is built around a *center sill* connecting the two trucks and the pockets for the draft gear and coupler assemblies which transmit pull and push ("buff") loads associated with motion of the train as a whole.

Freight cars rely on gravity to hold the car body in place on its trucks; a standardized *center plate* from 12 to 16 inches in diameter (depending on car capacity) on the car body extends one inch into a corresponding *center plate bowl* on the truck bolster whose rim keeps the truck moving with the car body. *Side bearings* spaced 4 ft 2 in. apart are the other points of contact between truck and car body; to allow the car to keep all its wheels on the rail on warped track, the side bearings have some clearance or are resilient.

Trucks on passenger-train cars are connected to the center sill by a locked center pin which can only be released from within the car. Its design, stout enough to maintain the truck/car body relationship in the event of derailment, is intended to use the weight of the trucks to increase the probability that the car will remain upright.

Truck Hunting

The center plate/side bearing system has conflicting requirements. It should let the trucks swivel freely on entering curves to minimize friction and wheel wear, but it should provide resistance to control *truck hunting* on tangent track. Truck hunting is a rapid oscillation occurring in empty cars at speeds of about 50 mph and above in which the wheel flanges zoom alternately from contact with one railhead to the other, with bad effects on both and generating damaging forces and wear in trucks and car body. As a result of this problem, there have been developed a number of proprietary designs for resilient side bearings, center-plate extensions, and bolster/side frame elements which are intended to delay the onset of hunting as speed increases; some also fight rock and roll. None of these designs has been universally accepted as fully meeting requirements for all classes of service at a satisfactory price.

The speed at which truck hunting may begin is lower in empty cars, with worn (hollow tread) wheels and with truck/bolster looseness allowing "out-of-square" oscillations.

Radial and Premium Trucks

In standard truck designs the two axles remain parallel as the train goes around curves. If they could move within the truck so that each remains radial with respect to the curve, wheel treads with the proper angle of "conicity" could steer the truck around the curve without flange contact or wheel slippage, reducing friction, wear, and lateral forces. Angularity of the axles must be linked to secure the proper radial orientation and yaw motions must be correctly damped to prevent hunting on tangent track.

101

A few hundred car-sets, representing competing designs aimed at providing significant radial action on curves of up to about eight degrees without unacceptably increasing truck complexity, weight, cost, and maintenance, were placed in service in the 1980s. Over routes with a high proportion of curved track, data from FAST and service tests indicate that, under cars in very high-mileage service, an investment in radial trucks may earn a satisfactory return. Savings in the same fuel and wear elements from extending railhead lubrication to tangent track (widespread as a result of similar tests in the late 1980s) tend to narrow the range of profitable radial-truck applications.

In the single-axle "trucks" that support the light weight intermodal "platforms" (Fig. 15-4) that have recently achieved some degree of acceptance in North American service for the four-wheel car, suspensions have always provided a degree of radial action. Sufficient to achieve full radial action only on the gentlest curvature, with proper damping this action does significantly improve overall performance in these vehicles where accommodating 48 ft trailers requires a wheelbase of over 30 ft.

Some less complex designs providing improved performance – particularly, higher hunting-threshold speeds – have achieved wider acceptance, especially in intermodal service. The frame-braced truck adds bolted-on diagonal cross-struts to maintain truck squareness. A heavy-duty version of the swing-motion truck long used for cabooses uses the side-frames as swing hangers to provide lateral cushioning and a transom-bolster combination increasing truck-frame rigidity.

The Rolling Bridge

The car body also must serve as a bridge holding up a load supported only at the truck center. The load is always heavy, may be concentrated in a short part of the car length, or may be dumped into the car with little regard for its feelings in the matter. To do this job with as little weight as possible, the car body is designed as a unit with the center still. This is why a boxcar may actually be lighter than a flat car of the same length and capacity – its sides, roof, and underframe form a box structure which is quite efficient structurally in comparison to the deck of a flat car designed to be as shallow as possible.

Critical parts of the car must be strong enough to take incidental loads that make it a more efficient carrier of freight, such as wheel loads of as much as 50,000 lbs from forklift trucks on boxcar floors and clamp loads from rotary dumpers that empty gondola cars by simply overturning them.

Car Body Materials

The body must also withstand the lading itself, which may be corrosive, abrasive, contaminating and/or flammable. As a result, most car bodies are built with many parts of copper-bearing low-alloy high-tensile steels; the extra cost of the premium material is counterbalanced not only by longer life and reduced cost of hauling dead weight but also by the smaller quantity required to do the structural job. Aluminum alloy car bodies are used in specific services where their corrosion resistance to a particular lading together with the extra load permitted by the weight saving will justify the extra cost.

Car Cost and Maintenance

Freight car purchases and construction, in past decades influenced far more by tax considerations and regulated car-hire rates than traffic considerations, fluctuate so much that both new-car price and average-life calculations based on year-to-year figures are meaningless; a car-buying binge in the late 1970s in which investors pumped as many as 95,000 cars a year onto the rails was followed by a decade in which traffic expanded but car installation fell to as low as 6,000 a year; limited demand held average new-car prices throughout the 1980s at less than $40,000.

In 1978, the last year for which accounting standards resulted in reporting detailed enough to separate car and locomotive expenses, annual average freight car maintenance cost was $800. This includes terminal and interchange inspection, running repairs to keep the car in serviceable condition, and heavy repairs in which such major components as coal-car side sheets may be replaced.

Based on long-term replacement history, the average life of a freight car is about 22 years, during which it will have had at least one major overhaul. Since components representing a major fraction of car cost (trucks, for example) are interchangeable, and fleet size to handle a given volume of traffic has been declining as utilization has improved, rebuilding including cannibalization (in railroad, owner, or contract shops) has been effectively used to avoid or postpone purchases while coping with shifts in demand for specific car types. Examples include the conversion of boxcars to skeleton intermodal units carrying recently legalized 53 ft trailers and the application of enclosed multi-level auto racks to 85 ft piggyback flatcars not readily convertible to handle a pair of 45 ft trailers. Major overhauls will also include upgrading to current component (safety appliance, brake, coupler, strength) standards. However, AAR regulations now prohibit unrestricted interchange of cars over 40 years old regardless of conformance with all other requirements.

Interchange and Inspections

Current FRA rules allow a train to operate a maximum of 1,000 miles between car inspections and brake performance tests provided that there is no change in the consist of the entire train. Establishment of responsibility for repairs and other aspects of operation requires inspection and acceptance of cars and their loads at the point where they are interchanged between railroads in an interline movement; for unit trains (Chapter 14), agreements are in force allowing interchange on the basis of inspections only at the point of train origin and as required by the 1,000 mile rule.

Periodic work legally required includes *in-date tests* of air brake performance and "COT&S" (Clean, Oil, Test and Stencil) disassembly and rework as necessary of the brake valve assemblies; for the current ABDW design the interval (on the basis of demonstrated reliability in service) of 144 months is long enough to take the car to its likely first major overhaul.

The Train

6

The business of the railroad is the selling and delivery of transportation. From an economic standpoint, it's the ability to assemble and move a large number of coupled cars as a unit that distinguishes rail systems, so the real name of the game is running *trains*. The rails and the flanged wheels guide the individual cars and let them roll with minimum friction, but action of the train as a whole is considerably more complicated than just the sum of the actions of its parts.

What's a Train?

The track is not known to be clear until *all* of a train has passed, so it's extremely important for safety's sake to identify each train and be sure that it's intact. For operating purposes, the Book of Rules defines a train very specifically as "an engine or more than one engine coupled, with or without cars, *displaying markers*." Basic markers are a headlight or other white light on the front of the consist and (in freight service) the red plaque (day) or blinking FRA light (night) of the EOT (end-of-train) device attached to the coupler of the last car.

Couplers

In order to have a train, cars and locomotives must be coupled together. The original coupler, an eyebar or a piece of chain connecting the train cars, evolved in two directions. In Great Britain and Europe it became a system with spring buffers at the corners of the cars (to make the thud less sickening as the engine stopped) and a short chain (freight) or tightened turnbuckle (passenger) tying the cars together. Since the buffers provide refuge room for the trainman as he stands between the rails to drop the link over the hook as the cars come together, this system is still in general use.

In the United States, the coupling evolved into the "link and pin" arrangement. A single loop of iron held by a pin through a vertical hole in the "draw-head" on one car was guided into a slot on the approaching car by the switchman and secured by dropping a loose pin in place through the link. While in theory it was possible to hold up the link with a stick, and some draw-head designs supposedly left room for the fingers as their striking surfaces came together, in practice the link and pin coupler was treacherous. Thousands of fingers, hands, and lives were lost due to its use.

The Federal Safety Appliance Act of 1893 required the adoption of couplers which would permit cars to be connected without requiring a person to go between them. Of the thousands of patented devices designed to do this, the swinging-knuckle design of Major Eli H. Janney was selected for standardization.

Es and Fs

The current standard coupler for general freight service is the Type E shown in Fig. 6-1. Like all Janney couplers, it works on the "clasped-hand" principle. To couple automatically, one or both of the knuckles must be open when the cars are pushed together; the knuckle swings to the closed position and a lock drops in place

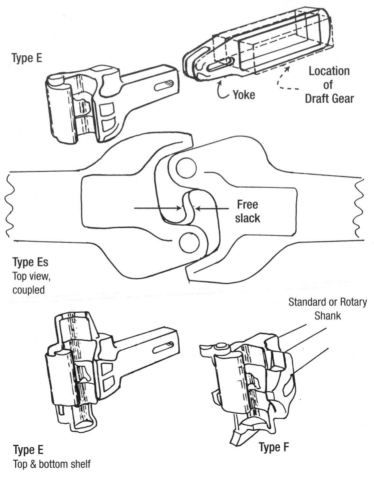

Fig. 6-1. Couplers

and holds it closed. Various internal features prevent the knuckle lock from jiggling or bouncing open under shock and vibration. To uncouple, the cars are pushed together enough to take the load off the coupler ("the slack is taken in") and the "cut" or uncoupling lever is turned by hand, lifting the lock pin. One knuckle opens as the cars move apart, and uncoupling has taken place.

The E coupler does not interlock in the vertical direction. Coupler height is maintained between 31½ and 34½ inches above the rail with the car either loaded or empty. The coupler knuckles are 11 inches high, so there is always a nominal engagement of at least 8 inches. Under extreme conditions it is possible for couplers to "slip by" in a moving train.

Interlocking Couplers

Passenger-train cars, hazardous-material tank cars and many other freight cars are now equipped with couplers which also interlock in the vertical direction. Fig. 6-1 shows some of these. The passenger Type H "Tite-lock" is similar to the Type F freight coupler but uses some machined parts to restrict free slack between mating surfaces to a minimum. F and H couplers do not allow the knuckles to slide vertically on each other and so must be hinged in the vertical plane to allow some up-and-down swiveling as cars move over vertical curves in the track and coupler carrier irons must allow vertical motion as well.

The E shelf couplers, like Fs and Hs, will tend in a derailment to reduce the severity of the accident by preventing the cars from disengaging, reducing jackknifing and the possibility of puncturing cars of hazardous materials. Shelf clearance is enough, though, to eliminate the vertical-swiveling complication. Also, if the shank of an E coupler mated to a shelf coupler should be pulled out, it will be prevented from dropping to the track and perhaps causing a derailment.

Rotary-shank couplers which allow a car to be rotated 180° to dump its contents without uncoupling are an important feature of cars for unit-train service where this form of unloading is used. They must be of interlocking design.

Couplers for long cars, such as 89-ft piggyback flats, must have extra long (60 in.) shanks and wide coupler pockets to allow enough coupler swing for sharp curves. On these cars in particular, it may be necessary to line up the couplers manually so they will couple.

Draft Gear

Even before the automatic coupler was invented it became clear that some controlled "give" between the drawhead and the car body could greatly reduce shock and strain on the cars. The importance of *draft gear* and the difficulty of meeting all its requirements is well illustrated by the fact that over 21,000 U.S. patents have been issued in this field. At first a stout spring was used, but it was soon found far better to use an arrangement which would dissipate the energy of a starting, stopping, or coupling impact in *friction* between its internal parts rather than springing back. Another essential feature of the draft gear was to provide relative motion or "slack" between the cars to help the locomotive start a heavy load, as mentioned in Chapter 4. With high-tractive-force, multi-unit diesel power this has become less important.

Impact Protection

The role of draft gear in protecting cars and lading remains and indeed has become more significant as train weight has increased. There is about ¾ in. "free slack" between a pair of Es and half that between two Fs; there is a total of somewhat over six inches of stretch per car in the head end of a heavy train being started. Management of this slack to avoid breaking the train in two is one of the biggest challenges to the engineer's skill.

Draft Gear Capacity

The space into which draft gear must fit has been standardized; most cars have draft gear pockets 24⅝ in. long, with total coupler travel of 5½ in. draft (pull) and buff (compression). In 1956 an alternate standard pocket 36 in. long was established, with maximum travel of 9½ in. The impact energy which can be absorbed at any given level of maximum force is directly proportional to the distance over which the impact can be spread out; improved rubber-friction or friction-hydraulic draft gears fitting in these pockets can keep car impact forces within the 500,000 lbs limit in loaded 70-ton cars striking at about 4 mph. Car center sills now have a compressive strength without serious distress of about 1.25 million lbs. The cars may take the punishment, but merchandise within may not, even if held in place with rugged load-restraining devices to prevent damage from internal impacts in the lading.

Cushion Cars

As a result, about one-sixth of all freight cars are equipped with longer-travel cushioning systems, either sliding center sill (Fig. 6-2) or end of car. Fig. 6-3 shows typical maximum-force curves for different lengths of travel as impact speed increases. Nobody *wants* to bang cars together this vigorously, but impacts in the range above the "safe coupling" limit of 4 mph do occur often enough to make the extra complication and cost of the cushion car a reasonable investment for carrying sensitive freight.

End-of-car cushioning devices have up to 15-inch travel, sliding-sill cars up to 30 in., with most providing 20-inch motion. The effectiveness in spreading out impact of the two types, within their limits of travel, is essentially the same. Action in the train may be considerably different. In the sliding-sill car, the two couplers and their regular, short-travel draft gears are held the same distance apart at all times by the sill; train slack per car is not increased. The end-of-car devices, acting like very long-travel draft gears, may let each car shorten by more than two feet.

Draft System Strength

As trains have become heavier and locomotives more powerful, all parts of the system, knuckles, coupler shanks, yokes (holding coupler to draft gear), draft gear parts, center sill lugs (against which the draft gear acts), and the center sills themselves have been strengthened. This has been done by increasing the size of parts where interchangeability is not affected and by using stronger alloys and heat treatment. However, the knuckle is deliberately kept weaker than the coupler shank, the

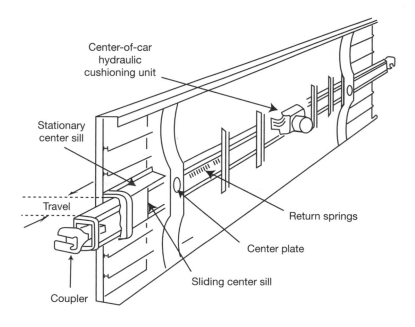

Fig. 6-2. Sliding Center Sill Cushioning. In the sliding center sill system, the car body, with its trucks, "floats" on the separate sill connecting the couplers, which are isolated from shocks by a center-of-car hydraulic cushioning device with travel of 15, 20, or 30 inches in either direction. A return spring recenters the sill between impacts. A regular draft gear is still needed at each coupler to prevent a blow from traveling through the cushioned car and hitting the next car, with the added mass of an uncushioned center sill. The sliding sill system adds about 3 tons to the weight of a 50-ft car.

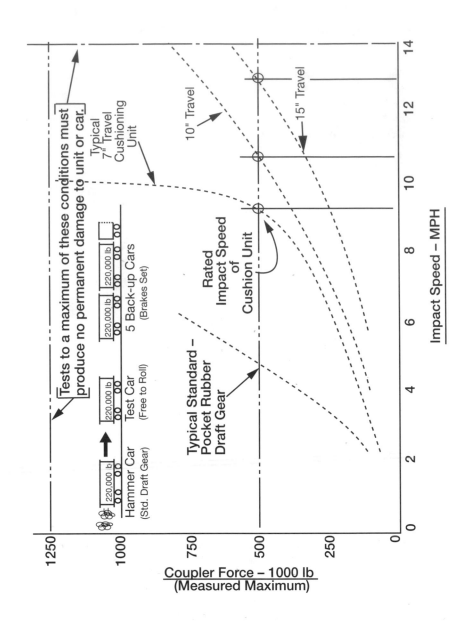

Fig. 6-3. Hydraulic Cushioning Performance and Requirements

shank weaker than the yoke, and so on. Thus, in case of failure out on the road, it will usually be the knuckle, which can be readily replaced by the crew, that breaks, and the likelihood of something serious such as a buckled center sill is remote.

Accordingly, coupler knuckles for general service are made of Grade B steel and have a strength of 350,000 lbs. For "captive" service where all cars in the train will be designed to the latest and strongest standards, Grade E knuckles with an ultimate strength of 650,000 lbs are available, giving the railroad much more leeway in adding tractive force on the head end.

Power to Stop

In moving traffic over a railroad, *power to stop* can be more important than tractive force, big cars, or strong couplers. If the motive power can handle only a few cars at a time, more trains can be run until the job is done, provided that a steady procession of them can move at reasonable speed without running into each other. That takes reliable braking power.

Before any train leaves its terminal, its crew must follow a specified test procedure to verify: that pressure at the rear end is within 15 psi of that being fed into its train line by the locomotive; that system leakage with brakes applied does not exceed 5 psi per minute; and that brakes on each car have applied and released properly.

The Air Brake

Since 1900, the common factor on all trains in American railroading has been the air brake – the most complex set of equipment on the freight car fleet, and the only one that has some components which could possibly be called "delicate."

Like wheel and coupler contours, air brake components have had to be standardized throughout the system. Despite the restriction of having to ensure that each innovation would work satisfactorily in a train with its predecessors, brake performance has continued to improve in major respects as the various systems have been invented, developed, tested, phased in, and phased out. Each of the features of the present ABD and new ABDW freight brake system has come about as a result of some limitation in earlier equipment which became enough of a problem to require improvements.

Brake Pipe Pressure

The chief function of the air brake system is to provide adequate, uninterrupted pressure from car to car. With the train assembled in the departure yard, the single air hose at the end of each car is manually connected to its neighbor, with all the angle cocks (shut-off valves), except at each end of the train, in open position. Automatic coupler assemblies which also make the air connection have been perfected and are widely used in rapid-transit service, but they are not compatible with the existing system, and the formidable job of making a changeover has so far not been judged worthwhile.

The brake system is charged, either by the air compressors on the locomotives or from a yard air supply (usually quicker), if available. Maximum braking power varies, within limits, simply by adjusting the feed valve on the locomotive. On a solid train of empties headed for a relatively level run, pressure would probably be set at a value near the lower legal limit of 70 psi, providing adequate braking with minimum chance of sliding any wheels flat. More demanding conditions would call for trainline pressure up to the 90 psi maximum for normal freight train operation. Passenger-train pressure is 110 psi.

Brake Pipe Gradient and Leakage

When the pressure throughout the train has built up, the brake valve on each car is in the "release" position (Fig. 6-4), with the brake pipe connected to the reservoirs and the brake cylinder exhaust connected to the atmosphere (via a special "wasp excluder" fitting that ensures that mud daubers can't frustrate brake action). There will always be some leakage, resulting in lower pressure at the rear end of the train. But the actual pressure in the reservoirs on each car is the system's reference, and its response to *change* in brake pipe pressure is unaffected.

By law, a train cannot leave its terminal unless measured brake pipe gradient is less than 15 psi. Leakage, with air supply cut off, must also be less than 5 psi per minute; air flow into the brake pipe of less than 60 cfm (as measured by a calibrated flow meter in the cab) has been accepted, subject to specific FRA conditions, as an alternate to the leakage test.

The End-of-Train (EOT) Device

Cabooses (and passenger cars) are equipped with a "conductor's brake valve" which can be opened to apply the train air brakes, primarily for use in emergency situations. The caboose also is equipped with an air gauge which can be used to measure the brake pipe pressure gradient and verify brake application on the last car as required in air brake tests.

Since elimination of the caboose on most freights in the late 1980s, such monitoring has been provided by the EOT device. In addition to serving as the rear marker, this device, via radio link, continuously displays the brake pipe pressure in the locomotive cab, not only allowing required brake tests to be performed without a long walk but also verifying proper transmission of the desired pressure reduction throughout the consist whenever train brakes are applied during the run. Most EOT devices also contain a motion sensor (pendulum or simple radar) to signal that "the rear end's moving" and advise the engineer that the slack has been taken out and full power can be applied to accelerate the train.

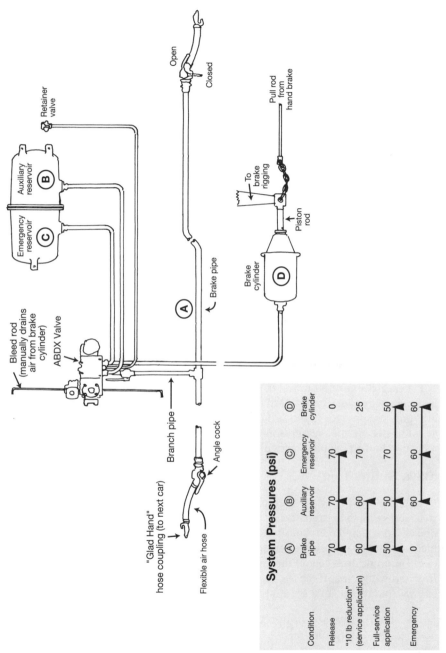

Fig. 6-4. The Automatic Air Brake

System Pressures (psi)

Condition	Ⓐ Brake pipe	Ⓑ Auxiliary reservoir	Ⓒ Emergency reservoir	Ⓓ Brake cylinder
Release	70	70	70	0
"10 lb reduction" (service application)	60	60	70	25
Full-service application	50	50	70	50
Emergency	0	60	60	60

113

If equipped with a two-way radio link, the EOT device can be used to initiate an emergency brake application from the rear end, a vital consideration in the rare event that some blockage in the brake pipe (behind which a brake application from the cab will be ineffective) has occurred subsequent to the last use or test of the train brake. This feature has been phased in as a requirement in any train service involving speeds and grades in which such a situation could be hazardous.

The Fail-Safe Principle

When braking is required, the engineer (on a locomotive with the current 26L equipment) moves his automatic brake valve handle to a position within the "service" range corresponding to the amount of retardation he wants. This *reduces* pressure in the brake pipe leading back through the train, at a controlled rate. This reduction causes the ABD valve on each car to use air from the auxiliary reservoir to *build up* pressure in the brake cylinder, applying the brakes.

This fail-safe, reverse action is the basis for the whole technology of the automatic air brake as it has developed from George Westinghouse's invention of 1872. With a supply of air on each car, a train break-in-two, a burst air hose, an air compressor failure, or any other situation causing loss of pressure will bring the train to a stop. The scores of improvements which have been and still are being incorporated into the system work to speed up, smooth out, fine-tune, and otherwise improve braking action throughout the train.

Service Application

For each pound of reduction in brake pipe pressure, the valve will build up 2½ psi in the brake cylinder, until a "full service" reduction of 20 psi from the 70 psi brake pipe pressure produces a full service application of 50 psi cylinder pressure (Fig. 6-4). At this point, the pressures in reservoir and cylinder are equal, and any further reduction in the pipe pressure will have no further effect.

Slack Action Control

In the days of hand brakes, in an emergency the engineer could only: set the steam brake on the locomotive drivers (or put the engine in reverse); whistle "down brakes" to signal the brakemen to start winding 'em up on the cars; and pray. The locomotive would start to slow down, and then the cars would run into it, one by one. The crude draft gear of the time would probably be enough to keep the impacts from throwing cars off the track, since the engine didn't have much braking power anyway, but it was not a graceful process.

With the first version of the automatic air brake, the brake on each car would begin to apply only after there had been time for the air in its section of the brake pipe to flow up toward the opening to atmosphere in the locomotive brake valve. This took time, time enough for the slack to run in before the brakes of the rear of a long train even began to take hold. With good braking power on the head end of the train, the result was quite violent – often enough to buckle the train.

Quick Service

The remedy was to add a "serial action" feature to the brake valve on each car. As the valve sensed the reduced pressure, it not only applied pressure to its own brake cylinder but also vented brake pipe air. This would in turn speed up the pressure reduction in the brake pipe of the next car. The modern valves use this basic idea in a variety of ways to move air among the various reservoir, brake pipe and brake cylinder volumes, and the atmosphere, not only to speed up and improve the certainty of brake applications but to speed up release as well.

Emergency Braking

For an emergency application, the brake valve opens the brake pipe wide (the big hole position). The resulting rapid rate of brake pipe pressure reduction causes the car valves to dump the contents of both auxiliary and emergency reservoirs into the brake cylinder (Fig. 6-4). This builds up a brake cylinder pressure equal to ⅚ of brake pipe pressure (as compared to ⅗ for full service). The rate of application back through the train is as fast as 900 ft per second, rather impressive considering that the speed of sound in air is only 1,100 ft per second, and that is the theoretical absolute maximum rate of "passing the word" pneumatically.

Brake Rigging and Braking Ratio

Braking ratio is the relation of the weight of the car or locomotive to the braking force; that is, the percentage obtained by dividing the braking force by the weight of the car or locomotive. Brake cylinder pressure is translated into stopping power at the wheel treads by the brake rigging and brake shoes. Most freight cars use a single cylinder on the car body, connected by levers and rods to one brake shoe per wheel. There is a single rod connection to the brake gear on each truck, and this is the only disconnection to be made in separating truck from car. The same rigging is actuated by a connecting chain from the geared hand brake, now used only in switching individual cars and to keep "parked" equipment from moving. An alternative to this standard "foundation" brake rigging used particularly on cars whose car body design would complicate the rigging (such as large-diameter tank cars where the tank serves as the car's "center-sill" structural element) is the use of two smaller brake cylinders on each truck which apply force directly to the brake beams.

The brake ratio is calculated by the following formula:

$$\frac{P \times L \times A \times N}{\text{Weight in lb}}$$

Where   P = Brake cylinder pressure (50 lbs)
        L = Ratio of brake levers
        A = Area in square inches of brake cylinder piston
        N = Number of brake cylinders

As an example, let's take a boxcar that weighs about 80,000 lbs and has a gross rail load of 220,000 lbs. This car has a brake lever ratio of 12.2:1, a piston area of 78.54 in., and one brake cylinder. Using the formula from above, we can determine the light weight ratio:

$$\frac{50 \times 12.2 \times 78.54 \times 1 \times 100}{80,000} = 59.89\%$$

For the gross rail load, we get the following formula:

$$\frac{50 \times 12.2 \times 78.54 \times 1 \times 100}{220,000} = 21.77\%$$

The calculated ratio is strictly theoretical, as it does not take into account such items as the force of the return spring in the brake cylinder and friction in the brake rigging from angularity, dirt, etc. The actual brake shoe force measurement is called the Golden Shoe ratio, and is usually about 65% of the calculated measurement. The Golden Shoe ratios are determined by a test mechanism which is substituted for the shoes on a car. The device has a digital display that gives a direct reading in pounds of brake force when air pressure is put into the brake cylinder.

AAR standards call for the following calculated ratios:

cast iron shoes	–	13.0% (gross rail load)
		53.0% (light weight)
composition shoes	–	6.5% (gross rail load)
		30.0% (light weight)

Slack Adjustment

The distance which the brake cylinder piston must travel to move the shoes against the wheels depends on the wear of all the parts of the rigging and particularly on the remaining thickness of the brake shoes. The longer the travel, the greater the volume of the brake cylinder and the lower the equalizing pressure in a full-service or emergency brake application. All cars are now required to have automatic brake slack adjusters which keep piston travel within limits.

Brake Force Ratios

The braking force applied to the brake shoes (expressed as its ratio to the car weight) results in a retarding effect with cast-iron shoes which is quite low at high speed (say 65 mph and above) but becomes as much as 2½ times higher as the train speed is reduced. The friction attainable between wheel and rail to slow the train also varies in the same direction with speed, but to a much smaller degree. In practice, the braking ratio could be about 150 percent for an emergency passenger-train application and no more than 70 to 80 percent for any empty freight car in full service. Otherwise, there would be too much likelihood of sliding wheels flat. This causes two problems.

Empty and Load Brakes

In freight service, the difference in weight between a loaded and empty car is now as much as 4 to 1. The same braking power for a loaded car will thus result in only one-quarter the stopping rate of the empty. At the higher speeds, the stopping distance will become very long; the most economical operating speed for a loaded train, considering the cost of energy against the cost of equipment-time, may not be practical because stopping distance becomes too long for the signaling system.

If the loaded to empty weight ratio of a car with composition shoes is greater than 4.6 to 1 (30% divided by 6.5%), the required minimum (loaded) and maximum (empty) braking ratios above can only be met by adding an "empty and load" braking function to change the brake force to match the light or loaded car weight. Any 100-ton car with a light weight of less than 57,000 lbs is thus required to be so equipped. Automatic empty/load systems have been available for decades, though only more recently in simplified and relatively less expensive versions; with more efficient car body designs (particularly, costlier but more productive aluminum-body coal-haulers) increasingly in vogue, this refinement is becoming commonplace.

High-Speed Braking

Early streamlined trains had to use elaborate speed-governor-controlled brake systems to allow very high braking ratios during the high-speed portion of a stop, progressively reducing it as the brake shoe friction increased. Individual wheel slip controls, similar to those on locomotive driving axles, acted to momentarily reduce braking on an axle that started to slide, avoiding the need for a reduced average braking force to take care of local adhesion problems.

Composition Brake Shoes

Many problem areas have been mitigated considerably by the development of composition brake shoes, first used extensively in the early 1960s. These have both a higher coefficient of friction (simplifying brake rigging and reducing the force it must generate) and one whose variation with speed better matches rail-wheel adhesion.

Release, Runaways, and Retainers

The freight brake systems can *apply* braking power in steps but does not have the *graduated release* capability which is practical in relatively short trains and is provided in passenger brake systems so that the engineer can make accurate station stops and come to rest without a "stonewall" effect.

In freight trains, once release is initiated by increasing brake pipe pressure, the brake valve completely exhausts the brake cylinder while recharging the reservoirs. The only way to reduce braking is to release the brakes completely and then re-apply them at a lower level. With the earlier systems, this could take a matter of minutes in a long train. If brake application was made at less than 30 mph in a long train, it was necessary to stop completely and allow all the brakes on the rear end to release before starting again. The ABD system largely eliminates this problem by its accelerated release (450 ft/second) and relatively rapid re-application capabilities.

Retainers and Pressure Maintaining

When air brakes were still in the early stages of development, there was always the chance that the train could run away while the brakes were being released prior to being re-charged to make up for the gradual leakage that eventually reduces brake cylinder pressure. This was initially overcome by the *retainer*, a valve on each car (manually turned up at the top of a descending grade) which retained some pressure in the brake cylinders after release. At the foot of the grade, the train would have to stop again while retainers were turned down.

In most cases, use of retainers have been eliminated by the *pressure maintaining* feature of the 26L locomotive brake valve. This maintains brake pipe pressure at a level that gives the desired degree of braking, making up for leakage by feeding air into the brake pipe. With the dynamic brake on the locomotive, to adjust for differences in train action, e.g., curves, it is usually possible to hold the train at the desired speed throughout a descent. Occasionally, retainers are still useful in holding heavy tonnage trains on grades while recharging after a stop, where the independent alone would not hold the train.

Braking Horsepower and Hot Wheels

Since it's effective on all the wheels of the train, air braking horsepower can greatly exceed locomotive horsepower, as well it should. A 13,000-ton train going down a two percent grade must dissipate 83,000 hp in heat to remain at a steady speed of 30 mph. Dynamic-brake horsepower may be about equal to the traction horsepower rating of the locomotive, perhaps 12,000 to 18,000 hp in this case. Every bit helps save brake shoes, which is why you'll see "helper" locomotives attached to trains going *downhill*, to contribute to dynamic braking capacity, though all railroads do not agree on this practice. In trains of less than 100 tons per operative brake, downhill dynamic brake helpers can cause undesired slack status changes. On a grade this steep, though, most of the work will have to be done by the brake shoes. If the grade is long, it may be necessary to stop and cool the wheels.

Since the brake heating environment is a wheel's toughest test, why not use a disc brake in which the thermal load has been taken off the wheel tread? Disc brakes are used widely in passenger service, but the relative simplicity, wheel-cleaning characteristics, minimum weight, and minimum cost of tread brakes has so far made them the most cost-effective system for general freight service. Even though brake shoe replacement is by far the most frequent item of maintenance on the freight car, it's also one of the easiest and quickest.

The Independent Brake

Brakes on the locomotive units themselves are controlled by the separate *independent* brake valve. This is a "straight air" system in which braking force can be applied and released to any desired degree without delay. It is used in switching cars when their brakes are not connected and is very important in train handling, allowing the engineer to gently bunch the slack, for example, before applying the train brake. Since retarding forces of independent and dynamic braking would be compounded and applied to the same wheels, they should not be used at the same time, as the wheels would slide.

Two-Pipe Systems

For special situations involving operation of loaded trains down steep grades the addition of a second brake pipe can eliminate stops to set up and turn down retainers and may be worth the extra cost on unit trains used intensively in a specific service. One option is to use pressure in the second brake pipe to set the retainers from the locomotive cab. In another system, the second brake pipe is connected to the brake cylinders on each car by way of a simple differential pressure valve which allows pressure from the regular brake system or the second pipe, whichever is higher, to enter the cylinder. The second pipe thus functions as a *straight air* system in which the engineer controls retardation directly. Since reducing pressure in this system will *reduce* braking, graduated release is provided and precise control during the descent is possible; at the same time, the standard automatic air brake system is fully charged and is available at all times should the straight air system fail.

Passenger-train cars have traditionally used a second train line for the *air signal* system allowing trainmen to communicate with the engine cab. The signal valves in each car reduce pipe pressure, blowing a whistle in the locomotive.

Electro-Pneumatic Braking

The speed of sound in air at normal temperature is about 1,000 ft per second; this is the maximum possible velocity at which the pressure reduction in the train line calling for a brake application can travel back from the cab. While a service application in the latest ABD system is propagated at somewhat more than half this speed, in a long train, the delay in braking at the rear end is many, many seconds. Furthermore, in a service application the rate of brake cylinder pressure buildup must be limited so that brakes at the rear have begun to apply before the head end has slowed enough to cause a destructive run-in of slack. At any particular train speed, the resulting extended stopping distance elongates the necessary spacing between trains, limiting line capacity.

Westinghouse himself felt at one point in the 1880s that only an electrically controlled brake transmitting the word at the speed of light instead of the speed of sound would be usable in long trains. However, he went ahead and improved the quick-service feature of his brake to the extent that it has served faithfully in general freight service for a century, postponing the complication of providing, maintaining, and hooking up reliable electrical connections between all the cars in a fleet numbering in the millions.

In rapid-transit and commuter railroad multiple-unit (MU) train service, where electrical connections between cars are required anyway, the electro-pneumatic brake has been in use in various forms since the early years of the 20th century.

Electronically Controlled Freight Braking

As the 21st century approaches, the availability of reliable, high-capacity two-wire communication technology has shifted the cost balance to the point that one of the most significant advances in train performance in recent history is taking place with the standardization of an electronically controlled pneumatic brake system for North American service.

The electronically controlled freight brake system completing development, in accordance with performance and physical compatibility standards coordinated and established by the AAR, incorporates a two-wire train line paralleling the existing train line, which then becomes basically an air supply line for the service and emergency reservoirs on each car which continue to contain the muscle to control train speed. An electronic control unit on each car, including battery back-up, takes over all braking control functions in accordance with digitally coded signals transmitted over the 230 volt DC train line from the locomotive cab.

The system has consistently demonstrated reductions in stopping distance, depending on load and gradient, of from 40 to as much as 70 percent. As we have noted, in conventional automatic air braking, once the brake pipe reduction triggers the brake application car-by-car, the buildup of brake cylinder pressure must be at a controlled rate to allow braking to the rear time to take hold and soften the slack run-in. With the simultaneous electronic braking throughout the consist, the brake cylinder pressure buildup can be unrestricted.

Graduated Release

The electronic brake also provides graduated release (and application) and release throughout the range of service braking because it is the electronic signal rather than the brake pipe pressure that is controlling the applied braking force. Since release can be stopped at any point there is no need for retainer valves. Brake pipe pressure is available at all times to recharge the reservoirs and compensate for brake pipe and cylinder leakage.

Circuit integrity the length of the train is monitored every second; in the event of loss of signal (through break-in-two or whatever) each car goes into emergency. Malfunction of the control unit on an individual car, on the other hand, results in that car alone ceasing all braking activity, sending a diagnostic signal to the cab advising the engineer of the loss of that proportion of the train's braking capacity.

Electronic Brake Introduction

Initial use of the electronic brake in revenue service has been on unit coal, solid double-stack and other captive-equipment trains – types now handling a major fraction of today's ton-mileage – which can be equipped and operated on a train-at-a-time basis. In such service the electric brake's benefits in safety, increased allowable speed, reduced slack action, reduced wheelset casualties (e.g., freedom from stuck brakes and shelled or slid-flat wheels) and costs (possibly, some increased brake-shoe wear when engineers find train handling with the train brake is smoother than with the locomotive's dynamic brake) can be assessed and realized without regard to compatibility for fleet-wide application. Charting an optimum path, whether selective, voluntary or mandated, toward general-service adoption of the electronic brake constitutes a challenge. Differences in performance between the two systems are so great that operation of mixed consists – nonequipped cars on the rear – during a transition may not be feasible.

Train Dynamics

A 150-car train of mixed loads and empties stretches more than a mile and a half. When starting up, the locomotive will move about 75 ft before the caboose even quivers. Drawbar pull in moving the weight of 9,500 tons on level track is about 25 tons, more than the weight of some of the cars in the train. However, most track is not level but is a series of ups and downs. When the rear of the train is on a 1.0 percent downgrade and the forward half is headed uphill at the same rate, there will be a net compression at mid-train of about 30 tons, pushing the slack in and compressing the draft gears. This compressed section of train must shift along the consist as it moves over grades. Add in the effects of curves, braking time lags, cars of different weight and with short- or long-travel cushioning, and the dynamics of this enormous snake becomes most complex. This is, of course, an extreme situation. When proper train handling methods are observed, when long car-short car coupling locations are regulated, and extreme "loads-rear, empties-forward" situations are avoided, then track-train dynamics problems can be minimized.

Ideally, a trainmaster would like to make up trains according to where the cars are going, rather than by where they must go in the consist to stay on the track. He or she would also like every engineer to have the experience and skill to be able to run any train smoothly, safely, and quickly over the division.

Train-Dynamics Analysis

Fortunately, it is now practical to study by computer analysis the effects of train make-up and handling by calculating the forces developed and absorbed by the components of each car as it moves along a representation of the grades and curves on any specific rail route. In-train forces developed can be determined with good accuracy, and the limits of train-handling technique in minimizing run-in and run-out forces can be worked out for favorable and unfavorable arrangements of light and heavy, short and long cars within the train.

Using test data on individual car behavior in Transportation Technology Center experiments with instrumented cars subjected to pull and buff forces up to 250,000 lbs between multi-unit locomotives while on curves and grades, the train forces can be interpreted in terms of the margin of safety against derailment.

The L/V Ratio

The key factor is the ratio of lateral forces on each wheel to the vertical load holding it down to the rail. This value reflects the combination of: the weight of the car; the bounce, rock and other dynamic effects on the truck suspension; weight shifts between axles from braking and train forces; brake shoe reactions; and (usually most important) the effects of lateral coupler forces as affected by the angle of the coupler shanks through which pull and buff forces must reach the car. Fig. 6-5 shows some examples of critical L/V ratios for a car with a high (98 in.) center of gravity. The rail-overturn figure is conservative since it assumes the rail has no stiffness against twisting (which would let the weight of other wheels help keep it upright).

With respect to rail climb, limits can be more closely determined under a variety of wheel and rail contours conditions with the AAR Track Loading Vehicle. This research car, riding safely on its two trucks, has a central wheelset which can be loaded to any desired combination of lateral and vertical loads to find the ratio at which it actually does leave the rail.

Vehicle/Track Dynamics – On the Road

To cope with increasingly severe train-dynamics problems associated with major increases in locomotive power and train tonnage associated with the general adoption of the 100-ton car in the early 1970s, a Train Track Dynamics Program coordinated by rail industry, supplier, and regulatory organizations in the United States and Canada developed train make-up and handling principles and practices based on state-of-the-art analyses, ongoing test programs, and the distilled experience of participating railroads. These have been widely disseminated and applied through "implementation officers" on individual railroads, often resulting in dramatic reductions in break-in-twos, derailments, and other incidents. Since 1987, industry-government research into this performance-critical matter of understanding and controlling interactions between train and roadway has continued under the Vehicle Track Systems designation.

Such programs have already proven extremely important in developing throttle and brake handling procedures compatible with the reduction or elimination of the *stretch braking* procedure long used to control train slack and prevent break-in-twos over difficult (undulating) track profiles. Applying locomotive power and train brakes simultaneously, often over a considerable portion of a run, obviously could rub away a lot of brake shoe metal, as well as burning up an amount of fuel totally unacceptable once the price went from a dime to a dollar a gallon; with the programs, working out ways to get over the line in one piece without stretch braking could be much more a matter of computation than full-scale trial and error than it would have had to be in the 1970s. With the aid of simulators for training, some

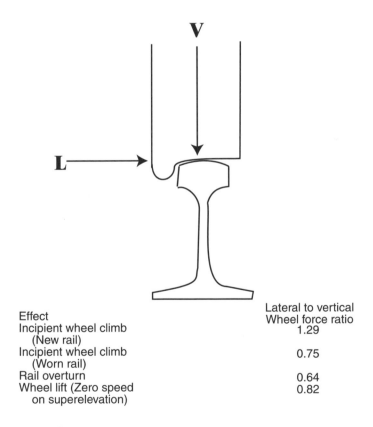

Effect	Lateral to vertical Wheel force ratio
Incipient wheel climb (New rail)	1.29
Incipient wheel climb (Worn rail)	0.75
Rail overturn	0.64
Wheel lift (Zero speed on superelevation)	0.82

Fig. 6-5. The L/V Ratio

modifications in train make-up, aids such as consist tonnage-distribution print-outs or displays, and detailed procedures for anticipating and minimizing slack action, many railroads were able to virtually eliminate stretch braking by the early-1980s.

Simulators. A sophisticated descendent of the relatively limited-performance simulators used by an increasing number of railroads since the middle 1960s to supplement road experience in locomotive engineer training is the FRA-financed RALES (Research and Locomotive Evaluator/Simulator) at the Illinois Institute of Technology Research Institute in Chicago. Built to be capable of conducting research on crew performance under fatigue and stress factors characteristic of a full over-the-road tour of duty, it supplements front/side/roadway cab-view displays with continuously programmable multi-axis cab motion and noise environment. It (and simpler versions incorporating route and signal displays based on more economical new technology such as laser-disk video) is being kept busy training and re-training engineers in routine and emergency train handling with consists and over routes realistically representative of any over which they may be called upon to drive trains.

Cab Displays. Many railroads have been providing each engineer with a print-out graphically profiling car-by-car weights along with consist length and tonnage figures affecting train handling. In common with the increasingly prevalent use of onboard microprocessors in conjunction with locomotive power control, diagnostics, and advanced train control, various computerized displays intended to enhance the engineer's ability to get over the road swiftly but smoothly are being introduced. One type continuously displays the consist as it moves across a profile of the railroad as well as data on train acceleration/deceleration and predicted braking pressure and draft gear forces throughout the consist.

An increasingly infrequent but still important use for the latest in-train performance programs is derailment analysis, a powerful supplement to track and wreckage inspection in assessing in-train forces and achieving probable-cause determinations precise enough to lead to effective preventive operating and maintenance practices.

Signals and Communication

7

The railroad is classified as a "single degree of freedom" mode of transport, that is, rail vehicles can only go back and forth along the "guideway." With only this one degree of freedom in which to maneuver, attaining high unit capacity and safety on an all-weather basis depends on a control system that keeps its vehicles in proper relation to each other. If paths cross or vehicles overtake each other from the same or opposite directions, a collision is inevitable.

The steam railroad was the first system where speeds could be high enough for stopping distance to exceed sighting distance; therefore, a clear track had to be assured by some means other than an alert driver. The railroad pioneered in the development of several principles and techniques which today form the basis for all successful traffic control systems.

Scheduling and Dispatching

American railroads quickly evolved to operation by timetable. Many of the lines were single-track affairs, so meeting points had to be established at stations where there were sidings, and the short trains of the time meant that traffic was rather dense in terms of number of trips per day. Delaying one train essentially paralyzed the line, since a train had no alternative but to wait until the train it was required to meet eventually showed up. In turn, it would delay all the following trains which couldn't move until it came through.

Timetable and Train-Order Operation (T & TO)

In 1851, Superintendent Charles Minot of the Erie used his recently installed telegraph line to issue the first *train order* – a message changing the meeting point between two trains, to the benefit of both, but doing it safely by first determining that the train being held at the meeting point had in fact "got the word." Minot had to run the train himself, since the engineer would have no part of disobeying the timetable. This organized system of train dispatching by "timetable and train order" (T & TO) was rapidly adopted due to the significant benefits. Procedures were standardized by committees of the Standard Rules Convention, forerunner of today's Association of American Railroads (AAR).

Train Orders – Revisited

While, in common with most railroads in the United States since the mid-1980s, the East-West has dispensed with train orders and now dispatches trains on lines not equipped with Centralized Traffic Control by Track Warrant Control (TWC) or Direct Train Control (DTC) rules, some background in the principles underlying T & TO and manual block signaling is necessary in understanding how these new systems work. Fig. 7-1 indicates the systems previously in effect.

Rules were developed over the years to specify the form of train orders and eliminate any uncertainty as to their meaning while ensuring accurate transmission, delivery, and observance. Train movements are authorized only by the current employees' timetable and orders issued by the *train dispatcher*. T & TO is safe but time-consuming; it takes about 35 pages in the Book of Rules to define the process, which until 1985 satisfied the E-W for moving a few heavy trains per day over its single-track line from W to C.

Superiority by Direction

Many of the rules governing T & TO operation must relate to "superiority of trains" – principally, which train will take siding at a meeting point. Misinterpretation of these rules can be a source of either hazard or delay.

Time Spacing

For trains following each other, T & TO operation must rely upon *time spacing* and *flag protection* to keep each train off the back of its predecessor. A train may not leave a station less than five-minutes after the preceding train has departed. There's no assurance that this spacing will be retained as the trains move along the line, so the flagman (rear brakeman) of a train slowing down or stopping will light and throw off a five-minute red flare ("fusee") which may not be passed by the next train. If the train has to stop, he must trot back with red flag or lantern a sufficient distance to protect the train, remaining there until the train is ready to move and he is called back (in pre-radio days) by whistle signal – four long blasts to return from west or south, five from east or north, plus one toot per track number if in multiple track territory, to be sure only the right flag comes in.

A fusee and two track torpedoes provide protection as he scrambles back and the train resumes speed. There is no reason the system can't work, but it depends on a series of human activities and is no fun in bad weather.

Safety and Capacity – Block Signaling

It is perfectly possible to operate a railroad safely without signals, and about half of the route miles in the United States make do without them; most of this mileage, of course, represents branch-line trackage, usually occupied by only one train at a

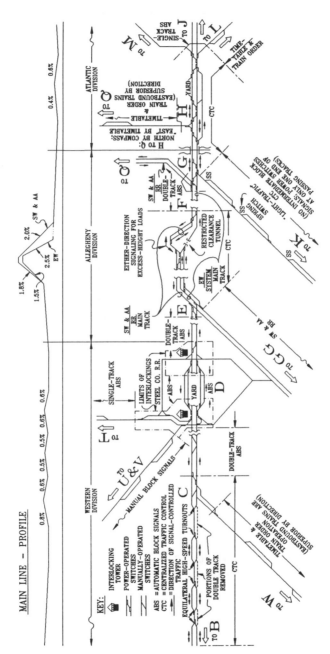

Fig. 7-1. E-W System – Track and Signaling Arrangement

time. The purpose of signal systems is not so much to increase safety as it is to step up the *efficiency* and *capacity* of a line in handling traffic. Nevertheless, it's convenient to discuss signal system principles in terms of the three types of collisions they must prevent – rear-end, side-on, and head-on.

Manual Block Signaling

Block signal systems prevent a train from ramming the train ahead by dividing the main line into segments ("blocks") and allowing only one train in a block at a time, with *block signals* indicating whether or not the block ahead is occupied. In *manual block*, the signals are set by a human operator. Before clearing the signal, he must verify that any train which has previously entered the block is now clear of it; a written record is kept of the status of each block, and a prescribed procedure is used in communicating with the next operator.

The degree to which manual block frees up operations depends on whether "distant" signals (Fig. 7-2) are provided and on the spacing of "open" stations, those in which an operator is on duty. If (as is usually the case these days) it is many miles to the next block station, trains must be equally spaced. Nevertheless, manual block does afford a high degree of safety, and federal rules allow a maximum speed of 79 mph in manual-block territory, as compared to 59 and 49 mph for passenger and freight trains, respectively, in "dark" (no signals) territory.

Our E-W System operated the line from V and U to D on this basis. This route, which is usually not very busy, experiences seasonal traffic "rushes," during which additional block stations were assigned operators to keep things moving.

Automatic Block Signaling (ABS)

The block signaling which does the most for increasing line capacity is *automatic* block signals (ABS), in which the signals are controlled by the trains themselves. Presence or absence of a train is determined by the *track circuit*. Invented by Dr. William Robinson in 1872, the track circuit's key feature is that it is *fail safe*. As can be seen in Fig. 7-3, if the battery or any wire connections fail, or if a rail is broken, the relay can't pick up, and a clear signal will not be displayed.

Vital Circuits

The track circuit is also an example of what is designated in railway signaling practice as a *vital* circuit, one which can give an unsafe indication if some of its components malfunction in certain ways. The track circuit is fail safe, but it could still give a "false clear" indication should its relay stick in the closed or "picked up" position. Vital-circuit relays, therefore, are built to very stringent standards: they are large devices; rely only on gravity (no springs) to drop the armature; and use special nonwelding contacts which will not stick together if hit by a large surge of current (as from nearby lightning).

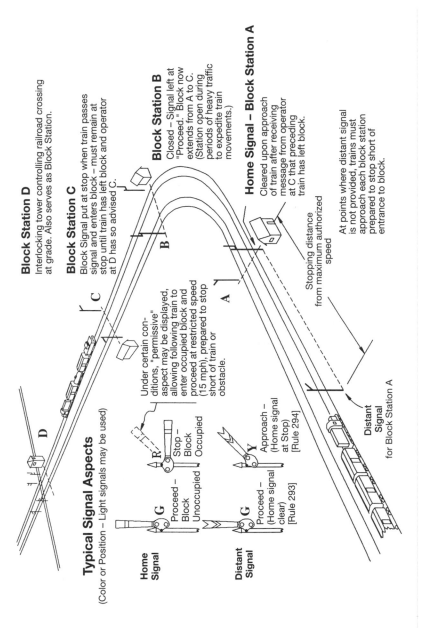

Block Station D
Interlocking tower controlling railroad crossing at grade. Also serves as Block Station.

Block Station C
Block Signal put at stop when train passes signal and enters block – must remain at stop until train has left block and operator at D has so advised C.

Block Station B
Closed – Signal left at "Proceed." Block now extends from A to C. (Station open during periods of heavy traffic to expedite train movements.)

Home Signal – Block Station A
Cleared upon approach of train after receiving message from operator at C that preceding train has left block.

Stopping distance from maximum authorized speed

At points where distant signal is not provided, trains must approach each block station prepared to stop short of entrance to block.

Distant Signal for Block Station A

Typical Signal Aspects
(Color or Position – Light signals may be used)

Home Signal
G Proceed – Block Unoccupied [Rule 293]
R Stop – Block Occupied
Under certain conditions, "permissive" aspect may be displayed, allowing following train to enter occupied block and proceed at restricted speed (15 mph), prepared to stop short of train or obstacle.

Distant Signal
G Proceed – (Home signal clear) [Rule 293]
Y Approach – (Home signal at Stop) [Rule 294]

Fig. 7-2. Manual Block Signaling

129

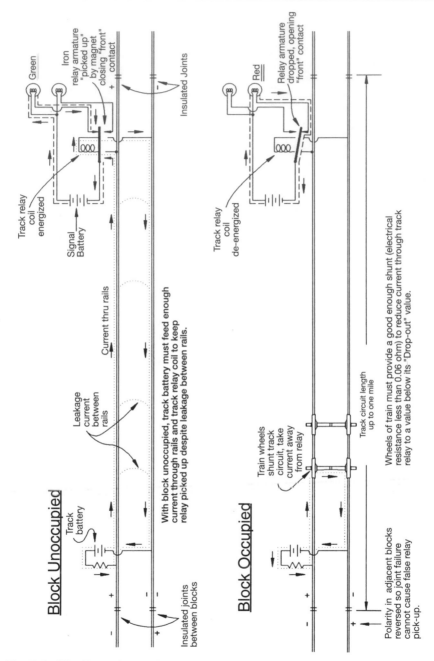

Fig. 7-3. The Track Circuit (Note: Symbols for Electrical Components Are Pictorial, and Are Not Those Used in Railway Signaling Practice)

130

Track Circuit Adjustment

Getting a track circuit to be absolutely reliable is not a simple matter. The electrical leakage between the rails is considerable and varies greatly with the seasons of the year and the weather. The joints in bolted-rail track are bypassed with bond wires to ensure low resistance at all times, but total resistance still varies. It is lower, for example, when cold weather shrinks the rails, and they pull tightly on the track bolts or when hot weather expands the rail to force the ends together tightly.

Battery voltage is limited to one to two volts, requiring a fairly sensitive relay. Despite this, the direct-current track circuit can be adjusted to do an excellent job, and false-clears are extremely rare.

The principal improvement in the basic circuit has been to use slowly pulsed DC so that the relay drops out and must be picked up again continually when the block is unoccupied. This allows use of a more sensitive relay which will detect a train, but additionally work in track circuits twice as long (about two miles) before leakage between the rails begins to threaten reliable relay operation.

Insulated Joints

The insulated joints defining block limits (usually used in dual sets in case one should get leaky) must be of rugged construction and are now frequently bonded with the toughest plastic adhesives available in addition to being secured with permanently crimped bolts. An alternative is the use of tuned audio-frequency track circuits which can do the job without insulated joints, which will be discussed later.

Signal and Train Spacing

Fig. 7-4 shows the situations determining the minimum block length for the standard "two-block, three-indication" ABS system. Since a train may stop with its rear car just inside the rear boundary of a block, a following train will first receive warning just one block-length away. By law, no allowance may be made for how far the signal indication may be seen by the engineer. So the block must be as long as the longest stopping distance (with a service, not an emergency, brake application) for any train on the route, traveling at its maximum authorized speed.

Track Capacity

From this standpoint, it is important to allow trains to move along without receiving any "approach" indications which will force them to slow down. This requires a train spacing of *two* block lengths – twice the stopping distance – since the signal can't clear until the train ahead is completely out of the *second* block. If heavily loaded trains running at high speeds, with their long stopping distances, are in the picture, block lengths must be long, and it may not be possible to get enough trains over the line to produce appropriate revenue.

131

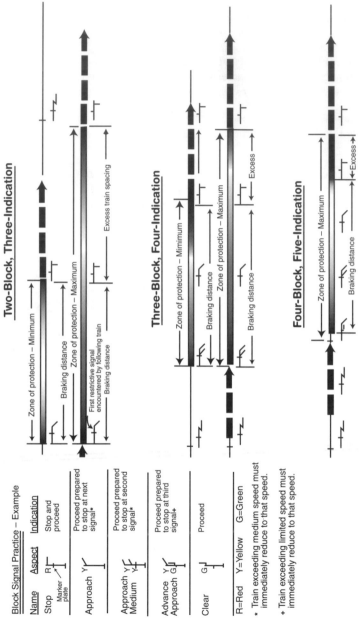

Fig. 7-4. Block Signaling and Track Capacity

Multi-Aspect Signaling

The "three-block, four-indication" signaling shown in Fig. 7-4 reduces the "excess" train spacing by 50 percent. With warning two blocks to the rear, signal spacing need be only half the braking distance. In particularly congested areas, such as downgrades where stopping distances are long and trains are likely to bunch up, four-block, five-indication signaling may be provided. Advance approach, approach medium, approach and stop indications give a minimum of three-block warning, allowing further block-shortening, and keep things moving.

Signal Aspects and Indications

Fig. 7-4 uses aspects of "upper quadrant" semaphores to illustrate block signaling. These signals, with the blade rising 90° to give the clear indication, began to replace the lower-quadrant semaphores in the early 1900s and are still used in diagrams to show available aspects on each signal head. Since World War I, when electric lamps and lens systems bright enough to be seen against the sun were developed, most new wayside signals have used the same aspects day and night, avoiding the maintenance of the moving semaphore arm which still must be supplemented with lamps and lenses at night.

Some of the systems developed by different railroads are shown in Fig. 7-5. Within the general rules discussed below, a railroad is free to establish the simplest and most easily maintained system of aspects and indications that will keep traffic moving safely and meet any special requirements due to geography, traffic pattern, or equipment.

Aspects such as flashing yellow for "approach medium," for example, may be used to provide an extra indication without an extra signal head. This is safe because a stuck flasher will result either in a steady-yellow "approach" or the more restrictive light-out aspect.

Special Aspects

System-wide aspects are illustrated in the Book of Rules. The signal-system rules in effect on each segment of line and each track (as illustrated on Fig. 7-1), along with rules for any special signal indications at particular locations, are established by the Employees' Timetable on a divisional basis. The important thing, of course, is that there be no uncertainty whatsoever as to the meaning of a signal.

General Design Rules

Some rules regarding signaling practices are established and enforced by the FRA as law. An example is prohibiting the use of white as a "clear" aspect – a missing colored lens would give a false indication. Other recommended practices come from the work of the Signal Section of the AAR. To abide by the "fail safe" rule, most two-light aspects are arranged so that the *absence* of *either* light will result in

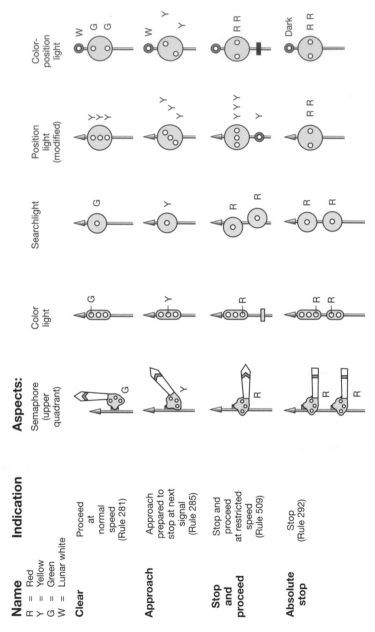

Fig. 7-5. Signals of Different Types – Examples of Indications and Aspects, Interlocking and Automatic Block Signal Rules

a more restrictive indication; if this is not the case, a filament-checking circuit must be used so that a burned out bulb will either cause the signal to "go red" or be completely extinguished. By rule, a dark signal must be regarded as being at the most restrictive aspect possible.

Absolute and Permissive Signals

Automatic block signals, whose purpose is to prevent rear-end collisions, have as their most restrictive indication "stop and proceed." Once the train has come to a stop, it is permitted to proceed at restricted speed (usually 15 mph maximum) but prepared to stop short of any obstruction, a train, broken rail, open switch, which has caused the red signal to be displayed. The permissive nature of a signal must be identified by the presence of a number plate on the mast or a second marker light in a staggered position (Fig. 7-5). A marker light or second signal head in vertical position with respect to the main signal is an "absolute" signal, such as at a junction or at the end of a passing track, which indicates that a conflicting movement has been authorized and requires that an approaching train stop and *stay* stopped. Such a "stop and stay" signal can be passed only by the authority of a specific train order.

Grade Signals

On an ascending grade, a tonnage train (one carrying its full rated load) will have a difficult time starting again if it's stopped by a block signal. Since its stopping distance on the grade is short, it can safely be allowed to proceed past a "stop and proceed" signal at restricted speed without a stop. Signals where this is the case are marked, usually with a "P" (for permissive) or "G" (for grade).

Cab Signaling

The earliest industrial use of electronics outside of communication systems was in the early 1920s in the form of *cab signaling* of "steam" railroads. By using a slow-pulsed AC, it was possible for the signal system to send a continuous message through the rails to a receiver/amplifier on the locomotive. Bringing the signal indication inside the cab where it cannot be obscured by fog and providing an audible alarm to further alert the engine crew to a restrictive indication increases the safety factor. The most attractive feature is that it allows a train to resume speed promptly when a block is cleared, even though the signal may not become visible for some distance. Subsequent improvements in electronic technology have allowed use of DC or audio-frequency transmission through the rails.

Automatic Train Stop/Automatic Train Control

Systems for automatically stopping the trains (ATS) were a popular subject for inventors even before reliable train brakes had gone into general use. Systems using a mechanical trip, moved out of the way only when the signal is clear, to hit a brake actuator on the train are successfully used in rapid-transit systems where: all the equipment is alike; the right-of-way is protected; and ice is not a problem. The first relatively satisfactory ATS for steam railroading was the intermittent inductive system of the late 1920s. In this scheme a magnetic device on the locomotive passes near and is actuated by an iron lineside "inductor," *unless* the effect of the inductor is nullified by an electromagnet inside. The magnet is energized only if the block signal is clear.

Since ATS provides only an on-off control, it must take effect at the first restrictive signal, where there is still stopping distance. Before passing the restrictive signal, the engineer has a few seconds to retain control of the brakes by operating a "forestalling" lever; if he fails to do so, or if he holds it down more than 15 seconds, a "penalty application" of the air brakes will occur.

ATC

More precise automatic supervision of train operation is available with continuous-coded *automatic train control* in which pulses at various repetitive rates in the rails are decoded by a receiver on the train and used to ensure that train speed is brought into accord with approach-medium, approach, or stop indications. ATC systems, usually in combination with cab signaling, are in use on several thousand miles of the most heavily traveled routes.

By ICC (now FRA) order of 1951, train speeds in excess of 79 mph are permitted only where ATS, ATC, or cab signals are in use.

Interlocking

Once turnouts and crossings were developed so that tracks could branch from or across each other, it became apparent that some way of assuring a clear route was needed if trains were to take advantage of their speed capabilities. The answer was *interlocking,* developed as early as 1857.

Railroad Crossings at Grade

At any crossing the law requires a "statutory stop" to verify that the way is clear before a train can proceed, unless the crossing is protected by an "interlocking plant." Operation was originally completely mechanical, with the levers in the control tower connected by long runs of "rodding" (actually, pipe) to cranks working the signal arms and track switches. In the "interlocking machine" (many of which are still in use), "tappets" and "dogs" on locking bars between the levers make it physically impossible to work the levers in clearing a route in anything but the proper sequence; signals must be at stop and derails open on the conflicting routes before the signal can be moved to "clear" from its normal stop position.

Throwing a track switch under a train had to be avoided, so a complex arrangement of detector bars was included which, when held down by the presence of wheels, impeded the movement of the levers. As soon as reliable circuits became available, they replaced the detector bars for this "occupancy locking" purpose.

Electric and Microprocessor Interlocking

Interlocking functions are now generally performed *electrically* by vital-circuit relays controlling power switches and signals, but the functions remain the same. To prevent all possible accidents a number of distinct types of locking are required. For example, the system must also assure that any train approaching at maximum speed has had time to stop clear of the route being set up before it can be cleared. This is handled by *time* or *approach* locking requiring an appropriate delay (typically up to five minutes) after opposing signals are at stop.

Since microprocessors can perform the logic functions of an interlocking at lower cost and in a minute fraction of the space required for relay systems, demonstrating that they can be at least equally safe in such *vital* functions has been a long-time goal of signal suppliers; continuous, enormously complex self-checking routines are required to ensure that no failure mode, including power loss and lightning surges, can allow the system to fail to "remember" the presence and status of every train, switch, and signal. The first vital microprocessor application was in a basic time-delay relay; the first complete "microprocessor" interlockings (which do include one vital relay to implement *system* fail-safety by cutting off all power to signals and switches should any of the digital logic checking turn up a discrepancy) went into service in 1985.

Junctions

To take care of junctions where trains are diverted from one route to another, the signals must control train speed. A train traveling straight through must be able to travel at full speed. Diverging routes will require some limit, depending on the turnout numbers (Fig. 3-6) and the track curvature, and the signals must control train speed to match.

Route or Speed Signaling?

One approach would be to have signals indicate which route has been set up and cleared for the train. American practice is to use *speed signaling*, in which the signal indicates not where the train is going but rather what speed is allowed through the interlocking. If this is less than normal speed, distant signals must also give warning so that the train can be brought down to this speed in time. Fig. 7-6 shows typical signal aspects and indications as they would appear to an engineer on the E-W approaching H from the west.

Once a route is established and the signal cleared, *route* locking must ensure that nothing can be changed to *reduce* the route's speed capability from the time the train approaching it is committed to enter until it has cleared the last switch. Additional

137

refinements to the basic system to speed up handling trains in rapid sequence include *sectional route locking* which unlocks portions of the route as soon as the train has cleared so that other routes can be set up promptly. Interlocking signals also function as block signals to provide rear-end protection.

Automatic and Route Interlocking

At isolated crossings at grade, an *automatic interlocking* can respond to the approach of a train by clearing its route, if there are no opposing movements cleared or in progress. Automatic interlocking returns everything to stop after the train has passed. Busy, complex interlockings, such as at the throat of a busy commuter-train terminal, may be handled by automated *route interlocking,* allowing one operator to take care of traffic which would require several levermen and a supervisor, if each switch and signal had to be thrown individually. Pushing a button at the entrance and exit of a route causes the machine to locate the best (highest speed) path that's available, set up all switches in that route, and clear the signal.

Other situations which must include interlocking protection if trains are to proceed without statutory stops or flag protection include drawbridges and "gantlets," sections of double track on bridges or in tunnels where the two lines overlap or are so close together that only one train can pass at a time.

Train Operation by Signal Indication

Where all trackage in a territory is controlled by block signals and interlockings, it is common practice to institute operation by signal indication, superseding the superiority of trains and eliminating the necessity for train orders in moving trains on designated tracks in the same direction (Rule 251) or in both directions (Rule 261). In effect, all trains become "extras," and instructions for their movement are conveyed directly by the signal system as supervised by the dispatcher, directly or through the block and interlocking station operators.

Centralized Traffic Control

When a system is so arranged that the dispatcher controls the throwing of switches and the clearing of signals for train operation by signal indication from a machine in his office, the terms TCS (Traffic Control System) and CTC (Centralized Traffic Control) are used to describe the system.

On many sections of double track, where trains move along under block-signal protection with few stops and rarely pass each other or encounter other interruptions, timetable and train order operation is satisfactory in moving heavy traffic without serious delay; in practice, only occasional train orders are needed. Such a section of the E-W System as that from C to E (Fig. 7-1) continues to be operated under double-track and block-signal and interlocking rules. Most trains travel in the "normal direction of traffic" on the right-hand track; train orders are issued when track work or serious

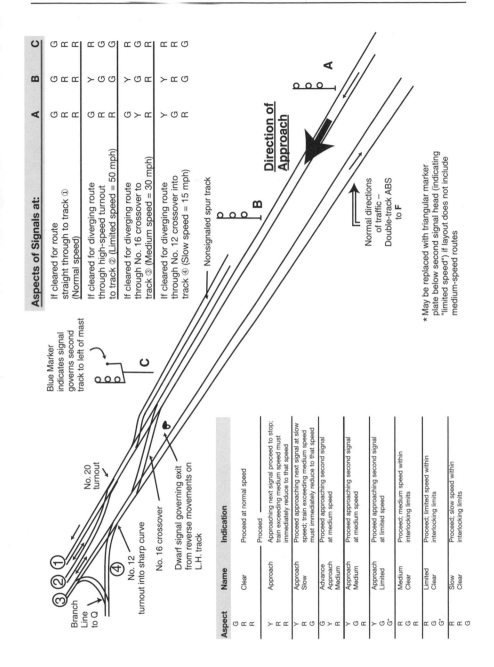

Fig. 7-6. Example of Speed Signaling in Approach to a Junction (East-West System, Eastbound at West End of H)

delay requires a left-hand movement. For heavily traveled single-track lines or congested sections of multi-track routes, however, CTC is usually the answer.

Single-track with CTC is considered to have about 70 percent of the traffic-handling capability of ABS double-track, so the E-W line between B and C, like thousands of miles of other main line in the United States, has been so converted. Pulling up some of the second track but leaving long "passing track" sections connected with high-speed turnouts reduces track investment, maintenance, and taxes while improving the flexibility of handling traffic which must move at much different speeds in the same direction (piggyback trains vs. ore extras). About 50,000 miles of line on U.S. railroads are so controlled.

CTC Controls

Controls for an extensive section of line are located on a panel with a diagram of the trackage. The dispatcher plans his moves based on lights which show the locations of all trains. He can implement his orders by sending instructions to what are, in effect, interlocking plants at the ends of each passing siding. The dispatcher gives instructions by turning a knob and pushing a button; when the switch points have shifted or the signal has cleared dozens or hundreds of miles away, a message is received that the action is complete.

Vital and Nonvital Circuits

CTC was originally made economically feasible, starting about 1930, by pulse-code technology making it practical to control all the signals and switches in an extended territory over only two line wires; today much CTC control goes by microwave. These are "nonvital" circuits, which can use up-to-date electronics to speed up, simplify, and reduce the cost of transmitting information because safety is not involved. The vital-circuit relays out in the field control and interlock switches, signals, and track circuits so that: the points cannot be thrown in the face of an approaching train; signal indications correspond to the route lined up; and so on.

Absolute Permissive Block

The CTC system on single track also usually includes APB (Absolute Permissive Block), a very ingenious arrangement of circuit functions among individual block signals between passing tracks. These circuits can determine the *direction* in which a train is moving and act to put all *opposing* signals from one passing track to the next at red as soon as a train heads out onto single track. At the same time they will allow signals *behind* the train to clear as it passes from block to block, allowing following trains to move along without delay.

The CTC machine is arranged so that it cannot send out conflicting messages, such as trying to clear signals in both directions on the same track. Should any such instructions get through, the local APB circuitry would prevent conflicting messages from affecting safety.

Control Centers

A logical, though not universally chosen, extension of CTC is to consolidate installations to the point where the entire railroad is dispatched from one room. Fig. 7-7 shows such a center, built "from scratch" to control all trains operating on more than 15,000 route miles of railroad, including both CTC and "dark" territory (see DTC/TWC below); its assigned personnel, computers, and communications systems also handle virtually all related operations-department functions such as crew calling and motive power assignment.

In common with modern CTC practice (where the nonvital "office" functions of maintaining control displays, generating commands, and communicating with the field interlockings have always used electronic technology of the current generation – from individual transistors through microcircuits to touch-control panels, microprocessors, and projection TV) the "big picture" of traffic throughout the railroad is displayed where all dispatchers and managers can see it, with detailed displays and controls for individual sections of line called up on each dispatcher's monitors for action as required.

Computer-Aided Dispatching

With the advent of digital minicomputers of lowered cost but steadily increasing computing speed and memory capacity, varying degrees of *computer-aided dispatching* have become more commonplace. The CTC system may, for example, recognize the need for a meet between two opposing trains, calculate the best meeting point on the basis of the trains' anticipated performance (based on hp per ton and route characteristics), check progress as the trains approach each other, and (subject to override by the dispatcher at any point) send switch and signal instructions to the field to execute the meet.

The computer may also free up dispatcher time for overall planning by taking care of much record keeping and paperwork, such as generating the "train sheet" record of all movements required by law.

Computer Control

For rapid-transit systems where trains making many stops are operated on extremely close headway, various degrees of "computer control" have been developed. Supervision of overall system performance, including regulation of the speeds and station-stop times of individual trains, may be provided, along with automatic spotting of the train at platforms, station announcements and so on, leaving the onboard operator in a monitoring and emergency manual control role. However, all successful systems of this type still separate the functions of automatic train op-

Fig. 7-7. Union Pacific's Harriman Control Center

eration (ATO) from those of ATC; that is, the computer-controlled ATO tells the train how to proceed, but it will only do so to the extent that the vital-circuit ATC has independently assured the computer that it is safe to do so.

Communications

From the very beginning of railroading, communication has been recognized as a key element. Superintendent Minot was so sure that Morse's new telegraph would be crucial in running his railroad that he had already put up poles and strung wire alongside the Erie and was prepared to make his own illegal instruments if necessary, before he reached agreement with the inventor on providing service.

Advent of telephone communication helped make operations a great deal more flexible; train crews could communicate with the dispatcher from wayside phone sheds without knowing Morse code. Allocation of VHF FM frequencies for railroad use after World War II and the development of portable radio equipment which could remain reliable under rugged conditions caused a rapid system-wide increase in radio communication between engine and caboose, and train and base stations.

Radio-Based Manual Block Control

Apart from the intermittent refinement in train-crew language caused by the need to observe FCC rules, use of radio has required great care in establishing procedures for its safe use. The dispatcher can plan meets much better when he can determine up-to-date positions and progress of a train from its crew rather than by calculations based only on the time reported at its last OS (train passing recorded "on sheet") point, but precluding disastrous actions based on mistaken identity or wrong assumptions from overheard conversations requires rigid rules.

Under proper safeguards established in the mid-1980s by individual railroads and subsequently standardized through the efforts of the AAR and inter-railroad rule-book coordination organizations, new forms of manual block control based on direct radio communication between dispatcher and train crew are in effect on most non-CTC trackage. As in the case of T & TO operation, in ABS-equipped territory the signals are a safety overlay to the dispatching system.

Direct Train Control. In DTC, fixed blocks (marked by wayside signs and often extending from one passing track to the next) are established. Train crews receive exclusive authority to occupy one or more blocks by radio in a standard-format transmission recorded by check mark on a pad form (Fig. 7-8); this authority takes effect only after being repeated back to and verified (names and numbers spelled out) by the dispatcher. Upon leaving the block, the crew releases it by a similar radio protocol.

Track Warrant Control. Under the TWC system, in designated territories, crews (including work crews and track motor cars) similarly can occupy main tracks only on the basis of possession of a "track warrant" covering a precisely de-

TRACK WARRANT E ⟨⟩ W *EAST-WEST R. R*

No. __*132*__ _____ *July 9* 19 *XX* ____

To: __*Extra 8172 West*__ At: __*Elmore Yard*__

1. ☐ Track warrant number _____ is void.

2. ☒ Proceed from __*Elmore Yard*__ To __*Lansford*__ On _____ track.

3. ☐ Proceed from _____ To _____ On _____ track.

4. ☐ Work between _____ And _____ On _____ track.

5. ☐ Not in effect until _____ M.

6. ☐ This authority expires at _____ M.

7. ☐ Not in effect until after arrival of _____ at _____ .

8. ☐ Hold main track at last named point.

9. ☐ Do not foul limits ahead of _____ .

10. ☒ Clear main track at last named point.

11. ☐ Between _____ and_____

    make all movements at restricted speed. Limits occupied by train or engine.

12. ☐ Between _____ and _____

    make all movements at restricted speed and stop short of men or machines fouling track.

13. ☐ Do not exceed _____ MPH between _____ and _____ .

14. ☐ Do not exceed _____ MPH between _____ and _____ .

15. ☒ Protection as prescribed by Rule 99 not required.

16. ☐ Track bulletins in effect _____ , _____ _____ , _____ _____

_____ _____ , _____ _____ , _____ _____ .

17. ☐ Other specific instructions: _____

_____

_____

_____

OK __*2108*__ M   Dispatcher __*EWK*__ .

Relayed to _____   Copied by __*D. E. Brainz*__

Limits reported clear at _____ M   By _____ .

(Mark X in box for each item instructed.)

Fig. 7-8. Track Warrant – Direct Communication by Radio From Dispatcher to Conductor

fined (by milepost, siding switch, or designated "control point") track segment of any length – often, to the next expected meeting point.

Advanced Train Control Systems

In a coordinated late-1980s effort by the Railway Association of Canada and the AAR to inspire the use of new technology to enhance train control capabilities across the spectrum of traffic densities while *reducing* system capital and maintenance costs, a team of railroad signal officers undertook the development of performance specifications for building-blocks – attracting, hopefully, competing suppliers' implementation ideas – from which advanced train control systems, matched to the needs of any route, could be assembled.

Subsequently, installations in service on individual railroads have tended to veer off toward functions of particular interest, such as reporting detailed locomotive diagnostics or coordinating local-freight work orders, items not usually considered part of C & S (Communications and Signals).

Although the march of technology – especially, computer power – has accelerated, and performance specifications guiding important functions such as integrating the ever-expanding array of electronic controls and displays in the locomotive cab and standardizing lineside radio communication protocol to facilitate its substitution for more costly line wires or buried cable are in effect, as of the mid-1990s, no extensive installations exactly in line with any one of the contemplated ATCS systems were in service.

A common basis for prototypes of advanced train control systems (ACTS) currently under test in Michigan, Illinois, Oregon, and Washington (U.S.), and Alberta (Canada) under a variety of names (all subject to change) and various railroad, industry, or government sponsorships is a location determination system on the locomotive. Without requiring a flow of information from the dispatching center, this "black box" must know, continuously, where it is with respect to key locations, characteristics, and circumstances on the line – passing tracks, permanent and temporary speed restrictions, maintenance work – affecting the train's movement authority to be displayed to the engineer. It must report this information to the dispatching center frequently, though not so often as to clog up the radio link. To do its job it must have in memory all details – track arrangements, curves, grades – of the railroad line; with today's cheap gigabytes, this is no problem.

Selecting and perfecting an affordable system to do this is the nub of the development. Continuing reductions in GPS (Global Positioning System) transponders, which prospectively can locate the train within as little as 50 ft (still not precise enough to tell which track it's on) make this satellite-based technology a strong competitor when teamed with locomotive interrogation of fixed lineside transponders or even, it has been proposed, inertial sensors which can "feel" which direction the train has taken at a switch. An onboard odometer periodically zeroed by similar interrogator/transponder inputs to maintain the required locational precision is a more down-to-earth alternative.

Positive Train Separation (PTS): The dispatcher's computer screens track-warrant authority to the locomotive's computer and cab display. Upon acknowledgement by the engineer, the warrant is read back (as in the case of any train order) to verify receipt and correctness, whereupon it takes effect. Failure to observe any speed restriction or the limit of authority results in a brake application. Another name for this class of system is Electronic Track Warrant.

Positive Train Control (PTC) and Communication-Based Train Control are names for similar system concepts in which various other features may be added to exploit the potential economic advantages of the continuous, precise train-location information provided in PTC. For example, in dark (unsignaled) territory the number of track-warrant segments can be increased, shortening them to ABS proportions and safely increasing line capacity without the expense of track circuits–one of the original goals of the ATCS program.

Railroad Communication Networks

Like any business geographically far-flung and with many customers, the railroad has a seemingly insatiable need for communication which has been augmented within the last two decades by the use of centralized digital computation for both operational and business aspects. Large railroads now find their long-haul communication load heavily weighted toward digital data traffic. The heaviest routes may equate to 1,200 simultaneous voice circuits, a minor load in terms of the capacity of the communications-company-owned fiber-optic cables now located on tens of thousands of miles of railroad right-of-way. While the economic advantages of railroad-owned microwave systems for long-haul communications have eroded – particularly where some of the cable right-of-way rental is in the form of copious transmission capacity – they may retain value for local traffic.

Because of the remote locations of some relay and signal installations, railroads have pioneered the use of solar-panel power sources.

Other Signal Devices

Among other devices or systems whose electrical or electronic nature places them under the responsibility of the Signal and Communications Department on most railroads are:

1. grade-crossing protection flashers and gates,

2. hot box and dragging equipment detectors,

3. wheel impact detectors, and

4. automatic equipment identification (AEI) readers.

1. Grade Crossing Protection Flashers and Gates

Except for the absolute safety of an underpass or overpass, flashing signals with automatic crossing gates provide the best available assurance against rail-highway collisions and continue to be added or updated at a rate of 1,500 or more per year. These installations require sophisticated circuitry to initiate the warning action sequence a safe distance ahead of the train but halt the sequence when the train has cleared the crossing. If nearby switching movements are common, manual controls are also needed to let the train crew start or release the warning and preserve their credibility and acceptability with the public.

With the wide-spread use of welded track the DC track-circuit installation requirement of four pairs of insulated joints has become an undesirable break in rail continuity. "Frequency Shift Overlay" circuits, operating in the low audio range around 1,000 Hz, are now likely to be used. Since current at these frequencies will travel only a short, predictable distance along the rails before fading out, and since different frequencies can be used to cause a receiving relay to pick up only in response to current from one source, these systems can do the job with uninterrupted rails. They can also detect the *rate* at which a train is approaching by how fast the current is being shunted by its wheels. A *grade crossing predictor* which lowers the gates a relatively constant time ahead of the arrival of trains traveling at widely different speeds is thus possible and now widely used.

2. Hot Box and Dragging Equipment Detectors

Fig. 7-9 shows a wayside infrared hot box detector which scans the journal bearings of trains passing at any speed. Such detectors are typically maintained at intervals of 20 to 50 miles on main lines. The heat profile of each bearing (compensated for ambient temperature) is measured, with such techniques as comparison with the opposite bearing on the same axle and a different threshold for plain and roller bearings (the rollers normally run somewhat hotter) used to determine if a bearing is dangerous. Also under development are defect detectors based on analysis of the sound spectrum emanating from the bearing, which typically will get noisy as failure approaches.

If defects are detected, predominant current practice is to have the detector automatically radio a message to the passing train identifying axle number(s) and side, a notification method compatible with cabooseless operation.

Reliability of detection with these devices is generally high, with false alarms more of a problem than missed hot bearings; *complete* protection is not economically feasible with wayside detectors because the cost (typically $35,000 to $100,000 per installation) precludes spacing them so closely that a disastrous failure cannot occur within the time between detectors. Sound-spectrum analysis of roller bearings approaching failure suggests that an acoustic approach, considering current advances in real-time data processing, may ultimately lead to a solution.

147

Fig. 7-9. Wayside Hot Box Detector

Hot wheels (statistically much more frequent than hot boxes), resulting from stuck or unreleased brakes and a hazard because of their potential for subsequent broken wheels, can be similarly detected and reported.

Dragging equipment detectors are located ahead of major bridges and interlocking plants where the potential cost of any resulting accident is high. *Rock slide de-*

tector fences alongside (and even overhead in vulnerable cuts) are connected to the block signal system to provide advance warning. High-water, earthquake-motion, shifted-load and high-car detectors are used in particular situations where the potential for hazard is high.

3. Wheel Impact Dectectors

Research has indicated that wheel-tread defects (not only slid-flat wheels readily detected by inspection but also wheels with built-up or otherwise out-of-round contours resulting in even greater impact loads) are highly damaging to the track structure, particularly if concrete ties are involved. Microprocessor analysis of impact force data from strain gages mounted on the rail can detect such axles; transmission of this data to the next inspection point is a required link in the chain leading to a reduced population of such mavericks.

4. Automatic Equipment Identification (AEI)

Keeping track of millions of freight cars has always been an expensive problem, basically handled for the first 130 years of railroading by clerks walking yard tracks with clipboards, a process in later years sometimes moved out of the weather and into the yard office by closed-circuit monitoring of illuminated incoming consists creeping by a TV scanner.

A 1960s AAR program mandated tagging of all cars in interchange with relatively inexpensive multicolor bar-code labels. Provided the car labels were kept reasonably clean, the optical scanning system, state of the art at the time, functioned reliably; but the comparatively high cost of reader installations resulted in less than universal use among major railroads. The label requirement was dropped and general railroad use of the optical system faded away in the early 1970s.

With the development of inert-transponder radio-frequency identification systems unaffected by grime and with the capability of reporting information in addition to reporting marks and car numbers, mandatory ACI tagging was reinstituted in 1992 and essentially completed on the existing freight car fleet within three years. With readers in service at more than 1,500 sites (Fig. 7-10) keeping tabs on locomotive units, end-of-train devices and some intermodal equipment in addition to the freight cars, AEI is also being used for such functions as checking equipment in and out of repair facilities as well for its basic use in updating train consists and expediting interchange reporting. To reduce costs, readers are often co-located at defect-detector sites.

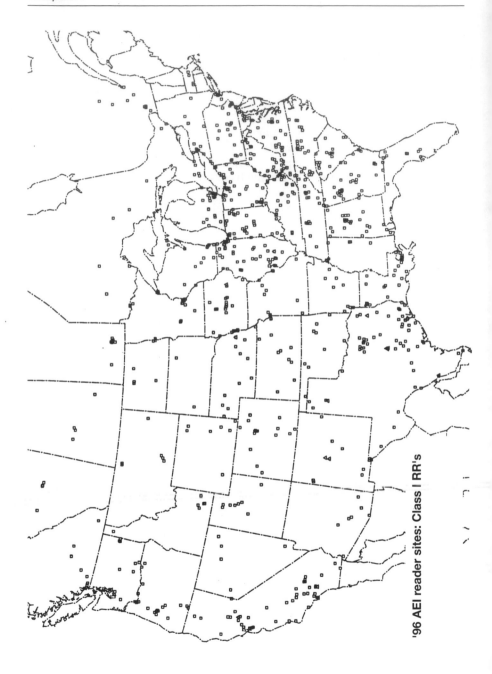

Fig. 7-10 Automatic Equipment Identification (AEI) reader sites

Railroad Operation
Moving From Here to There

8

During every business day, approximately 100,000 freight cars are loaded in the United States, Canada and Mexico. Some are loaded with bulk commodities while in motion and without being uncoupled from their trains, and others have their loads placed aboard in piggyback trailers or sealed containers which started their journey by highway or water. Somewhat more than half of these carloadings, however, are represented by shipments of an individual car or a small group of cars, loaded at a specific point where the contents were produced or processed, and destined for a consignee hundreds or thousands of miles away. The shipment may start its journey alone or coupled to other cars loaded at the same time or place but headed in other directions; the shipment will finish its trip at an unloading point where the contents [will be] consumed, processed, distributed or sold.

While mega-mergers since 1980 have consolidated more and more long-haul traffic onto two and three systems, respectively, in the western and eastern halves of the rail network in the United States, with the proliferation of regional and shortline spin-offs of important secondary and branch lines, interchange between railroads will remain typical of many shipments; in 1994, an estimated 30% of all carloads (producing almost 50% of rail freight revenues) traveled over more than one company's lines. Frequently, a shipment will travel in a car belonging to none of the railroads over which it is routed.

The "Average" Freight Train

Statistics as to the average freight train – 65 cars (37 loaded) carrying 2,750 revenue tons of lading at an average speed (including all terminal and enroute delays) of 22.4 mph to produce 61,000 net ton miles and $1,525 gross revenue per hour on Class I roads in 1994 – of course, don't begin to describe the variety of operations involved in railroad freight movements. Unit trains carrying 12,000 net tons in 110 cars may travel over 1,500 miles without a change in consist; intermodal trains may run at allowed speeds up to 70 mph over connecting railroads, stopping only at hub terminals to pick up and set out large blocks of cars. On the other hand, a car in a local freight may travel only a few miles at a jump and start out as the entire train consist. A large part of the railroad system's profitability depends upon arranging its operations so that most of the travel of individual shipments (average haul is 800 miles) is in trains of average or better proportions and performance.

Obviously, the labor and energy involved in a specific shipment will vary with the tonnage, distance, route, and handling involved. *On the average* in 1994, earning the carload's $1,400 in gross revenue (unchanged from five years earlier because of a 9.4% decrease in freight rates) required the expenditure of 20.6 hours of railroad-employee time (down 25%) in total – including maintenance-of-way and equipment, bringing back the empties, debugging computer programs, quoting freight rates, and so on. Total diesel fuel consumption for all movements – switching and road – amounted to 144 gallons (down 3.4%) for that hypothetical average revenue carload, or about nine miles per gallon for the loaded portion of the movement, which may not sound like much until you remember that it's for moving about 95 tons of car and lading.

Follow One Carload

To get some idea of how this task of moving freight is accomplished year in and year out, we can examine in sequence the process of handling a carload from receipt to delivery, with later digressions discussing rules and practices common to earlier regulatory circumstances and other classes of traffic.

Contract Rates

It should be noted that, in accordance with partial deregulation of railroad traffic in the 1980 era, most freight (an estimated 67% of all tonnage in 1994) now moves under rates and terms set by contract between the railroad and shipper rather than on the pre-1980 basis of published tariffs and conditions proposed by railroad rate bureaus and approved or set by the Interstate Commerce Commission. Since the terms of a contract (not public information, except that summaries of the terms for those covering agricultural commodities must continue to be published) still need to cover the same matters as a tariff: exactly who will do what for whom for how much and when – the functions remain, though the terminology may be different. By the terms of the ICC Termination Act of 1995, remaining regulatory aspects of rate setting and tariff publication for nonagricultural commodities were eliminated. Authority for review of the competitive consequences of, and setting conditions for, railroad merger proposals was retained by the Surface Transportation Board which has succeeded the ICC as an independent agency, now housed within the Department of Transportation. Consequences of a century of regulation aimed at enforcing common-carrier access and equal treatment of small and large shippers, including rigid prohibitions regarding the extension of credit or anything else that could look like a railroad "rebate" to a favored customer, tend to live on in the form of business practices that may seem archaic. The ancestry of some of these will be traced later as historical background.

The Paperwork Path; EDI

Tracing a single carload from origin to destination should provide some feeling for the "paperwork" that must accompany the physical transportation of the goods as well as some appreciation for the degree to which it may now be represented by computer displays and print-outs rather than by typed forms. Much of the process as described here has already been superseded by later technology (the twilight of the "IBM card") and references to local agents should be interpreted loosely, since the function is now more likely to be accomplished remotely by fax or PC network.

As was the case a century earlier in the establishment of the system of Standard Time Zones, the railroad industry was a leader in the development and use of Electronic Data Interchange (EDI) standards for transmitting data from computer to computer, a protocol which has been widely adopted throughout the nation's commercial establishment.

Jones Cannery is located on the East-West Railroad at city B (*see* system map, Fig. 2-4). Jones contacts the E-W's freight agent to request a car to ship 100,000 lbs of canned goods to their customer, Smith Company, in the port city of AA. The E-W's Car Service Division will then pick out the appropriate car for placement at Jones Cannery's railroad siding. With a west to east shipment, such as this, the Car Service Division will select an eastern line car, so that the car will be heading back towards its home railroad.

They select a boxcar (identified as PR 123456) belonging to the Peninsular Railway, as AA is in the same general direction as Peninsular trackage. While the E-W is using this particular boxcar, they are paying "rent" to the Peninsular in the form of mileage and per diem charges, much the same as one would pay when renting an automobile.

After the car is obtained and inspected by the mechanical department to see if it's mechanically fit for loading, the car is then spotted by the switching crew to Jones' siding (more about switching in Chapter 11). On the E-W, the car is processed through the yard by the continuous inventory car location system with IBM cards or CRT display, rather than physical checks.

Demurrage

Once the car has been delivered to Jones, it is subject to the Demurrage Rules. Demurrage is a tariff established and assessed by the railroads and enforced by the ICC to encourage shippers to load and unload quickly to get the cars back in revenue service. The customer generally has 24 hours to load and 48 hours to unload. The amount of time varies according to commodities, rate, and tariff applications. After the allotted time has expired, the customer is subject to a demurrage charge. The demurrage bill is issued by the local freight agent to the customer and is paid at that point.

Bill of Lading

Following receipt and loading of the car, Jones presents to the railroad a straight bill of lading. The bill of lading is a contract of carriage between Jones and the E-W. It is also Jones' receipt that states the customer has issued the railroad a carload of goods and a bill of lading. In most cases, the shipper pays the freight charges, so the bill of lading is marked "Prepaid." If the consignee is to pay the freight bill, the bill of lading is to be marked "Collect." Once the bill of lading is signed by the shipper and the railroad, it is a legal contract, admissible in a court of law, in the event of any contention about the shipment. The legalities concerning bills of lading and agreements between shippers and transporters are spelled out in the law of bailments, often summarized in the "fine print" on the back of most bills of lading.

There are several different types of bills of lading, but they all fall into one of two categories, "open or straight" and "order." The open bill of lading is used for most collect and prepaid shipments. The order bill of lading comes into use when the shipper wants to be paid for his goods before the shipment is released to the consignee. The finances are taken care of by the shipper's and consignee's respective banks. Freight charges may be prepaid or collect. Other types of bills of lading include individualized forms used by the federal government and some private industries and export bills of lading.

Rating the Shipment

If the shipment is to be transported under a contract between railroad and shipper, its terms will determine the rate charged. In other cases, where deregulation means that a published, ICC-approved tariff is not involved, if it is to do business, the railroad must establish and provide equivalent price information. This is most likely to be made available through the centralized, computerized REN (Rate EDI Network), which can be accessed by anyone with EDI data exchange capability. As discussed below under "Tariffs," determining the cost of a shipment is still not necessarily a simple matter.

Compiling a Waybill

When the E-W receives the bill of lading from Jones, the local E-W rate clerk will rate the shipment, that is, he or she will check the various tariff documents to find out the actual rate for the products Jones is shipping. From all the information received and determined to this point, the E-W makes up a waybill to help keep track of the car and shipment and to inform the rest of the railroad that the shipment is moving on the E-W system. A waybill contains the following information:

Car initial and number
Waybill number, which is assigned to the freight agent by the railroad
Waybill date

Origin station

Name of shipper

Consignee, or customer at destination

Destination city

The route the car will travel

The Standard Transportation Commodity Code, a seven-digit number as
   signed by the ICC to a particular commodity

Physical description of articles

Weight of shipment

Applicable rate

Total freight charges (weight x rate = freight charges)

Prepaid or collect

Whether the shipment is perishable; if so, perishable instructions will be
   included

All of this information is fed from the yard office into the E-W's computer in
headquarters, which keeps track of all cars on the system, the freight being carried
and its destination.

The waybill is a contract between the railroads moving the shipment. The junction stamps applied to this document as it travels between carriers determine the divisions which will apply and provide the basis for misroute claims between carriers. The last handling road-haul carrier takes the waybill into account and is responsible for collecting the freight charge and allocating it among the handling
lines. The handling lines match up waybill numbers in interline settlements to assure they have not been left out of the payments for any car they handled on a road-
haul. Thus, the waybill is a great deal more than a simple movement instruction.

The original waybill will travel with the car from its origin to destination and is
carried by the train conductor. One copy will be sent to railroad headquarters; several copies are kept on file at the local freight office. Other copies of the waybill may
go to other departments or offices in the railroad depending on individual practice.
Under the Interchange Settlement System (ISS), an AAR procedure put into effect
in 1996, any waybill involving interchange is entered electronically into a central
file, where it is assigned a unique identification number; copies are automatically
sent to all carriers on the shipment's route.

Other Computer Operations

Several steps involving the use of the continuous inventory car location system
and the railroad's computer operating database follow the preparation of the waybill. These procedures vary from railroad to railroad in their details, but in most
cases, several events will be reported to the computer plus changes made in the continuous car inventory, whether in the form of IBM cards or in the mini-comput-
er/CRT systems. These events include the set, release, and pull of the car, any bad

155

orders (cars that have defects that may prevent their safe movement over the railroad), weighing or inspection movements, and holding for billings. The car inventory system produces the switch lists used in picking up and in classifying the outbound load.

While the waybill is being prepared in the yard office, a switch crew goes to Jones' siding to pick up the car and take it to the classification yard, where the car will be switched into the proper outbound train. All the waybills for the particular train are gathered together, and a wheel report is compiled for the conductor. The wheel report is a list of cars in a train showing destination, weight, load or empty status, etc., for each car, and which the conductor updates as the train picks up or sets out cars enroute. The wheel report is used by the conductor for the haul over his territory, in this case from city B to city C. At city C, the wheel report is turned over to the conductor on the haul from C to D, and so on. Wheel reports are turned into headquarters and are sometimes used to figure mileage on the cars.

Many roads no longer use the conductor's wheel report to figure mileage, but rely on computer-generated wheel reports and computation programs. The mileage calculations are for interline settlements of the mileage charges on cars which the railroads are "renting" from each other.

The next report entered in the computer, just prior to train departure, is the consist report. This report now lists only time, date, location, and car numbers, since on any sophisticated system, waybill data was previously entered, and train symbol itinerary is already established in the computer. The division point will now be aware of what train is coming in, what's on it, and whether they will have to add or cut out cars. When the new crew comes on at the division point, the old crew hands over the waybills for the cars continuing and the wheel report.

Interchange

In order to get Jones' shipment to Smith in city AA, the car must be turned over to the SW & AA Railroad at city G. Before the train gets to G, the E-W yardmaster in G has already received a consist report from the computer. From this report, he makes up a switch list for his switching crews, so that they will know whether each car stays with the train, stays in the area for local delivery or, as in this case, interchanges to the SW & AA Railroad to continue on to city AA.

The switching crew brings car PR 123456 and any other cars being interchanged to the SW & AA yard to be made up into a train heading for city AA. The E-W yard office personnel must enter into the computer an interchange delivery report which confirms that the car(s) has been turned over to the SW & AA. The report includes the initial and number of the car, its contents, destination and the time and date it was delivered to the SW & AA. As soon as the car is turned over, the E-W's per diem and mileage charges end, and the SW & AA's charges begin.

The waybill that was filled out in city B and that has traveled with the car to city G is turned over to SW & AA yard personnel, who make waybill entries into their computer to advise their people of the destination, contents, etc., of this car. They also will make a wheel report for their crew.

Arriving at Destination

The SW & AA train then continues on to city AA. When the freight agent in city AA receives the waybill, he/she will notify Smith Company that the car containing their shipment of canned goods has arrived. Smith will either order the car to be sent to their siding as soon as feasible or will order it in by number, i.e., a specific sequence of cars. The SW & AA switch crew will then bring the car to Smith, if it has established credit with the railroad or the freight bill has been prepaid. If not, Smith must pay for the freight charges before car delivery.

Car PR 123456 then goes on to Smith's demurrage. Smith has an allotted amount of time to unload the shipment and notify the SW & AA to pick up the car. If Smith goes over the allotted time, then the SW & AA charges and collects the demurrage fee.

The local freight agent prepares a freight bill for the consignee which is made up from the information on the waybill. Smith remits its check for these charges to the SW & AA Railroad, unless the charges have been prepaid.

Order Bill of Lading

If the shipment carries an order bill of lading, the last road-haul line cannot turn over the shipment to the consignee or to the switching company making final delivery until it has proof that the goods have been paid for. Proof of payment includes: order bill handed over by the bank that has made payment; a consignee bond that is on file with the railroad's credit and collection department; or a certified check of 125% of the value of the shipment. Mistakes can sometimes happen. Improper communication between railroad employees may allow the shipment to be delivered before proof of payment is received. Should something go awry, and the consignee cannot pay for the goods, the last road-haul company is responsible for the cost of the merchandise.

Regardless of who pays the freight charges, the company has 120 hours (not including weekends and holidays) to pay the charges. U.S. government agencies have 30 days to pay. If the railroad does not show evidence of attempting to collect, it could be found in violation of the Elkins Act. The railroad may also be liable to fines if it unduly denies credit to shippers. Credit regulations are spelled out in Section 1320 of the ICC Act.

Rate clerks are entrusted to accurately rate shipments and supply the proper data for freight bills. In the event of undercharges or overcharges due to errors on the bill, the railroad is not absolved of the responsibility of refunding the overcharges, nor is the shipper excused from paying to the railroad the difference between the undercharge and actual charge. The originating carrier must make the refund or collect the difference when the shipment is prepaid. For collect shipments, it's the delivering line's responsibility. The payee has 30 days to make payment to the railroad after he has been notified of undercharges.

The Complexities of Switching

The road-haul freight that brings a car into town usually doesn't deliver it to the consignee's siding, but must rely on switching to get the car to its final destination. Basically, there are three types of switches – intra-plant, intra-terminal, and inter-terminal. Intra-plant switching involves the movement from one track to another or between two points on the same track within the same plant or industry. Intra-terminal switching is the movement from a track, industry, or firm to another track, industry, or firm on the same road within the same district. Inter-terminal switching covers movements from a track of one road to a track of another road within the same district.

When an inter-terminal switch is called for, things can get complicated. Inter-terminal switching involves complex agreements between the railroads in every city. Each railroad establishes a switching district (*see* Chapter 11) in which it will arrange to have a car delivered, regardless of whose tracks the siding is located on. Railroads establish reciprocal agreements ("we'll switch your cars, if you'll switch ours") to ensure that cars are delivered.

Switching Charges

The road handling the switch will be paid a switching charge which is determined by each railroad within each switching district. These charges are computed via careful analysis of crew time, fuel cost, etc. The rates are then published and usually approved by the ICC. They can be determined by any basis the railroad selects – commodity, weight, distance, type of car, or any combination.

Settlement of charges among railroads is taken care of by monthly switching settlement statements based on lists provided by the freight agent. The accounting department arranges for settlement of charges via a process similar to interline settlements which follows.

Interline Settlements

In order for the E-W Railroad to collect its share ("division") of revenue from the shipment it must get its money from the SW & AA Railroad, which collected the freight charges from Smith. Under ISS, the central computer advises each railroad in the route of its share; each has an opportunity to approve or question its share electronically. If all concur, that's it and the customer is billed; any railroad's objections must be resolved by negotiation within a fixed time frame or the matter will be settled arbitrarily. Once a month, the participating railroads settle their net balances with each other by transfer of funds.

Railroad Regulation–Some History

Since it would be virtually impossible to obtain a right-of-way through settled country without the back-up capability of invoking the government's power of *eminent domain* to set a reasonable price, railroads must, in practice, be chartered by public authority. These charters, in turn, require that railroads operate as *common carriers*. Since the railroad by its very nature can carry just about anything that's worth transporting, this isn't just an academic matter. Most of the federal regulation of railroads in the United States is based on the Interstate Commerce Act of 1887 and subsequent extensions; these in general were established at a time when railroads were in a monopoly situation in land transport and have had the primary thrust of keeping the overall level of rates low and equalizing access to regulated transportation among shippers and consignees in different locations and situations.

Since rates have been regulated by the Interstate Commerce Commission, railroads have been exempt from the antitrust provisions of the Clayton Act and allowed to propose rates and establish standardized tariff provision (and formats) collectively through the workings of *rate bureaus*.

Although the steady growth of the state and, later, federally-financed highway systems and the federally-constructed and maintained internal and coastal waterways systems have made the monopoly aspects of rail transportation a thing of the past for most commodities, regulation of railroad (and common-carrier trucking except for any commodities however remotely related to agriculture, which were exempt) continued in full flower until the passage of significant *deregulation* legislation in 1980.

Full effects of the Staggers (deregulation) Act of 1980 (which followed the "4R" Railroad Revitalization and Regulatory Reform Act of 1976, a less far-reaching piece of legislation whose effects were largely postponed by ICC interpretations), can only be assessed with the passage of time as they are interpreted by litigation, and the thought patterns and habits of railroaders, shippers, and regulators ingrained over the years adapt to the shifts in philosophy implied. A few of the provisions of the act:

- Railroad pricing is subject to antitrust law; rate-bureau functions are severely limited, with only railroads participating in an interline (joint) rate allowed to vote in establishing its level.

- Within broad limits, especially on traffic for which other modes of transport provide an alternative to the shipper, individual rail rates may be raised and lowered rapidly in response to the competitive situation from unregulated carriers, seasonal factors, and other service and cost effects. Intermodal ("piggyback") and some boxcar traffic has been totally deregulated.

- "Blanket rate" changes under the ex parte procedures are phased out, except for limited changes directly related to specific cost increases.

- *Contract rates* between railroad and shipper guaranteeing a rate basis for a specified volume or proportion of the shipper's business over a specified period of time under agreed-upon conditions are specifically made legal (subject to antitrust law); not all aspects of the contract are public information.

- *Surcharges* may be applied by a railroad to a specific commodity or route or to its division of a joint rate to bring revenue up to the cost of handling the shipment, potentially eliminating the cross-subsidization of unprofitable traffic associated with the regulated rate structure evolved over the years.

In general, the major effects of the first 15 years of this partial deregulation has been a dramatic improvement in railroad stability and profitability (though industry "return on investment" has not reached "cost of capital" levels), virtual elimination of such historically important ratemaking principles as "processing in transit" and – with continuing competitive pressures such as those associated with private trucking – a broad lowering of constant-dollar rail rates (in some commodities, exceeding the rate of inflation).

Though now likely to be reflected primarily in the provisions of rate contracts rather than rulings and tariffs, legacies of the regulated years nevertheless live on, showing up inter-community (especially inter-seaport) conflicts and pressures for legislative adjustments to the extent that a discussion of some of these historical factors is included.

Equal Access

Since most rail shipments now represent fairly regular movements from quantity producers to their customers, they usually originate at private side-tracks. As common carriers, railroads are required to provide a track connection to any customer who wants it, unless it can be shown that it is physically impractical. The railroad can require financial arrangements appropriate for the volume of business involved, but the same rules must apply to all. The railroad will place a car for loading and pick it up as part of the freight charge, but since equal service to all is the rule, there must be a charge, specified by tariff, for intra-plant movements; a large company with its own network of track will probably do its own switching.

Public Loading Facilities

The railroad must also provide places where shippers and consignees who don't have their own sidings can load and receive carload freight. The simplest of these are "team" tracks, sidings located and spaced so that teams and wagons (now trucks, of course) can back up to the cars. More elaborate railroad-owned facilities range from a small gantry crane up to the huge port terminals handling coal, ore, grain, and other bulk cargoes between car and barge or ship, with provisions for intermediate storage. For each service provided by these facilities a schedule of charges must be established by published tariff, subject to regulation to assure that the rates are not unduly discriminatory to those who do not opt for all services. Fig. 8-1 is an example of the "new look" in team-track facilities.

Shortline Railroading

Shippers who are some distance from a "line-haul" railroad may reach a line-haul road via a connecting line. If it is a plant-built and -owned facility only, the owner saves switching charges; if it is a common carrier, the shortline receives a "division" of the freight rate (typically, considerably more than just the percentage of the mileage involved, since the costs of an originating or terminating carrier are recognized as being disproportionately high). In return, the shortline must be prepared to accept freight from all comers, including competitors, and its divisions will be scrutinized closely to see that profits from them don't constitute, in effect, a rebate on the freight rate as compared to what's available to others.

The Commodities Clause

Since 1906 it has been illegal for a railroad company to transport any commodity (except timber and materials used in railroad operations themselves) which it owns. That is, a railroad cannot own a coal mine or a steel mill and transport its output for general sale. This act was intended to equalize the situation between producers by requiring the carriers to divorce themselves from subsidiaries that could profit by manipulating freight rates. By raising rates exorbitantly, the railroad with captive mines could presumably put the squeeze on its competitors while using the freight income to offset the price paid on its product.

The converse is not prohibited; a nonrailroad company such as a big steel producer can build and own a railroad to serve its needs, but this line, as a common carrier, must provide equal service and charge equal rates to its parent's competitors. These are matters which, presumably, can be more readily controlled by the regulatory authorities.

Tariffs

What is the freight rate on a shipment? Unfortunately, that isn't an easy question for the friendly local freight agent. Tariffs are complicated, to say the least, when

161

you multiply the thousands of stations by the dozens of routings by the hundreds of commodities, which results in millions of different combinations. Over the period of a hundred years, the tariff bureaus, acting for the "Trunk Line" (Eastern), Southern and Western lines, have developed a system of published tariff documents which, by cross-referencing against each other, reduce the problem of presenting all needed combinations from being hopeless to merely challenging. The answer is contained in those documents, but is derived only by tracking down, adding, subtracting, multiplying, and dividing a number of different numbers which together reflect all the factors that go into a rate, factors far more numerous than simply how much the shipment weighs and how many miles it has to go. Examining a few of these and hinting at the rest may provide some insight into the philosophies underlying the system.

Class and Commodity Rates

One-of-a-kind or occasional shipments, such as a car of granite curbstones going to a small town in the Midwest to surround its new fountain in the park, are covered by *class rates*, rates determined by finding the classification which includes "granite, rough finished" (with some other characterizations and qualifications) in a list of hundreds of other items of generally equivalent density, value, and nature with respect to handling care required. Class rates have become so high that, in general, even for a single shipment, application will be made to quote a commodity rate, which is usually done. Class rates move less than one percent of traffic. Commodity rates move the rest.

More or less regular shipments (the bulk of the business) are likely to be covered by *commodity rates*, rates for one particular commodity or item from one specific point or area to another, such as raw copper ingots from a smelter town in Arizona to a processing plant in Illinois or washing machines, boxed in accordance with another reference specification, from a plant in Kentucky to a distribution center in the state of Washington. These rates, lower than corresponding class rates, have been set up, for example, to let an area compete in various markets with sources elsewhere in the country or world, to make it economically possible for a particularly bulky commodity to travel that far, or to recognize economies possible from centralizing a particular manufacturing, processing, or distributing function at one point.

Ex Parte Changes

All of these class and commodity rates in turn may be changed (in inflationary times, raised) by the effects of across-the-board ex parte changes authorized from time to time by the ICC to recognize changes in costs affecting the whole level of rates. In turn, these are usually modified by "hold downs" on particular items for which raises are not requested for competitive or technical reasons.

Incentive Rates

To encourage shipments in amounts, forms, or under other conditions which will make more economical handling by the railroads possible, "incentive" tariffs (merely one form of commodity rate) may be established in return for the acceptance of such requirements as loading cars to more than the minimum carload weight. These are discussed in a little more depth in connection with unit-train operations.

Processing-in-Transit Rates

While the general level of freight rates generates a great deal of discussion, controversy, and litigation, the matter of freight rate comparisons between different sections of the country, different port cities, and even in different directions for the same commodity between the same areas is ever more controversial. Over the years thousands of such matters have been determined by Congress, the ICC and the courts, and are reflected in current tariffs.

In the case of our East-West System, for example, consider the matter of the farmers at A vs. those on the branch leading west from U (both in the west-central area of Fig. 2-4). There is a flour mill at A, so grain processed there can go directly to the bakeries in the metropolitan area of J on the east coast. Wheat grown in the U area would be at a disadvantage as there is no mill in the area. It would have to be shipped as grain to the processor at F and re-shipped to J, at greater freight cost since two shipments are involved. The answer, so far as the miller at F and the wheat growers at U are concerned, is the "milling-in-transit rate" established many years ago which treats the two "legs" of the trip from U to J, with a stopover at F where the grain becomes flour, as a single movement, accorded a rate equal to the through A - J flour rate. The flour mill at F can stay in business despite dwindling local supplies as shopping centers and apartment developments take over the wheat fields.

163

Fig. 8-1. Team-Track Loading Facility

Car Types and Carloadings

9

To get any load from origin to destination, there has to be a suitable car. The technology of standardization, as previously shown, makes it possible for any car to go anywhere. But what kinds of cars are needed; who is going to buy them; how do you find the one you need; and how do the empties get back?

Freight Car Types

The freight car fleet in the United States in 1996 consisted of the following types of car, with ownership as indicated;

Type	Total	Class I Railroads	Other Railroads	Car Companies and Shippers
Boxcars:	156,284	97,022	28,363	30,899
Plain Box	*39,155*	*10,941*	*9,299*	*18,915*
Equipped Box	*117,129*	*86,081*	*19,064*	*11,984*
Covered Hoppers	350,611	151,583	15,885	183,143
Flatcars	131,840	81,187	6,878	43,775
Refrigerator Cars	31,103	25,478	2,713	2,912
Gondolas	179,046	103,918	15,624	59,504
Hoppers	166,980	105,718	16,087	45,175
Tank Cars	215,482	,985	,024	214,473
Others	9,227	4,974	1,790	2,463
TOTAL	**1,240,573**	**570,865**	**87,364**	**582,344**

Source: *Railroad Facts,* 1997 Edition. AAR Publications.

Cabooses are not included in the preceding table; EOT (end-of-train) monitor devices having taken the place of most of the 19,000 that were on the roster in 1980, only a fraction remain active in local freight or other services where operating conditions such as long back-up movements warrant their use.

Traffic Distribution

For each principal class of commodity *going from one producer to one receiver,* there is one preferred freight car design to carry it. Many variables govern the type of car needed: available loading and unloading gear; the size, shape, and nature of the commodity; its value and need for protection; and the customary unit quantity of shipment. All these variables make a difference, large or small, in how satisfactory a particular car can be. Since there can't be an infinite number of different types of car, the one actually used will represent a compromise between what's ideal and what is practical for the car builders, railroads, and shippers.

Carloadings are reported in 18 major "commodity groups" which in total represent about 96% of the total loadings, exclusive of intermodal traffic (trailers or containers loaded on railcars, as discussed in Chapter 11); the number of trailers and containers loaded is now reported separately, without regard to the commodities involved, since the lading in most intermodal traffic is identified only as "Freight – All Kinds."

The following section presents these commodity groups in terms of the approximate carloads, tonnage, and revenues of each in traffic originated on railroads in the United States in a reasonably typical year in the mid-1990s. Percentages (some of which, grain in particular, may vary significantly from year to year) contributed by each commodity group are with respect to total traffic, intermodal included.

Grain

Fig. 9-1. LO "Jumbo" Covered Hopper Car

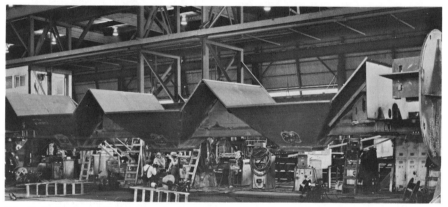

Fig. 9-2. Hopper Slope Sheets that "Funnel" Lading Out of Car

Carloadings per year:	1,320,000 (5.7%)
Tons originated:	121,000,000 (8.2%)
Gross revenue:	$2,100,000,000 (6.4%)
Examples of preferred car:	"Jumbo" covered hopper
AAR Mechanical Designation	LO

"Jumbo" covered hoppers are built with cubic capacities up to 5,700 cu ft to suit the density of the particular grain involved. They have superseded the boxcar (which must be equipped with temporary "grain doors" in its doorways to withstand the pressure and prevent leakage of the contents) as the principal carrier of grain, almost doubling tons per load and providing for direct loading and unloading by air or gravity.

167

Other Farm Products

Fig. 9-3. RP Mechanical Refrigerator Car

Carloadings per year:	150,000 (0.6%)
Tons originated:	11,100,000 (0.5%)
Gross revenue:	$310,000,000 (0.9%)
Example of preferred car:	Mechanical refrigerator
AAR Mechanical Designation	RP

The mechanical refrigerator car, with diesel-powered cooling unit and fuel capacity for as long as two weeks unattended operation, was developed to meet the sub-zero requirements of frozen food products which could not be met by the time-honored ice-and-salt-cooled cars. Now, most refrigerator car cooling systems are mechanical and are of general-purpose type, also capable of maintaining temperatures required by various fresh or frozen products. Most are also equipped with cushioning and load-restraining devices.

Metallic Ores

Fig. 9-4. HMA Ore Hopper Car

Carloadings per year:	440,000 (1.9%)
Tons originated:	40,400,000 (2.7%)
Gross revenue:	$380,000,000 (1.2%)
Example of preferred car:	Ore hopper
AAR Mechanical Designation	HMA

Ore is very dense, loading as heavily as 170 lbs per cu ft, so cars used exclusively in this service are of small cubic capacity. Cars in processed taconite pellet service have an added collar to increase cubic capacity and carry the same tonnage of this lower density product.

Coal

Fig. 9-5. Rapid-Unloading Aluminum Quintuple-Hopper Car

Fig. 9-6. Bethgon Coalporter Unit-Train Gondola Car

Carloadings per year:	5,680,000 (24.7%)
Tons originated:	574,000,000 (39.1%)
Gross revenue:	$7,021,000,000 (21.7%)
Example of preferred cars:	Unit-train hopper
AAR Mechanical Designation	HT / GT

Coal (cont.)

Most coal tonnage goes to generating stations, to export docks, and to steel mill coking plants, often in unit trains. Choice of bottom-dump hopper or high-side solid-bottom gondola depends upon unloading facilities at receiving point. Cars unloaded by overturning them in rotary car dampers may be equipped with a rotary coupler at one end which allows emptying without uncoupling; bottom-dump cars, which may also be unloaded in a rotary dumper, may be equipped with power-operated hopper doors for unloading in motion. Approximately 4,000 cu ft capacity is required for 100-ton load.

Crushed Stone, Gravel, Sand

Fig. 9-7. HM "Aggregate" Hopper Car

Carloadings per year:	760,000 (3.4%)
Tons originated:	70,000,000 (4.8%)
Gross revenue:	$460,000,000 (1.4%)
Example of preferred car:	"Aggregate" hopper
AAR Mechanical Designation	HM

Midway in density between ore and coal, crushed rock, gravel, and sand require about 2,000 cu ft capacity for a 100-ton car. Where steady traffic is not expected, these commodities are often handled by partial loading of coal hoppers, but lower costs in regular service may warrant compact, quick-discharging cars of this type.

171

Nonmetallic Minerals

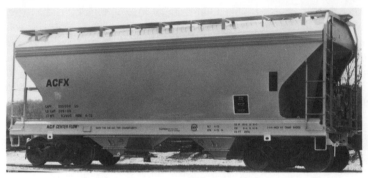

Fig. 9-8. LO Small-Cube Covered Hopper Car

Carloadings per year:	380,000 (1.7%)
Tons originated:	36,000,000 (2.4%)
Gross revenue:	$400,000,000 (1.4%)
Example of preferred car:	Small-cube covered hopper
AAR Mechanical Designation	LO

Many minerals such as salt or phosphate require protection from the weather and cannot be shipped in open-top cars. Special car linings may be needed to protect contents from contamination; most minerals are dense and load to 70- or 100-ton car capacity in twin-hopper cars of 2,500 to 3,000 cu ft capacity.

Grain Mill Products

Fig. 9-9. XF Food-Service Boxcar

Carloadings per year:	710,000 (3.1%)
Tons originated:	45,000,000 (3.1%)
Gross revenue:	$1,120,000,000 (3.6%)
Example of preferred car:	Food-service boxcar
AAR Mechanical Designation	XF

XF cars have special seamless plastic linings to prevent contamination and "plug" doors which are forced inward by the operating mechanism after sliding into the closed position to provide a smooth interior. These cars are reserved for processed and packaged food service; carriers contaminating XF cars are subject to a special penalty charge.

173

Food and Kindred Products

Fig. 9-10. RB Insulated Refrigerator Car

Carloadings per year:	670,000 (2.9%)
Tons originated:	43,000,000 (2.9%)
Gross revenue:	$1,310,000,000 (4.1%)
Example of preferred car:	Insulated refrigerator car
AAR Mechanical Designation	RB

RB "bunkerless refrigerator" cars have the equivalent of at least 3-inch insulation on sides and 3½ inches on roof and floor but no cooling system. With plug doors and, usually, load-restraining devices (designation RBL), these cars can maintain the temperature of many food products within satisfactory limits throughout an extended trip without the expense of mechanical temperature control.

Lumber and Wood Products (Except Furniture)

Fig. 9-11. FMS Center-Beam Bulkhead Flatcar

Carloadings per year:	260,000 (1.1%)
Tons originated:	14,000,000 (1.0%)
Gross revenue:	$520,000,000 (1.6%)
Example of preferred car:	Center-beam bulkhead flat
AAR Mechanical Designation	FMS

The bulkhead car is now preferred for transporting finished, packaged lumber because of the ease with which such lading can be handled by forklift trucks. The efficient carbody structure provided by the central girder or truss against which the bundles are secured allows a car long enough to hold 100 tons of lading to remain within axle-load limits.

175

Coke

Fig. 9-12. CSX Transportation Steel Triple-Hopper Car

Carloadings per year:	290,000 (1.3%)
Tons originated:	20,000,000 (1.4%)
Gross revenue:	$380,000,000 (1.2%)
Example of preferred car:	Coke hopper
AAR Mechanical Designation	HTC

Coke, used primarily in blast furnaces in the smelting of iron ore, travels relatively short distances from coking plants to the steel mills. Much lighter than coal, coke is shipped in hopper cars built to larger cubic capacity or equipped with "coke" racks to accommodate its volume.

Pulp, Paper, and Allied Products

Fig. 9-13. XL Equipped Boxcar

Carloadings per year:	650,000 (2.6%)
Tons originated:	37,000,000 (2.5%)
Gross revenue:	$1,510,000,000 (4.7%)
Example of preferred car:	Equipped boxcar
AAR Mechanical Designation	XL

Rolls of newsprint are subject to flattening from impacts of shifting within the car, with subsequent problems in the printing press and damage claims. The cushion-underframe car equipped with load-restraining devices adaptable to its particular load is indispensable in handling such commodities. Paper products are also subject to damage if loaded in cars contaminated or roughed-up by previous loads.

177

Chemicals and Allied Products

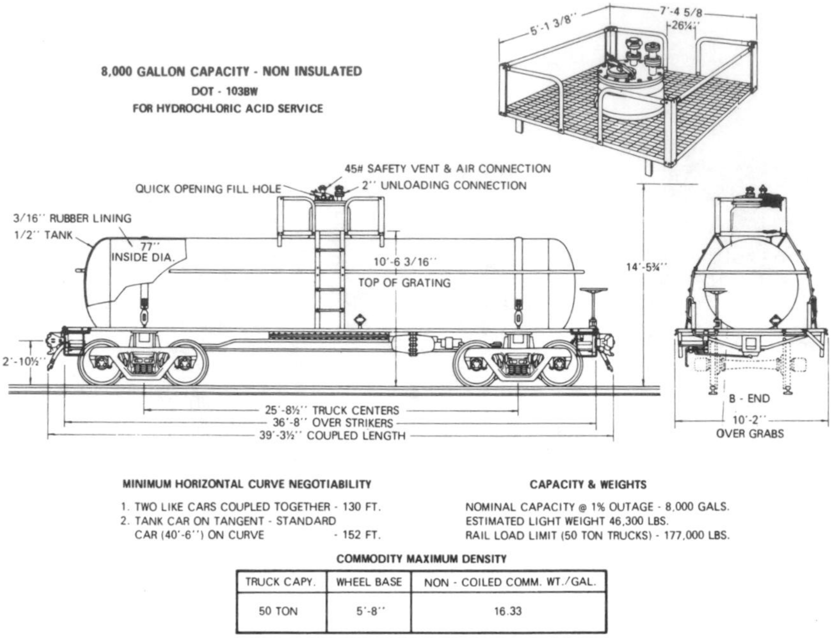

8,000 GALLON CAPACITY - NON INSULATED
DOT - 103BW
FOR HYDROCHLORIC ACID SERVICE

QUICK OPENING FILL HOLE

45# SAFETY VENT & AIR CONNECTION
2" UNLOADING CONNECTION

3/16" RUBBER LINING
1/2" TANK
77"
INSIDE DIA.

10'-6 3/16"
TOP OF GRATING

5'-1 3/8"

7'-4 5/8"
26¼"

14'-5¾"

2'-10½"

B - END
10'-2"
OVER GRABS

25'-8½" TRUCK CENTERS
36'-8" OVER STRIKERS
39'-3½" COUPLED LENGTH

MINIMUM HORIZONTAL CURVE NEGOTIABILITY

1. TWO LIKE CARS COUPLED TOGETHER - 130 FT.
2. TANK CAR ON TANGENT - STANDARD
   CAR (40'-6'') ON CURVE   - 152 FT.

CAPACITY & WEIGHTS

NOMINAL CAPACITY @ 1% OUTAGE - 8,000 GALS.
ESTIMATED LIGHT WEIGHT 46,300 LBS.
RAIL LOAD LIMIT (50 TON TRUCKS) - 177,000 LBS.

COMMODITY MAXIMUM DENSITY

TRUCK CAPY.	WHEEL BASE	NON - COILED COMM. WT./GAL.
50 TON	5'-8''	16.33

Fig. 9-14. Nonpressurized Chemical Tank Car

Carloadings per year:	1,720,000 (7.5%)
Tons originated:	142,000,000 (9.7%)
Gross revenue:	$4,590,000,000 (14.1%)
Example of preferred car:	Chemical tank car
AAR Mechanical Designation	T*

* Tank construction and testing covered by numerous Department of Transportation [DOT] safety specifications for different commodity classes.

Tank car size has increased rapidly in recent years since elimination of requirements for running boards and use of tank itself as "center sill" strength member of car has allowed tank diameter to increase to clearance limit. Since many chemicals require special tank linings or materials, heater coils for unloading, etc., most cars are leased, owned by, or assigned to individual shippers and carry only one class of product. Capacity ranges up to 150 tons (with six-wheel trucks) in some cars.

Petroleum Products

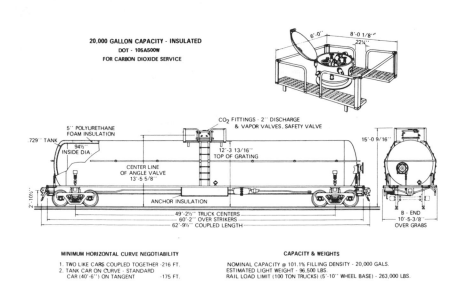

20,000 GALLON CAPACITY - INSULATED
DOT - 105A500W
FOR CARBON DIOXIDE SERVICE

6'-0'' 8'-0 1/8''
22¼''

CO₂ FITTINGS - 2'' DISCHARGE
& VAPOR VALVES, SAFETY VALVE

5'' POLYURETHANE
FOAM INSULATION
.729'' TANK

94½''
INSIDE DIA.

15'-0 9/16''

CENTER LINE
OF ANGLE VALVE
13'-5 5/8''

12'-3 13/16''
TOP OF GRATING

ANCHOR INSULATION

2'-10½''

49'-2½'' TRUCK CENTERS
60'-2'' OVER STRIKERS
62'-9½'' COUPLED LENGTH

B - END
10'-5-3/8''
OVER GRABS

MINIMUM HORIZONTAL CURVE NEGOTIABILITY

1. TWO LIKE CARS COUPLED TOGETHER -216 FT.
2. TANK CAR ON CURVE - STANDARD
   CAR (40'-6'') ON TANGENT   -175 FT.

CAPACITY & WEIGHTS

NOMINAL CAPACITY @ 101.1% FILLING DENSITY - 20,000 GALS.
ESTIMATED LIGHT WEIGHT - 96,500 LBS.
RAIL LOAD LIMIT (100 TON TRUCKS) (5'-10'' WHEEL BASE) - 263,000 LBS.

Fig. 9-15. Pressure Tank Car

Carloadings per year:	290,000 (1.3%)
Tons originated:	22,000,000 (1.5%)
Gross revenue:	$550,000,000 (1.7%)
Example of preferred car:	Pressure tank car
DOT Class	112A

One of the principal petroleum products carried by rail is liquified petroleum (LP) gas, which must be kept under pressure to remain liquid at ordinary temperatures. Special restrictions apply to the construction, handling, and equipment of cars in this "hazardous material" service. Capacity 33,000 gallons.

Stone, Glass and Clay Products

Fig. 9-16. Typical Load-Restraining Device Used in DF Car

DF cars are boxcars with special loading devices that prevent damage to the lading. Often, the cars are prominently marked with the letters "DF" to indicate their special purpose.

Stone, Glass and Clay Products (cont.)

Fig. 9-17. DF Boxcar

Carloadings per year:	580,000 (2.8%)
Tons originated:	42,000,000 (2.9%)
Gross revenue:	$1,010,000,000 (3.1%)
Examples of preferred cars:	Gondola - stone DF Boxcar - glass and clay products
AAR Mechanical Designations	GB XL

Primary Forest Products

Fig. 9-18. HTS Woodchip Hopper Car

Primary Forest Products (cont.)

Carloadings per year:	510,000 (2.2%)
Tons originated:	43,000,000 (2.9%)
Gross revenue:	$900,000,000 (2.8%)
Example of preferred car:	Woodchip hopper
AAR Mechanical Designation	HTS

Largest of all hopper or gondola cars by far are those used in carrying woodchips from the forest to paper plants; it takes over 7,000 cu ft of some varieties to approach the 100-ton mark, so new cars built for this service are at the prescribed limit of height, width, and length. "Shakeouts" (portable machines attached to the car which develop an oscillating force causing the car to vibrate on its springs) are often needed to encourage the load to flow out the hopper doors. Gondolas are used where suitable car dumpers are available.

Metals and Products

Fig. 9-19. ATSF Two-Cover Coil Steel Car

Finished steel in sheet or coil form requiring protection from the weather is shipped in gondola cars with removable covers allowing it to be loaded and unloaded from above by gantry cranes. The concentrated weight of coils requires heavy-duty load-securing devices, aided by sliding-sill or end-of-car cushioning. Structural shapes, pipe, and other long products travel in open-top "mill gons" of 52 to 65 ft length, with drop ends to allow overhang above an "idler" flatcar for exceptionally long loads.

Metals and Products (cont.)

Carloadings per year:	616,000 (2.7%)
Tons originated:	48,800,000 (3.3%)
Gross revenue:	$1,165,000 (3.6%)
Example of preferred car:	Coil Steel Car
AAR Mechanical Designation	GBSR

Motor Vehicles and Equipment

Fig. 9-20. FA Enclosed Tri-level Auto Rack

Carloadings per year:	1,135,000 (5.7%)
Tons originated:	27,800,000 (1.9%)
Gross revenue:	$3,174,000,000 (9.8%)
Example of preferred car:	Enclosed tri-level auto rack
AAR Mechanical Designation	FA

The low rates made possible by carrying 12 to 18 automobiles per car not only regained the majority of this traffic for railroads but have allowed the auto manufacturers to concentrate assembly of particular makes and models at single plants because of the greater distances over which shipping finished cars is economically attractive. Increasing vandalism and pilferage claims have caused the development and adoption of the enclosed rack car despite the additional investment, which may amount to as much as $900 million for the 30,000 cars involved.

Waste and Scrap Materials

Fig. 9-21. GB Gondola Car

Carloadings per year:	604,000 (2.6%)
Tons originated:	37,000,000 (2.5%)
Gross revenue:	$655,000,000 (2.0%)
Example of preferred car:	Gondola
AAR Mechanical Designation	GB

The relationship of freight rates for "recycling" materials to those for shipping ores, minerals, etc., used in the alternative process of meeting current needs by the use of new raw materials (and leaving the scrap to clutter up the environment) has become a considerable social issue in recent years. Scrap is not a time-sensitive commodity requiring expedited handling, but the volume fluctuates widely with changes in price, tending to cause alternating shortages and surpluses in car supply, both of which are costly to the railroads. This gondola, suitable for scrap and other heavy loads, is also equipped with lading strap anchors for commodities requiring tie-down.

All Other Carloads (Except Intermodal)

Fig. 9-22. BCOL Combination-Door Boxcar

Fig. 9-23. XM "Free-Running" Boxcar

This category (excluding intermodal loadings) includes merchandise and machinery of all types not falling within the other commodity categories. Since cars equipped for handling specific loads are usually assigned to such shippers, a typical car found in this service is the unequipped (XM) boxcar.

All Other Carloads (Except Intermodal) cont.

Fig. 9-24. FM General-Service Flatcar

Carloadings per year:	920,000 (4.0%)
Tons originated:	55,000,000 (3.7%)
Gross revenue:	$1,140,000,000 (3.6%)
Examples of preferred car types:	Unequipped "free-running" boxcar Combination-door boxcar General-service flatcar
AAR Mechanical Designations	XM XM FM

Versatility has remained a goal of the car designer for at least a century and a half. In particular, a house car with flat floor and side doors capable of hauling "boxcar" traffic in one direction but also with roof-loading hatches and self-clearing hopper bottom for handling a bulk load on the return has been repeatedly invented and re-invented but not yet overcome cost, weight, cross-contamination, ruggedness, and convenience problems to the extent leading to widespread acceptance; in 1990, at least one current design was under test.

The "combination-door" boxcar has been perhaps the most widely used example of a car with worthwhile if more modest claims to versatility. With "grain doors" across its regular sliding center doors it can handle granular bulk commodities, while packaged or palletized items are easily loaded or unloaded through the wider opening provided by the extra set of "plug" doors. The vulnerability of the latter to damage unfortunately results in restriction to "narrow-door" use whenever its operating mechanism becomes unserviceable. The general-service flatcar has a wood deck for nailed-down blocking of the load, standard-size stake pockets and concentrated-load capacity to handle a wide variety of loads.

Intermodal Equipment

Evolving from standard but extra-long (75 ft) flatcars built for moving bulky but light wagons from town to town (since they were charged a flat rate by the car, the circus owners naturally wanted to do the job with as few vehicles as possible), piggyback car design has been driven by the height and length of highway trailers allowed by the most favorable laws the trucking interests have been able to push through Congress and state legislatures. The result has been a unique variety of railcar configurations, as illustrated here and in Chapter 11.

TOFC (Trailer on Flatcar) traffic generally requires accommodating the maximum cubic capacity, as represented by trailer lengths which have grown from 35 to 40 to 45 to 48 and even 53 ft; with the highway axle load at 18,000 lbs vs. 55,000 lbs for a "70 ton" railcar, emphasis has been on two-trailer/car or four-wheel single-trailer configurations. With COFC (Container on Flatcar) traffic by 1990 rising from a long-term minor role to more than equal volume with TOFC, the economies of stacking have put the railcar emphasis back on load-carrying capacity; 20 ft containers, in particular, are likely to be loaded with some dense commodities.

While the 125-ton truck has not been generally accepted for unit-train service where every axle is pounding away at the track with a full load, in double-stack COFC cars where the heavy ones are relatively few and far between (and articulation tends to result in somewhat lower dynamic wheel-rail forces) the heavier axle-loads have become routine on many main lines.

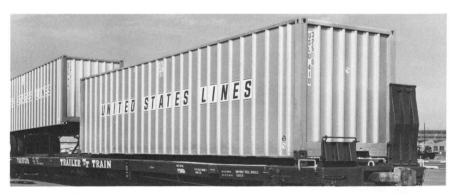

Fig. 9-25. TOFC/COFC FlatCar.

Fig. 9-26. Heavy Double-Stack Car

Car Ownership and Distribution

10

Each railroad wants to have just enough cars available for the shippers on its line, not too few, since that sooner or later means lost business, and not too many because the cost of providing freight cars (purchase, depreciation, maintenance, and rental, without counting the expense of returning empties) is – after transportation labor – the railroads' largest single cost item. Despite a continuing trend toward improved utilization, such car costs amount to about 15 percent of total expenses.

Some roads are primarily *originating* carriers, located in areas where more products are mined, grown, or otherwise produced than are consumed; they will tend to be short of cars and under pressure to buy more. Predominantly *terminating* carriers can depend upon cars made empty on line as their supply for loading, to the extent that the cars are suitable for carrying the commodities they originate with reasonable efficiency. But they may have large, unfavorable balances of car rental payments, if they don't own their share of the fleet. Much traffic is seasonal; the "value" of a car to the shipper and the railroad fluctuates with demand at a particular time and region. For the best use of the entire fleet it must operate as a pool from which cars are available and can be drawn in response to market forces.

Car Rental Systems and Rates

Car Hire Systems. As they compare to the cost of owning cars, the conditions and rates for using and paying for cars belonging to another railroad or a private car owner are crucial factors in ensuring an efficient level of supply of cars of needed types. As of the mid-1990s, these terms remain in a state of flux; for the first time in U. S. history, the number of privately owned cars (*see* Table in Chapter 9) in the fleet exceeded the total of those owned by Class I and smaller railroads.

Bi-lateral Agreements. Somewhat similarly to the shift of rail traffic rate-making from rigid Interstate Commerce Commission-controlled tariffs to negotiated shipper-railroad contracts, as permitted by the Staggers Act of 1980, car rental rates and conditions are now in many cases established by bi-lateral agreements between railroads covering their interchange of specified types of car. These are permitted by the Car Service and Car Hire Agreement with the Customer Operations Division of the Association of American Railroads, to which all railroads are signatories and under whose terms all car interchange takes place. Car-hire rules and rates directly under this agreement are discussed further.

As in the case of contract freight rates, the terms and rates of bi-lateral agreements (in the interest of mutually advantageous car utilization, generally more "liberal" to the parties involved than the alternative – otherwise, they wouldn't be set up) are private. The task of keeping track of all individual car movements and interchanges and resulting car-hire charges, followed by calculating inter-railroad balances for monthly settlement, is handled on the AAR computers on a strictly confidential basis.

Car Hire – Per Diem. Use of railroad-owned cars, which are identified by 2-, 3-, or 4-letter AAR-assigned "reporting marks" not ending in "X" (usually the initials of the railroad's name), is paid for on the basis of what is still often referred to as "per diem," although it is now on hourly instead of daily time intervals and also includes a charge for each mile run. Regulated by the ICC for a great many years in the 1920s through the 1930s the charge was a flat "dollar a day." This charge was gradually raised after World War II; eventually, the prevalence of more specialized, productive, and sophisticated cars and the disproportionate increase in new-car prices (which increased six-fold between 1950 and 1980) caused the rental to be based on the initial car cost less depreciation for age.

Under daily rentals, the road on which a car was physically located at midnight each day owed the fee to its owner; hourly car-hire rates were substituted in 1979 to remove any incentive for a mad scramble (perhaps resulting in inefficient scheduling and operations) to shove cars onto connections just before the daily deadline.

What Should the Rate Be?

The objective is to set the rate high enough that there will be a net return to the owner (to encourage an adequate total car inventory) and a strong incentive for railroads to keep "foreign" (rented) cars moving, but yet low enough to encourage a receiving road to hang onto an empty long enough to find a return load and thus improve overall car utilization.

During the long period of railroad regulation, ICC authority for setting the rate rested on the principle that car rental is part of the cost base on which a level of freight rates providing a "fair return" would be allowed. In matters of car distribution, the ICC also acted as guardian of the principle that a "commodity" (empty cars) in short supply should be doled out to claimants in even-handed, nondiscriminatory fashion, with shippers and communities of all sizes receiving equal consideration. This was, of course, in conflict with the idea of reducing the severity of a car shortage by allowing the assignment of cars to multi-car, quick-turnaround (unit-train) service.

The ICC could also prescribe higher incentive per diem rates to encourage acquisition of car types expected to be in shortage during certain times of the year. This it did for plain boxcars in the late 1970s – setting a rate that was high enough to make a new boxcar out there earning per diem an extremely profitable investment. The result was an unprecedented spurt in boxcar production, followed, not long thereafter, by a huge car surplus and virtual cessation of all boxcar production for a dozen years.

Who Prescribes Car-Hire Rates?

In line with the partial deregulation of railroad rates by 1980, the prescription of car hire rates was shifted from the ICC to the railroad industry itself. What is now known as the Equipment Assets Management Committee within the AAR, with membership broadly representing large and small carriers, establishes rates for recommendation to the ICC (since 1995, the Surface Transportation Board), which retains oversight because of such matters as the antitrust implications of such an industry-wide process. Mileage and per-hour rates for each car type are prescribed by formula from the car's original cost and age.

Typical prescribed car-hire charges as of 1990 range from 18¢ per hour plus 5.4¢ per mile for an elderly 40-ft plain (unequipped) boxcar to $1.17 per hour plus 7.1¢ per mile for a relatively new, expensive multi-level 89 ft flatcar.

Deprescription

After a considerable period of discussion, since it could affect railroads of differing sizes owning smaller or larger car fleets of differing age in radically different ways, a 10-year process of deprescription for railroad-owned cars not moving under bi-lateral agreements or freight contracts was instituted by law in 1992. Cars with the reporting marks of Class III carriers (some of which had fleets of a size, greatly disproportionate to their own limited mileage out there on the main lines somewhere) are exempt from deprescription and continue to earn car-hire at a rate frozen at a 1990 level. New cars are deprescribed; owners can deprescribe one-tenth of their fleet each year, until at the end of the 10-year process all cars owned by the larger railroads will be earning car-hire at market rates – rentals set by a bidding process reflecting their value at the time and place.

Private-Owner Cars

Private-owner cars, owned by shippers or leased from a car company, are identified by reporting marks ending in "X." If they are moving under the terms of a contract, the freight rate negotiated with the railroad reflects the value of the shipper-furnished car. In "tariff" service they are paid for on the basis of loaded miles run. In effect, the railroad compensates the shipper for saving it the cost of supplying a car.

The shipper must make arrangements, similar to interchange rules regarding inspection, etc., for the car to be accepted by the originating railroad. The railroad retains the option – of concern in situations of car surplus – of supplying a suitable car of its own if available.

Car Service and Distribution Rules

As part of the partial railroad deregulation process, direct ICC control of car distribution was eliminated, leaving car service rules and their enforcement up to the industry itself. Car distribution not under bi-lateral agreement is regulated by the Customer Operations Division (COD) of the AAR under the previously mentioned car service agreement to which all railroads subscribe. They thus contractually agree to follow its rules, directives, and orders for car handling and routing, under penalty of assessment (subject to arbitration) for violations.

Car service rules – established and amended by letter ballot of the subscribers, with votes in proportion to the number of cars owned–have two underlying objectives: first, ensuring the timely movement of empties to where they are needed for loading; secondly, reducing empty-car mileage. An example of a change aimed at the second objective is the revision of Car Service Rule 1 covering the loading of empty "foreign" (owned by another railroad) cars.

Rather than requiring that such cars may be loaded only for a shipment routed in the direction of the home (owner) road, they may now be loaded "without regard to route or destination," recognizing that a short detour away from home toward a more likely source of long-haul traffic may result in a higher proportion of loaded mileage. Considering the unbalance between overall traffic flow in opposite directions, this system does fairly well in encouraging loaded backhaul. Nationwide, general-service, "plain" boxcars averaged 64 percent loaded mileage in a recent year.

How Does an Empty Get Back?

If no load is likely to be available soon, the empty will be sent back "via the service route" (Fig. 2-5), retracing the route it took on its last loaded trip. Thus the railroads that got a piece of the revenue will bear the corresponding burden of the empty mileage.

However, if the demand for a type of car in an area is building up beyond that supplied by normal movements, a railroad may ask the COD to issue a Car Quota Directive requiring that its connecting roads route a daily quota of unassigned empties to it for loading. Grain cars may thus, for example, be diverted toward the Southwest in anticipation of the winter-wheat harvest.

Assigned Service Cars

Cars specially equipped to handle specific commodities or products are in assigned service to cover the traffic between specified shippers and consignees. They

192

are in effect in a pool making regular trips over a specific route. Car ownership is often shared by the railroads making up the route in proportion to the mileages involved. This may result in an empty owned by the terminating railroad being sent back empty to a "foreign" line for loading, but the car hire will balance out.

Cars in assigned service usually return empty; equipped boxcars, for example, which are usually in this service, average only 54 percent loaded miles, but railroad and shipper benefit from the more certain supply of suitable cars.

"Free-Runner" is a term used by transportation people to describe cars that may be loaded in any direction (in accordance with the current version of Car Service Rule 1) rather than being returned empty reverse route.

Railbox-Railgon

To provide access to a fleet of cars of types not otherwise available in sufficient quantity at the time, Trailer-Train (now TTX Corp.– itself owned by a large number of major railroads) subsidiaries were established to acquire large fleets of "Railbox" and "Railgon" standardized plain boxcars and gondolas, to be available to railroads as free-runners on demand at rates generally lower than the ICC incentive rates in effect. Although many were later shifted to individual-railroad ownership, about 14,000 RBOX and GONX cars remain in service; despite the "X" in their reporting marks they operate under railroad-owner rules. TTX itself owns and leases out a fleet of some 90,000 cars – all specialized, including five-platform piggyback spine and double-stack well cars along with 89 ft flatcars welded to railroad-owned multi-level auto racks.

How Do You Find an Empty?

In filling the order of a shipper for an empty to load, the traffic department of a railroad has its own computerized record of its own and foreign cars on its line. For major traffic movements to be handled in nonassigned cars, however, it's not good enough to be seeking out suitable empties *after* the order has been placed; suitable cars should already be moving toward the loading points. Several major communication, display, and data processing systems now aid the railroads, COD, and shippers in doing just that.

Car distribution itself is directly controlled by the Operations Department of the railroad; orders are received through agents, who are operating employees, matched by car distributors and filled by transportation officers and yardmasters.

UMLER

The Universal Machine Language Equipment Register is a data file updated daily by car owners to reflect car availability: added, retired, bad order – maintained on the AAR computer in Washington, D. C. Data, which can be addressed to varying degrees of depth depending upon need, include reporting marks, number, capacity, weight, mechanical designation, interior and exterior dimensions, special equipment, cost, periodic inspection, and maintenance status, and so on, for all freight cars, piggyback trailers, and containers in interchange service – a total of almost 4 million units. (UMLER also covers locomotives, maintenance-of-way equipment, and end-of-train reporting devices.)

It is a self-policing system since only cars registered in UMLER may be accepted in interchange and be entitled to car-hire payments. In addition to its car fleet management functions, UMLER data is also used for such operating functions as determining the length of specific train consists in planning single-track meets.

TRAIN II

This second-phase version of the "Telerail Automated Information Network," continuously upgraded since going into operation at the AAR in 1975, receives information from all railroad car interchanges in the United States and Canada; since 1992, all interchange data is received by EDI (Electronic Data Interchange) transmission from the interchange point. Its databank on the location and status of every freight car is updated hourly. Other data, most of which is received or updated no later than one day of the event, includes such matters as the time of placement for loading, release time after unloading, previous loads (important for determining suitability for planned next load) and current routing. It serves as an automatic message routing system sending advance information from the originating road's computer to the computers of all bridge and connection's lines so they can plan car handling.

Car Tracing

Shippers are even more interested in the location, status, and time of arrival of cars loaded with their goods, and railroad traffic departments have long maintained communication and office systems for providing such information on a timely basis. Increasing computational capability has extended and automated the process; starting in 1980, the AAR has provided a SAM (Shipper Assist Message) service whereby a shipper with high-speed data communication capability can direct a query to the AAR's computer in Washington and automatically receive data on any of the cars carrying his shipments from the computers of all participating railroads. "Third-party" agents will provide such service (for a fee) to shippers who do not have such message-transmission capability.

Car Routing Optimization

In a system with more than a million items moving throughout a network as complex as the North American rail map, the overall effect of a car service rule on the overall efficiency of fleet utilization is far from intuitively obvious. When it was responsible for car distribution, the ICC took steps toward understanding the way cars actually moved by basing studies on a more manageable database obtained by collecting a one percent sample (still over 200,000 a year) of all waybills. This database collection (for the Surface Transportation Board and the FRA by the AAR) continues.

On the basis of such inputs and mathematical network models of rail routes compatible with evolving computer capabilities, a variety of AAR and other studies with extensive participation of various university researchers have generated computer programs which have been and continue to be used to evaluate the net effect of car service orders and directly improve car utilization strategies of railroads and car fleet managers.

Multi-level Reload projects, implemented by the railroads and United States and Canadian automobile manufacturers in the mid-1980s to direct rack cars made empty at distribution terminals to the most advantageous reloading point rather than assigning cars to assembly plants, are a case in point. By 1985 empty-car mileage was reduced by an estimated 200 million miles per year by raising the loaded-mile percentage from 50 to about 63 percent.

Terminal Operations

11

The first step in the actual rail movement of our shipment occurs when the switch or local freight crew, which also brings and sets out incoming loads and empties for loading, picks up the car. The actual operation of picking up a load is simple and quick, though there are some important things to be remembered (such as closing the derail and releasing the hand brake). Often the car to be picked up will be sandwiched between partially loaded or unloaded cars which will have to be re-spotted. As Fig. 11-1 shows, it does make quite a difference which way the siding is connected to the main track.

In total, however, the switching involved in originating, terminating, and interchanging shipments is a very expensive part of railroad operations. Industries outside of terminal limits are served by road crews, and much yard switching is in connection with forwarding trains through intermediate yards. In a recent year, approximately one-quarter of all transportation expenses (principally, train crew wages and benefits) on Class I railroads was chargeable to yard operations. Since only the roadhaul brings in revenue, the ability of yardmasters and trainmasters to provide reliable, timely service with a minimum number of switch and local crews and locomotives has a lot to do with whether the railroad makes money or not.

The Switching District

For a simplified but representative bird's-eye view of some of the ways such operations may be arranged, consider our East-West System's situation in the metropolitan/port area of J. Fig 11-2 shows the principal trackage in the "J Switching District," an area within which a shipper located on any one railroad is in effect served by all. The basic rate to "J" applies for shipments (from all points beyond a certain minimum distance) to any point within the area, whether it's directly on one of the line-haul railroads such as the E-W System, or can only be reached via the J Terminal and a car-float trip across the harbor to Port Island.

The tangle of trackage in Fig. 11-2 looks complicated, and it is, but it's not even in the same league as the actual situation in such areas as New York, Chicago, or Minneapolis-St. Paul. It will serve to illustrate some typical arrangements for getting freight into the line-haul system.

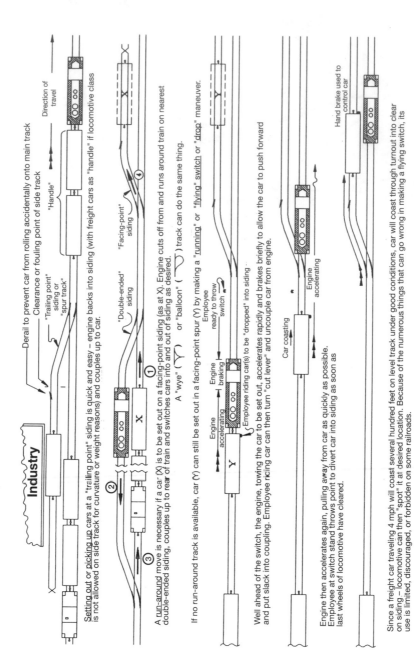

Direction of travel

Derail to prevent car from rolling accidentally onto main track

Clearance or fouling point of side track

"Handle"

"Trailing point" siding or "spur track"

Industry

Setting out or picking up cars at a "trailing point" siding is quick and easy – engine backs into siding (with freight cars as "handle" if locomotive class is not allowed on side track for curvature or weight reasons) and couples up to car.

"Double-ended" siding

"Facing-point" siding

A run-around move is necessary if a car (X) is to be set out on a facing-point siding (as at X). Engine cuts off from and runs around train on nearest double-ended siding, couples up to rear of train and switches cars into and out of siding as desired.

A "wye" (Y) or "balloon" (O) track can do the same thing.

If no run-around track is available, car (Y) can still be set out in a facing-point spur (Y) by making a "running" or "flying" switch or "drop" maneuver.

Employee ready to throw switch

Engine braking

Engine accelerating

Employee riding car(s) to be "dropped" into siding

Well ahead of the switch, the engine, towing the car to be set out, accelerates rapidly and brakes briefly to allow the car to push forward and put slack into coupling. Employee ricing car can then turn "cut lever" and uncouple car from engine.

Car coasting

Engine accelerating

Engine then accelerates again, pulling away from car as quickly as possible. Employee at switch stand throws point to divert car into siding as soon as last wheels of locomotive have cleared.

Hand brake used to control car

Since a freight car traveling 4 mph will coast several hundred feet on level track under good conditions, car will continually move onto siding – locomotive can then "spot" it at desired location. Because of the numerous things that can go wrong in making a flying switch, its use is limited, discouraged, or forbidden on some railroads.

Fig. 11-1. Set-Outs, Pick-Ups, Run-Arounds and Drops

The Base of Operations

The East-West System's principal operating base in J is its "77th St. Yard," (1) in Fig. 11-2. Trains to and from the west start and end their runs here, and most switching crews working within the J district work out of 77th St., where complete servicing facilities for locomotives are available.

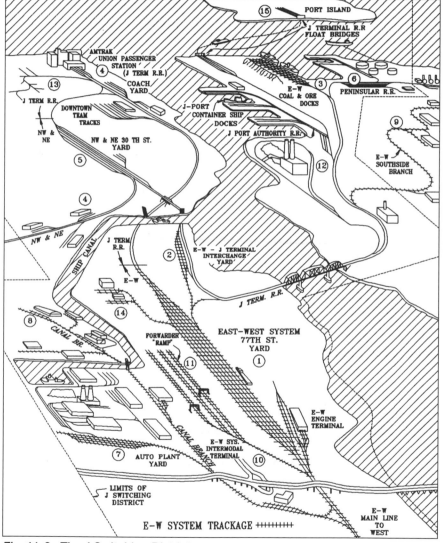

Fig. 11-2. The J Switching District

Switching and Terminal Companies

Much of the trackage in the J area is owned and operated by the J Terminal Railroad, which as we noted in connection with the system network map (Fig. 11-2) is a "joint facility" owned by the line-haul railroads serving J. The E-W System "interchanges" cars for points on the J-T at a small yard (2) switched directly by 77th St. yard crews. To reach its huge export-import coal piers at (3), the E-W has trackage rights over the J-T and its key bridge across the harbor. Inter-city passenger trains operated by Amtrak over the line-haul railroads continue without pause onto J-T trackage and into the Union Station downtown at (4).

Interchanges Large and Small

As our E-W System map (Fig. 2-4) shows, the E-W and the NW & NE are mostly competitors in the J area, but there is some freight originating on one of them destined for points on the other which will be interchanged at J. This traffic, a few cars each way a day, is handled by the J-T crews which pick it up at (2) and deliver it to the NW & NE's principal J Yard at "30th St." (5). This, unfortunately, is not likely to be a quick process since there isn't enough business to make it a principal factor in scheduling the various trips that make up the short cross-town connections.

The interchange between the E-W and the Peninsular Railway, on the other hand, is a big one, with many cars of feed for the farming country south of J coming in on the E-W. Interyard "transfer runs" from (1) to (6) handle this traffic on schedules closely tied to the arrival and departure of connections at both ends.

Reciprocal Switching

A shipper on the E-W "Canal Branch" at (8), one on the J-T downtown in the congested old warehouse area at (13), and one on the NW & NE at (5) with something to ship to the west can all choose either E-W or NW & NE for its initial segment of its line-hauling routing, and, under tariff rules prevailing under the ICC until partial deregulation in 1980, he will get the same rate. In one case, the E-W will: order an empty from the NW & NE, to be delivered to them via the J-T; place it for loading; pick it up when released by the shipper; and deliver it to the J-T for transfer to the NW & NE for the roadhaul. In the other case, the situation is reversed. Within the switching district where these reciprocal arrangements apply, the origination line-haul road will "absorb" the switching and "per diem reclaim" charges payable to the other lines involved, giving up a chunk of its "division" of the through line-haul rate in exchange for being able to compete for the traffic from shippers not located on its tracks. Much of this balances out, of course, and the extra moves involved make it likely that service, speed, and reliability will cause the shipper to tend to route his freight via the line he's on. "Freedom of choice," uninfluenced by *rate* differences, is preserved.

Under post-1980 Staggers Act conditions, with most regular shipments moving under contract terms more closely tied to the cost of handling individual classes of traffic, such absorption of switching charges is no longer a common practice.

Marine Railroading

Port Island's industries are served by car floats, barges with tracks on their deck which receive strings of cars pushed aboard over "float bridges," mating sections of track arranged to rise and fall with the tide. A tug then moves the float across the channel where its cars are offloaded and moved by switch engines to industry and dock trackage. Once a widely used method of serving harborside industries and of bridging gaps in the mainline rail network, this flexible but expensive method of reaching across the water is now limited to a few operations in ocean and Great Lakes port areas. As here at J, services by individual line-haul railroads have been consolidated into joint operations.

Shifters, Locals, and Turns

The huge automobile plant at (7) is the principal source of traffic on the E-W "Canal Branch" that extends to (8), serving numerous industries within the J Switching District. Auto plant traffic requires several trips a day from 77th St. to the small Auto Plant Yard, where the plant's own locomotives and crews take over for the extensive intra-plant rail operations.

Names for a particular crew assignment tend to have a strong local flavor, and what one line calls a "shifter" might well be dignified by an entirely different title on another railroad. All these crew assignments extending outside a yard but within a switching district have the common goal of picking up and delivering loads and empties as efficiently as possible, considering the constraints of long-standing work agreements, difficult physical track arrangements, congestion grade crossing, and drawbridge interference.

Thus, what the E-W employees mean when they refer to the "docks shifter" is not a single 1,000 hp switch engine puttering around the waterfront but a set of up to five six-axle diesel units which leaves 77th St. with a massive train of coal which it hauls over the J-T to the docks and exchanges for equally heavy loads of ore, also rearranging loads and empties at the pier that may be required to let the giant ship/car/stockpile stacker/unloader do its work.

Local Freights

Outside of yard limits, local freight crews handle industry switching as they work their way along the line. Since the E-W's "Southside Branch" (9) extends beyond the J Switching District, its daily switching is accomplished by such crews. The branch is short but so busy that two crews are often used, one leaving 77th St. and working its way out to the far end, where a second crew takes over its locomotive, caboose, and papers for the trip back.

Out on the main lines (Fig. 2-4), local freight crews are assigned segments of line long enough so that normal levels of traffic can be readily handled in a day's work, and occasional overtime. One such run is from H to K, a fairly long distance but with relatively few plants to be switched; it is worked westbound on Monday, Wednesday, and Friday, eastbound on the alternate days.

Turns

Branches such as that from T to S may be handled by "turns," runs which go out to the end of the line, turn, and come back. Through lines, such as between J and P, may be run as two shorter turns; one crew will work from H to M and back, meeting its counterpart (which is doing the same thing starting from P) at the midpoint and exchanging trains. This gets everybody back to the home terminal at the end of the shift, and the meeting point can be changed as necessary to equalize the time required on the two turns if the relative amount of business changes.

Classification
and Blocking

12

The next step in the terminal operations is to assemble the cars from various sources into *blocks* (blocks of cars, not to be confused with track "blocks" in the signal system) headed for individual destinations; these blocks will then be combined into trains for the linehaul. There are two principal ways the switching can be done – flat and gravity – and the E-W, like most of the larger railroads, uses both.

Flat Switching

Fig. 12-1 is a condensed and shortened diagram of the E-W's 77th St. Yard at J. In actuality, a yard serving this large a metropolis would have many more tracks, but the operating scheme would be the same. Locomotive and car movements in any yard on a railroad are much the same, but the pattern and purpose of the operation is part of the railroad operating scheme as a whole, and each yard may be distinctly different in that respect.

Yards, Subyards, Tracks, and Leads

In reality, yards of this size and complexity are also located in areas as sparsely populated and seemingly remote as J is densely populated and strategically situated. The logic for this is the FRA-mandated 1,000-mile inspection. All trains, regardless of commodity, terrain, or climate, must be thoroughly inspected every 1,000 miles or less for safety-related defects by qualified railroad personnel. It is also quite convenient to perform major switching operations at these yards.

Within any major yard, the tracks will be arranged in several subyards, each with a somewhat more specific purpose. At 77th St. there is an engine terminal with tracks where hostlers: fuel, sand, and water the diesels; separate and rearrange units into new combinations, making up suitable locomotives for outgoing runs; and move engines into and out of the diesel shop for inspection, running repairs, and heavier maintenance work by the mechanical department's specialists. Car repairs are performed on the rip track, in the car shop, and in the car shop yard on freight cars found to need it. To the east is the E-W System, J Terminal RR Interchange Yard, arranged so that cars placed by one road's switching crew can easily be picked up, after acceptance by the car inspector, by the other road's crew.

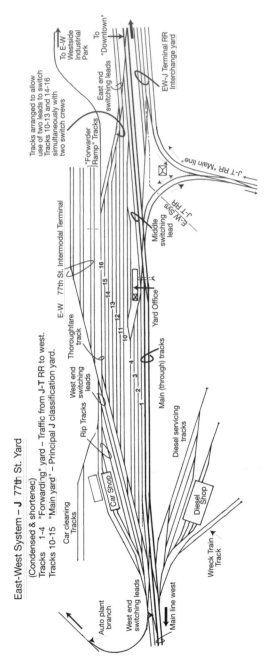

Fig. 12-1. East-West System – J 77th St. Yard (Condensed and Shortened)

There are two classification yards in the 77th St. complex, Tracks 1 through 4 being known as the "Forwarding Yard" and Tracks 10 through 16 as the "Main Yard." Each consists of a group of parallel body tracks connected by ladders (Fig. 3-7) at each end to switching leads extending from each end. Crossovers connect the switching leads to main tracks (the main line to the west and to downtown, the auto plant branch) leading to the outside world. These are all hand-throw switches, operated by the switch crews themselves or, in the case of trains entering or leaving the yard in completing or starting their runs, by switch tenders. Some tracks, designated as thoroughfare tracks, are normally kept free of standing cars so that yard and road engines can use them to get from one end of the yard to the other freely without fouling the main tracks.

Shuffling the Deck

To take one example of all the car-flows in which 77th St. is involved, consider the matter of getting empty cars to industries along the E-W's main line between J and I. There are plenty of cars available which have come into the J area from the west under load, and consigned to team tracks, distribution terminals, and consuming industries all over the J Switching District. They come back into 77th St. from various switch runs, directly and via the J-T interchange, and will be found on tracks in the Main Yard assigned as "arrival tracks" by the yardmaster.

The Switch List

Yard and computer generated data received on all empty cars entering the 77th St. yards is analyzed by the division's car distributor who will identify suitable empties (in regard to ownership, type, special equipment, etc.) to match against empty car orders received from agents on the line. Based on this information, the yard office will generate a switch list which tells a yard crew on which tracks and in what order cars currently sitting on other tracks are to be placed.

The objective in this particular case is to make up the today's "I Peddler," the local freight which runs from J to I, serving the lineside industries enroute. In the process, of course, the switch crew, a yard conductor or foreman, engineer, and several yard brakemen or switchmen, will handle many cars as part of their travels in other directions on other missions. When the I Peddler is complete, it will have both empties and loads for its industries, including cars that have come from the Peninsular, from the docks on Port Island, and even from *eastbound* trains. It may be quicker to bring a car destined for a point just west of J into 77th St. on a fast freight from the west and then take it back on the local rather than having it come all the way east from I in local service.

Station Order

To speed up the local's work, its train will be arranged in "station order," with cars to be set out at the first station at the head end followed by those for the next station and so on. Blocking cars by station order is particularly important in the case of through freights which make set-outs and pick-ups at only a few specified points and whose schedules aren't compatible with any additional manipulating enroute.

Batting 'em Out

To carry out the work put on paper by the switch list, the engine takes a cut of cars from one of the yard tracks, hauls it back onto the switch lead, and then proceeds to shove or kick the cars into their assigned tracks. A capable, experienced crew will often have several cuts of cars moving at one time, coasting slowly toward the cars already on the body tracks after being cut from the string attached to the engine. The brakemen will think ahead so as to be in the right position to line up a switch for the next cut or to ride the car and work the uncoupling lever to cut it loose, all with a minimum of lost time and a maximum of riding rather than walking. The crew will kick cars with due regard for their weight, the distance to be traveled, and any grades in the yard (yard leads are sometimes just a bit higher than the center of the body tracks so that a slight grade helps keep the cuts rolling) so that they do not impact at more than walking speed (4 mph or less). Cars with especially sensitive loads are moved all the way into coupling with engine attached and other cars are not dropped onto them, as called for by the rules.

Nevertheless, flat switching is a relatively slow and consequently expensive process if there is a lot of rearranging to be done. After the cars are in the proper tracks for their destination, they probably will not be in station order, so it will be necessary to pull them back out and shuffle them again. In flat switching a long train, the switch engine may take short cuts of cars and classify them, moving rather snappily in the process but having to go back several times to get more, or take longer cuts and have to accelerate sluggishly in making each move. Either way, the engine will move the equivalent of many train-lengths in getting all cars into their assigned positions.

Gravity Switching

Because of the time and money consumed by flat switching, the E-W System (like most fairly large railroads) does as much of its classification as possible by gravity. It has built what it likes to call "electronic classification yards," often simply known as "hump" or "retarder" yards, at D and H. The yard at H, on the basis of system traffic-flow studies, provides hump classification of westbound cars only, while D Yard, located between the two main tracks, has separate gravity yards for handling eastbound and westbound traffic.

System-Wide Effects

Due to the capability for thorough classification of westbound trains at H, the J 77th St. Yard simply places into trains in any order all westbound cars arriving from every connection, branch, and station in the area (except for those going out in the I Local) and sends them off to H. Cars coming into H from the west are already blocked for the various connecting railroads, docks, yards, and major industries in the J area. As a result, about half the trackage in the main 77th St. classification yards was removed to make room for the new Intermodal Yards handling the E-W's steadily increasing piggyback traffic.

Very little eastbound traffic comes onto the E-W between D and H, so trains are blocked at D so thoroughly that they can go to their destinations without further classifications and bypass the H Yard; what little eastbound work must be done there can better be done by flat switching.

The Hump Yard

Fig. 12-2 shows a gravity yard arrangement typical of that built by the E-W System at H. The basic idea, of course, is to push the cars being sorted over an artificial hill or "hump" and let gravity push them into the classification tracks. It is the most efficient classification method if the traffic pattern is such that most of the cars passing through are headed in different directions from their neighbors in the incoming trains. Running the whole train over the hump just to get one or two groups of cars headed in the right direction would not be worthwhile. But where the cars are really scrambled, the hump comes into its own; the hump locomotive need travel only one train length in classifying the entire consist.

Receiving Yard

Incoming trains stop in the *receiving* or *arrival* yard, which must have enough tracks to accommodate trains coming in from all principal lines over a period of a few hours. Road locomotives and cabooses are removed, and the humping engine, often a six-axle unit with a slug attached, couples up to the rear of the cars on one track.

Other hump yard facilities include an inspection pit, often provided on the single track approaching the hump itself so that each car's running gear can be thoroughly inspected for defects, which will get in-train or rip-track attention depending on the nature of the problem. Receiving yards may also be set up with track spacing and runaways so that inspectors can examine cars from small utility vehicles.

Before being pushed over the hump, air must be bled from brake cylinders so that the cars will roll freely. A switch list is provided to the "pin-puller" standing at the right side of the hump so he will know where the cars are to be separated. The upgrade leading to the hump ensures that the slack is in so the cut lever can be operated.

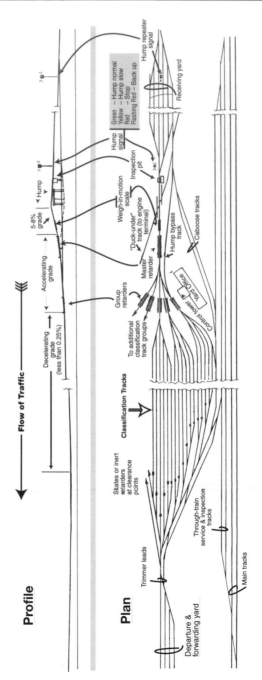

Fig. 12-2. Gravity Classification Yard

The Classification Bowl

The classification tracks themselves, often called the "bowls" because of their concave profile, fan out from the base of the hump in groups of five to nine tracks; the total number depends on the size and function of the yard and available land but may be as many as 60 to 70.

Coming over the hump, the cuts of one or more cars first encounter a steep grade, which quickly accelerates each cut so that there will be enough space between it and the next one for switches to be thrown. There is usually a "weigh-in-motion" scale which automatically takes care of the requirement that each car loaded on-line must be weighed before it enters interchange or reaches its destination.

Car Retarders

Electric or electro-pneumatic car retarders regulate the motion of the car during its descent; it is the computerized control of the switches and retarders that gives the modern hump yard its "electronic classification yard" title. The retarder is a set of powerful jaws on each side of and a few inches above the railhead which grasp the car wheels, slowing the car to the computed exit speed. This process produces loud squealing, and some yards located in populated areas now must meet environmental requirements by providing noise baffles alongside the retarders to reduce, to an acceptable level, noise radiated sidewise.

The retarders are arranged so that each car passes through only two, a master retarder at the foot of the hump and one group retarder on the track leading into each group of classification tracks. Through the group retarders, the tracks are on enough of a grade to accelerate the cars and make sure that they will move through the turnouts into the classification tracks. Beyond that point, they flatten out to a grade that isn't quite enough to keep a free-rolling car moving at the speed at which it enters the track.

At the far end of the classification tracks there is usually a slight up-grade which will tend to slow cars as they approach the turnouts and tracks leading to the departure tracks. Skates (wedge-shaped shoes placed atop the rail by a remote-controlled skate-placing machine) or inert retarders (spring-loaded versions of the master or group machines) are used to keep the cars from rolling too far and fouling the exit trackage.

Retarder Control

In the most modern electronic yards, the retarder and switch control system accepts "switch list" data telling it which track each cut is to take, along with waybill information on the weight of each car, and a count of the cars already in each track. Its memory includes such information as the length, grades, and curvatures of each track and its approaches. It gets individual data on the speed and "rollability" of each cut – on both curved and straight sections – from trackside radar devices, and keeps track of the wind velocity affecting car movement.

On the basis of this computerized information, the retarders are controlled to cause each car to leave the group retarder at a speed which will let it roll just far enough up the track to which it is being sent to couple with the cars already there. The hump tower operator monitors the whole operation from his vantage point where, day or night, he can watch each cut roll down into the bowl. He can override or modify the automatic operation should any problem threaten to develop.

Distributive Retarders

Another type of coupling-speed control is provided by the distributive retarder system. A small forest of hydraulic cylinders located close alongside the rails in the classification tracks contain mushroom-shaped pistons which must be depressed by the wheels of a car as it rolls by. An orifice restricts the rate at which the piston may be pushed down so that a car traveling at more than four miles per hour will be retarded to that speed. Spaced along tracks on a slightly accelerating grade, these cylinders act, without the complication of any centralized control, to maintain the desired constant speed up to coupling. As an option, units provided with an air supply can also push up to nudge a car traveling too slowly up to the set speed. This system, which trades system and installation costs for the upkeep of hundreds of spread-out mechanical units, has gone into service in North America in a few relatively small yards. In the interest of minimum wear on the retarders, these are double-ended yards in which locomotives need not enter the classification tracks and cars routinely pass the retarders only once.

Trimming

At the lower end of the yard, one or two trimmer engines take care of such chores as pushing cars together if they didn't quite come together, re-arranging cars within a classification and re-humping any misclassified cuts.

Cars go over the hump at a rate of about 3 mph, which works out to one 50 ft car every 10 seconds or 300 cars per hour. With two hump locomotives on the job so that a second train can start over the hump as soon as the first has cleared, and with a reasonable allowance for trimming and other delays, a single hump can classify up to 1,500 cars per eight-hour shift. Traffic is rarely distributed evenly around the clock to fully utilize hump capacity on all three shifts, but processing of 3,000 to 3,500 cars per day is often achieved.

High-Capacity Yards

Since all the cars being classified into a single bowl must go over one track, yards which must handle more cars than this must either have two hump tracks which – at least during some times of the day – can function as two separate subyards, each distributing cars into the tracks on its side of the bowl, or the speed over the hump must be increased. This can be done by providing a third set of *tangent-point* retarders (located at the point where the cars enter the individual classification tracks) making the final speed reduction. Cars can then travel through the turnouts and group retarder area at higher speeds, increasing the rate at which the train can go over the hump without having the cuts too close together.

Departure

In some hump yards, trains leave directly from the classification tracks, but in most cases classified cuts are pulled forward into a departure and forwarding yard. Here they are combined into trains (perhaps by the road locomotive if agreements permit) with blocks in station order, fitted with the rear-coupler-mounted EOT (end-of-train) device that has generally superseded the caboose, and subjected to mandatory pre-departure mechanical inspection and air brake tests.

Line-Haul
Operation

13

Everything discussed to this point is just the prelude to the primary railroad operation that must bring in all the revenue to support the whole system: moving trains along the line, from one point to another. The average mile of line in the United States operated in freight service carries 8.1 trains per day, which doesn't sound like much activity. However, since more than two-thirds of all ton-miles are carried on less than 20 percent of the mileage, the typical main line will see several times that many trains. As we have seen, traffic will tend to concentrate itself at certain times of the day, so planning, scheduling, and dispatching trains so that each uses its "track space" to generate its share of transportation is important.

Scheduled, Advertised, and Extra Trains

Fig. 13-1 is a highly condensed "schedule" of westbound through-train operations on our East-West System for part of one particular day. There is no official timetable that shows all these train movements on one page; "employee's timetables" show only trains operating on the particular division which they cover. Also, in the E-W scheme of things (typical but by no means the way it is done on all railroads), only First Class trains appear in the timetable with schedules which actually confer timetable authority for their operation.

First Class schedules include only Train Nos. 17, 19, 151 and 153 westbound. In accordance with standard practice, trains that are west- or southbound by timetable have odd numbers, while east- or northbound trains have even numbers. On the E-W, all trains are either east- or westbound; the timetable arbitrarily designates that H to K, K to F, and T to D are westbound directions.

Nos. 17 and 19 are passenger trains operated over the E-W System by Amtrak; Nos. 151 and 153 are piggyback freights permitted to run at passenger-train speeds and also accorded first-class status. On the E-W, all other trains are technically "extras," which must be given specific authorization to run each trip and are designated by the number of the locomotive unit leading the consist and the direction of operation (Extra 5411 East, for example). Thus, it is possible for any employee to tell immediately the direction of a train's movement. One exception to this is a "work

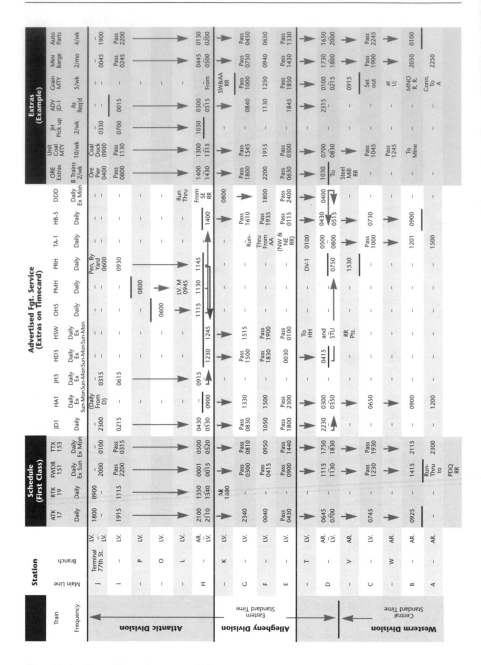

Fig. 13-1. East-West System – Westbound (Partial Schedule, Local Freight
Runs Not Shown)

extra," usually a maintenance-of-way train performing duties which may require moving back and forth over a section of track more than once. Work extras are given authority by train order to work between two designated points for a period of time and do not have a specified direction.

Advertised Freight Service

At another point in the employee's timetable are the "Advertised Freight Service" schedules, accompanied by a note that "the times shown convey no timetable authority." Nevertheless, these trains are usually the backbone of the railroad's service, and their schedules are the ones that the traffic department's freight solicitors publicize. They are variously known as "symbol" or "manifest" trains, often given formal or informal "name train" status reflecting their speed, purpose, or other attractive attribute. Their operation, particularly in making connections with other trains, is closely watched. Taken as a whole, the advertised freight service constitutes the network of services which can move a car to any point on the main lines of the system in reasonably predictable fashion.

Fast and Not-so-Fast Freights

Each advertised freight, often identified by a symbol including the initials of its origin and destination, has certain functions to perform and will be so scheduled. In general, the more business a line has, the more specialized the purpose of its "hotter" freight trains. If there is only one sizable train-load of through freight moving over a particular route per day, the daily fast freight on that line will have to make stops at each operating point to set out and pick up cars for and from the local freights working the area; it will probably do some "work" at major industries as well. Its average speed may not be impressive, but if it can receive most freight loaded by the end of the day and move it to its destination in time to catch the first available connection, it has done its job.

Other trains may have to be provided with extra horsepower, skip major stops, and accept only high-rated traffic to their connections, hundreds of miles farther on, to reach principal destinations at the most desirable time, very early in the morning, so that cars may be placed for unloading at the start of the business day. A closer examination of Fig. 13-1's schedules (shown in "24-hour" time to save space here, although "A.M. Lightface" – "P.M. Boldface" is more likely to be used in timetables in the United States) will show examples of both fast and not-so-fast freights.

Extra Trains

Also shown on Fig. 13-1 are examples of the extra trains which will normally handle much of the traffic. Many of these, which run only when the business is there, are on just as fast and exacting schedules as the advertised or timetabled trains; the dispatchers, yardmasters, and trainmasters know what treatment each warrants and will act accordingly. An ore extra is going to take a long time to get up

215

the big hill between F and E and back down to fairly level ground again (Fig. 7-1), so all the more nimble trains will be allowed to run ahead of it at this point. But its overall time may not be much longer than that for some arranged trains which do intermediate work and are reclassified at the major yards.

Keeping the Line Moving

Other extras, such as "Advance JD-1," are just that, additional trains run to handle the periodic overflow of traffic which would otherwise clog up the railroad. When it becomes apparent that JD-1 will not be able to handle all the traffic available by its scheduled 0330 departure from J and still be able to pick up its cars originating at I, an extra, unofficially known as its "advance section," will be created at I, to run ahead of JD-1 and relieve it of enough tonnage and work so that it can maintain its schedule and make connections at D. In the process, Advance JD-1 will "fill to tonnage" with any westbound empties which may have accumulated. Running the advance in the same "time slot" as JD-1 from H to D affects other trains less than if it were sent out at some intermediate time.

Balancing Power

Then there are those extras that no one really wants to run but which may actually improve productivity overall. There will often be periods in which traffic is much heavier in one direction than the other and the normal method of "balancing motive power" – simply adding the extra diesel units to the locomotives heading back in the slack direction with their trains – will not get enough units back fast enough to handle tonnage in the heavy direction. Since locomotives running "light" (without train) can make much better time, in traveling over a heavily graded line such as this one over the mountain, there may be no alternative but to run groups of units back to the other end of the railroad from time to time.

Moving Those Blocks

The job of the advertised freight service is to move quickly and efficiently the blocks of cars assembled in the various yards by the classification process to their destinations in train-size lots. This process becomes a matter of scheduling, taking into account not only the cars, but motive power, train and yard crew, yard space, and main-track availability as well. For a brief look at a little bit of what's involved, consider one group of one day's trains on the schedule of Fig. 13-1 – specifically, OH 5, PMH, PRH, HB 5, and a "Unit Coal Mty Extra."

PRH is a key schedule; it is the principal carrier of through traffic which has come up from BB and CC and intermediate points on the Peninsular Railway, leaving in the evening and arriving at the Peninsular's J Yard early in the morning. "Normal" interchange at this point would call for a transfer run taking the cars for the E-W over to its 77th St. Yard where they would be classified and put into the next train west. This process would take the better part of a day, so the two line-haul railroads have set up a "run-through" arrangement.

Pre-Blocking

The Peninsular "pre-blocks" cars for the E-W interchange in three classifications – a block for I, a block of cars for points in the Southwest via the E-W and the SW & AA to HH, and all other cars for points on the E-W; this is about all the classifications it can make without delaying its overnight train. The E-W, in turn, runs PRH out of the Peninsular yard in J rather than 77th St. and inspects and accepts the cars from the Peninsular at that point.

Motive power and cabooses are not pooled on this particular run-through because changing them loses no time, and the utilization would not be improved. But PRH, once its inspection is complete, moves out over the J Terminal RR with a J-T "shuttle" train crew. As it passes 77th St., the E-W crew climbs aboard, the J-T crew drops off, and the train continues on its way to H. At I the Peninsular block is set out, and any cars from I which have accumulated since JH 3 left are picked up.

Synchronized Arrival

OH 5 (from O), PHM (from P and M) and PRH all arrive at the westbound receiving yard at H within a 30-minute period; JH 3 has finished going over the hump, so tracks are available. The Southwest block from the PRR is immediately cut off the rear of PRH, run over the hump first to put its cars into the proper blocks of cars from earlier trains which are to go out in HSW, and within an hour they are on their way. HSW is the hottest train off the E-W to the Southwest; it is pre-blocked and runs through to the STU RR intact from H. A one-hour connection including some classification is not normally possible, but the traffic pattern is such that the Peninsular cars almost always go into no more than three different blocks of HSW. With this special attention, the transfer is made, saving a day's time.

Cars from OH 5, PMH and the rest of PRH go over the hump in normal fashion, and priority cars are blocked in HB 5 for its 1400 departure. The hump classification process at H on these three trains is sufficiently thorough that HB 5 need not go into the yards at D or B. Its cars have not just been blocked as those for C, for B, and connections west from B, but rather into cuts for particular major industries at B, for particular locals working out of C, and for individual cities and yards all along the PQR.

Assigning Motive Power

Between H and D are the Alleghenies. While considerable poetic license was used in the energy-per-ton discussions of Fig. 2-6 in making this eastern railroad go over a pass 5,000 feet high, they are still a formidable obstacle. The E-W has some 20 miles of 2.0 percent (compensated) grade going up the Big Hill on the westbound track and long stretches of 0.3 percent in approaching the mountains. Fast freights, such as HSW, carry very few empties and run about 90 cars, usually grossing about 80 tons a car, for a trailing tonnage of 7,200.

To make the schedule, the train will have to run up to 60 mph on the level stretches and not less than 30 on an 0.3 percent adverse grade. Fig. 4-10 shows that about 1,800 tons can be assigned to a 3,000 hp unit on that basis, so four such units will provide enough power until the train reaches the mountain. What will happen then? At 1,800 tons per unit on 2.0 percent, a four-axle unit simply won't hack it; speed will fall below 22 mph. To prevent slipping, its power-matching circuitry will reduce horsepower output. There won't be enough tractive force, and the train will stall.

Three six-axle 3,000 hp units will have sufficient tractive force to lug the consist up the grade at about 10 to 12 mph, but the continuous tractive force rating of the traction motors will be exceeded unless they are low-geared, with 65 mph maximum speed. Experience has shown that scheduling train speed so close to the locomotives' rating results in high traction motor maintenance, since there will be occasions when speed will briefly exceed the established limit by a few mph. Twenty miles at 10 mph will take a very long two hours. Now what?

Helpers and Doubling

On lines where a single grade is the problem and very few trains are run, a standard practice is to "double the hill." The crew takes half the train to the summit, sets it out and goes back for the rest, too slow a process for main-line trackage. Maintaining 20 mph up a 2.0 percent grade requires reducing the load to about 900 tons per unit. This would require eight units to haul the 7,200 tons over the route. If there were several such grades along the line (a very unfavorable situation, fortunately found on only a few main lines), reduced tonnage or the use of radio-controlled units would be the best solutions. Most doubles are unplanned, due to such factors as locomotive failure.

As it is, the E-W uses helper units to assist its fast freights over the Alleghenies between F and E. Four on the rear end plus the four road locomotives "on the point," will provide the required one unit per 900 tons; as Fig. 4-10 shows, at the required 20 or 22 mph speed, either four-axle or six-axle units will do about equally well. Since the west slope of the Big Hill is almost as steep and even heavier tonnage moves eastward, helpers (if that is the solution chosen) will be needed eastbound in even greater numbers. Therefore, HB 5 might keep its helpers all the way to E so that their dynamic braking power will allow the train to descend more rapidly without overheating the train wheels. The pushers will then be in position to help the next eastbound.

Heavy Freight Service

As our schedule sheet shows, a "Unit Coal Mty" extra left H just 45 minutes ahead of HB 5. This is a train similar to the one considered in Figs. 2-7 and 2-8, 100 empty gondolas weighing only 25 tons each, rolling back toward the mines at 45 mph. Eastbound the train weighs 12,500 tons with its load and is powered to make 35 mph on level track, which takes only 5,300 hp. It rates just two 3,000 hp units. It's on an exacting schedule in each direction, since the whole operation depends on the train's making a round trip every 72 hours.

Westbound up the hill the empty train has 1,250 trailing tons per unit. Fig. 4-10 shows that two six-axle 3,000 hp units can maintain about 14 mph with that load; it can get up and over without assistance. With adroit dispatching, HB 5 with its helpers will overtake and pass the empty train on the hill west of F where there is a second westbound track (Fig. 7-1) for just such maneuvers.

Right behind HB 5 leaving H is one of three westbound Ore Extras carrying a shipload of iron from the docks at J to the steel mills of D. Grossing 13,000 tons each, they are powered by three 3,000 hp six-axle units and can make 35 mph on level track, hogging down to about 18 mph on a long 0.3 percent grade. What will they need to get up the hill?

Locomotive Selection

The ore trains *can* take the time to lug up the hill at 10 mph, so they can be loaded to 1,800 tons per unit, which means a total of 7.22 units. Since 0.22 of a unit is not available, in practice the E-W will add five units to the two already on each extra and expect to make it. Train dynamics analysis is very appropriate in determining how many units can be put on the head end and how many on the rear end without exceeding the coupler or center-sill strength of the cars or approaching a hazardous L/V ratio (Fig. 6-5) on any of the curves on the hill.

From this sampling of motive power assignment problems on the E-W, at least two factors are apparent that will determine the types of locomotive the railroad should have on its roster. For pusher service, it will have six-axle units; they are essential for the ore drags and will do as well as four-axle units in assisting fast freight. For fast-freight, over-the-road service, the E-W will prefer four-axle units. They're lighter and cheaper to maintain and, even with fast-freight gearing, will do well pulling their share of the load up the mountain because the speed is not allowed to drop too low.

Computerized Scheduling

From this sample, which doesn't begin to cover all the little interactions between trains, tracks, signals, laws, and people that must be considered in figuring out the best way to run the railroad, it should be clear that scheduling is a complicated process. A standard way of handling it, particularly on single-track lines where trains can only meet each other where there are passing tracks, has been with string. Strings stretched across a board marked out with the hours of the day on two sides and with mileage and station locations at its ends represent the train schedules. The strings are then shifted until they cross each other only at passing points, keeping the slope of each string correct at all points since it represents the speed of the train.

Today, computer programs, including individual train performance routines, offer a way of refining the process of working out the best pattern of traffic, making quick changes in conditions, and trying out new ideas before disrupting the railroad itself.

Car Scheduling

The nuances of train scheduling are important to the railroad, but the shipper couldn't care less how the trains move. The important thing is when will the carload be delivered at the consignee's plant. Therefore, computerized *car scheduling* programs based on network optimization principles have been developed which, given a railroad's routes and train-schedule structure, tell how each car should be handled (picked up, blocked, moved over the road, classified, and set out at destination) to provide the best overall balance of cost, speed, and (particularly) reliability of service. Then it is up to the railroad to get the word to each employee concerned so that the cars are handled and do move accordingly.

Unit-Train Operation

14

From the earliest days of railroading there have been large-scale movements of single commodities from one point of origin, a mine, for example, to a single destination, such as a port or processing mill. In effect, trains have shuttled the same cars back and forth in handling the traffic, and the relative efficiency of handling a nonbreakable item at economical speeds in heavy trains has been reflected in the rate established.

Multi-Car Rates

However, as a matter of public policy, the railroads were for many decades prohibited from establishing any rates or rules which provided lower rates in return for requiring that a commodity be shipped in quantities larger than a carload at a time. This was on the basis that such rates would favor large shippers. This consideration became increasingly unrealistic, since unregulated bulk barge operators on the government waterways were under no such restrictions. The fact that the big shipper had no incentive to ship or receive in large lots did not encourage working with the railroad to explore lower costs possible with an integrated large-scale loading/transporting/unloading system.

Changes in governmental opinion on the matter – in Canada in the 1960s and several years later in the United States Congress, with ultimate confirmation by repeated court decisions – permitted the establishment of multi-car or trainload tariffs. In the United States, deregulation by the Staggers Act of 1980 permitted individual-shipper contracts further broadening volume/service/pricing options.

The Unit-Train

The *unit-train,* a system including efficient, rapid loading and unloading facilities matched up with whole trains (or large blocks) of cars (and often, locomotives) assigned to the service, has resulted. A long-term contract for transportation under specified conditions of volume and scheduling assures a high degree of equipment utilization and thus allows an attractive freight rate, with benefits to all concerned.

Fig. 14-1. Unit Coal Train Being "Flood Loaded"

While the largest-scale application of this principle has been in the movement of coal from mine to power plant (over 98 percent of which moved under contract rates by 1994), it is also used in handling such commodities as semi-finished steel, orange juice, hot liquid sulfur, grain, crude oil, fertilizer, double-stacked "landbridge" containers and even (in at least one situation) salt water. Fig. 14-1 shows a typical coal train being "flood loaded."

Equipment Specialization

The amount of money and the long-term commitments involved require extensive study of each unit-train system. As a result there is considerable specialization in particular equipment used. Coal-carrying cars, for example, may be owned by the mining, railroad, or power company, or may be leased. They may be unloaded by overturning the cars in a dumper (without uncoupling the cars if one end of each is equipped with a special rotary coupler) or by manual or automatic bottom-dump, depending to a considerable extent on the space available at the receiving end of the movement. Motive power may be shipper- or railroad-owned and may be all at the head end or include mid-train remote-control units if the route profile makes that work out best.

Equipment Utilization

The utilization of dedicated cars achieves mileage-per-day averages from 3 to 20 times that of the general-service car. The train travels directly from origin to destination on a single waybill without being switched at intermediate points. At its destination, it is immediately unloaded and started back for a similarly quick reloading. Turnaround-cycle time may range from 1½ hours (for some automated within-plant operations covering a few miles) to 96 hours for a 2,000-mile round trip which may include crossing major mountain ranges.

Since the benefits of overall transportation efficiency, however derived, may be equitably distributed *over the life of the contract* by negotiation between the railroad and the train sponsor (usually, the buyer of the product), paying substantial premium for lighter-weight aluminum-body coal cars which can carry a few additional tons per car within axle-load limits (and thus move the total annual tonnage with fewer cars and trips) may result in assured savings; such cars, difficult to justify in general service, have become dominant in coal-car acquisition programs; a goal in the continual car-design refinement process taking place in the 1990s is a light weight of 40,000 lbs, enabling a "100-ton" vehicle to transport a 223,000 lb load within the 263,000 lbs weight on rail limit.

Mini-Trains

A related system possibility brought about by multi-car ratemaking is the point-to-point "mini-train" carrying a commodity such as crushed rock or grain in 5- or 10-car units directly from a loading to a delivery point. They operate under tariffs requiring special "while-we-wait" loading and unloading and work rules allowing a reduced-size (two-man, for example) train crew not restricted by normal divisional or yard/road limits.

The mini-train becomes, in effect, a 500- to 1,500-ton truck which can take grain from a country elevator to a terminal on demand without tying up expensive covered hoppers for days in the "normal" local freight set-out/load/pick-up/classify/road haul/yard switch/set-out/unload and return car cycle. As the unit train's low rates have made producers of low-value commodities competitive over distances previously impossible, the mini-train can make railhaul truck-competitive on short hauls.

A further refinement introduced in 1988 is the patented "Dump Train" developed by the Georgetown Railroad of Texas, a dedicated string of 10 to 15 or more special hoppers which unload in sequence onto a continuous conveyor belt powered by a transfer car at one end. Capable of unloading 1,000 tons or more of aggregate, coal, or other bulk commodity to order in less than an hour, in some services one has made as many as three revenue trips per day.

Intermodal Traffic

15

In 1885, the Long Island Rail Road established a short-lived service in which loaded farm wagons, horses, and farmers were carried into Long Island City on flatcars, boxcars and a passenger coach, respectively, thus saving two transfer operations in getting the produce to market. This was by no means the earliest "piggyback" operation, so the idea of intermodal through shipments without reloading is not new. After long periods of little activity, however, the idea really started to catch on in the early 1950s, sparked by several factors: improved rail equipment for carrying more than one trailer per car was developed; the ICC decided that a railroad wouldn't have to obtain a truck-route certificate to carry freight over its own rails in its own trailers; and containerization of ocean freight began to change the shape of the merchandise-carrying fleets of the world.

COFC/TOFC Traffic Levels

What is most widely called piggyback, technically labeled TOFC/COFC (Trailer on Flatcar or Container on Flatcar traffic), has continued to expand, to the point where it now represents about 23 percent of the carloadings on U.S. railroads, passing the 8 million mark in revenue trailer/container loadings (including dual-mode trailer-rail movements) in 1994.

The Intermodal Transfer

The unique feature of intermodal traffic is transfer from one mode – rail, sea, or highway – to another. Where rail is involved, there are three principal methods in use.

Circus Loading, so named for its use for over a hundred years in getting the wagons of traveling shows (or the vehicles of an Army group) on and off the flatcars taking them from town to town, requires only an end-of-track ramp. Fold-down bridge plates on the ends of the flatcars (Fig. 15-1) form a temporary roadway over which the trailers (or containers on chassis) are backed – ramp-to-car and car-to-car – in loading a string of cars. Ramp loading is the only suitable method for use at locations where only a few transfers a day are made, but has become virtually obsolete with the concentration of transfers at a small number of high-volume terminals where the delay and cost of loading trailers in series would be uncompetitive. Bridge plates have been removed from most TOFC cars.

Gantry Loading, suitable for either containers or trailers, uses a traveling overhead crane straddling roadway and track to make the transfer or "lift." Gantries have become bigger, faster, more versatile, and more expensive as the business has developed. Since loaded containers must be lifted by the top corners while trailers must be supported from below during the lift, a crane handling both must be equipped with two types of adapter slings.

Side Loading of containers involves sliding the box from road chassis to flatcar, originally with specialized gear peculiar to the particular container/car system in use. Its chief problem has been the failure of any one system to achieve wide enough acceptance to become standard. Potentially, such side loading could be the quick, flexible, and low-capital way for handling transfer of containers.

However, the dominant equipment used in side loading, adaptable to both TOFC and COFC and known by a variety of names of which "piggypacker" is typical, is the mobile side loader. Essentially a gigantic, relatively high-speed forklift, it simply picks a container or trailer up bodily, drives to the appointed spot and sets its burden down on flatcar, chassis, roadway, or storage-area stack.

Intermodal Terminals

While most early intermodal transfer points (once estimated to number 1,500) were simple ramps (fixed or portable) suitable for circus loading of trailers or containers on chassis, all but about 75 of the 300 or so intermodal terminals (still often referred to as ramps) were mechanized with gantries or mobile-lift units by 1989.

The E-W System's 77th St. Intermodal Terminal started out as such a ramp but has long since been expanded and equipped for gantry loading. Its location (Fig. 11-2), however, illustrates some of the points necessary for a successful facility. Its tracks connect directly with the main line so that incoming and outgoing TOFC/COFC trains, the hottest on the railroad, do not have to work their way through the yards. Since its gantries can place the trailers and containers directly on flatcars designated to go to their destination, there is no further "classification" of the railcars necessary after loading. Within the metropolitan area it serves, the terminal is located for easy highway access (Fig. 11-2) but west of the Ship Canal drawbridge which could seriously interfere with reliability.

Piggyback Equipment

Fig. 15-1 shows the dimensions and characteristics of intermodal components as they became standardized in the late 1970s when piggyback traffic became significant and when 40-foot trailers and the 8 ft x 8 ft x 40 ft International Standards Organization (ISO) containers were the longest in general highway service.

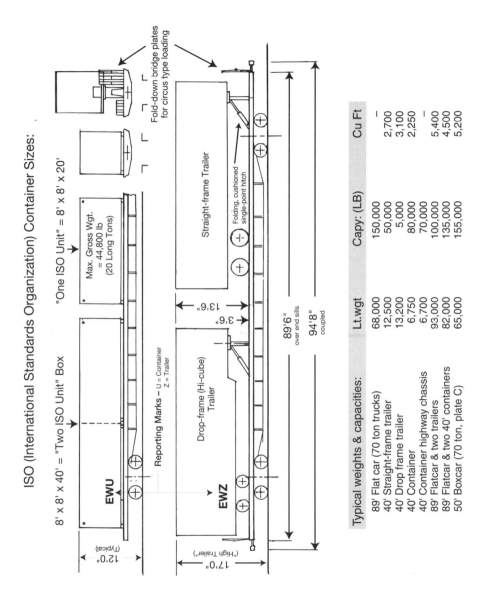

Fig. 15-1. TOFC/COFC Equipment

Typical weights & capacities:	Lt.wgt	Capy: (LB)	Cu Ft
89' Flat car (70 ton trucks)	68,000	150,000	–
40' Straight-frame trailer	12,500	50,000	2,700
40' Drop frame trailer	13,200	5,000	3,100
40' Container	6,750	80,000	2,250
40' Container highway chassis	6,700	70,000	–
89' Flatcar & two trailers	93,000	100,000	5,400
89' Flatcar & two 40' containers	82,000	135,000	4,500
50' Boxcar (70 ton, plate C)	65,000	155,000	5,200

227

Although galloping nationwide increases in U.S. highway vehicle limits brought about by the Surface Transportation Act of 1982 and the "double-stack revolution" discussed later have brought about rapid changes in the piggyback fleet, some 47,000 of the 89 ft "standard" flats (many converted to handle two 45 ft or three 28 ft "pup" trailers, and/or 20 to 45 ft containers "102 inches wide") remained in service in 1994. Most of the rest were converted to fully enclosed multi-level auto racks.

Trailer vs. Container vs. Boxcar

Compared to boxcar traffic, TOFC traffic is more expensive to move over the road because of the extra tare weight represented by the trailer and its wheels, greater wind resistance of the high cars, and (sometimes) restrictions associated with the high center of gravity. Terminal expenses are greatly reduced, as the cost and delay of moving individual cars through crowded switching trackage and classifying for linehaul is replaced by one-man/one-trailer movements which can be taking place simultaneously all over town as the time for train loading and departure approaches.

COFC avoids the height, wind resistance, and extra-weight problems of TOFC at the cost of the logistic problems of having chassis available when and where needed; until double-stacking increased the attractiveness of COFC sufficiently to make solving the chassis-supply problem worthwhile, containers tended to travel piggyback only on chassis, diluting potential savings.

In general, intermodal transfer costs in conventional rail service have required a trip length of 500 miles to make the three-to-one fuel consumption saving of rail movement and the labor saving of carriage in trains competitive with road haulage. Concentrating traffic at large-scale, well-located points served by fast, quick-turnaround, reduced-crew, cabooseless trains operating at low enough cost to permit frequent (several departures per day) service has proved sufficient to capture traffic in some shorter-haul markets.

Intermodal Plans

Once the capability for through freight movement on an intermodal basis has been established, the number of combinations of "who does what for whom" rapidly expands. Prior to the deregulation of piggyback traffic following the Staggers Act of 1980, a railroad could not start hauling trailers without approved tariffs. Most traffic moved under the seven TOFC/COFC "plans" illustrated in Fig. 15-2, typically in about the 1980 percentages stated. While these "Plan" designations are no longer needed nor familiar since deregulation, they do illustrate the ways in which intermodal traffic continues to be solicited, priced, and moved by railroads, truckers, water carriers, shippers, and third-party operators (transportation brokers, package express companies, and forwarders). As a business organization the railroad must seek service and price combinations that can be provided profitably without disproportionately affecting its other (boxcar) traffic.

228

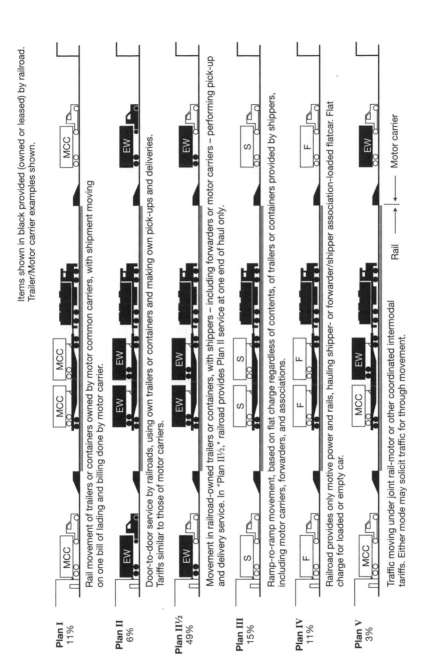

Fig. 15-2. TOFC/COFC Plans (Items in Black Provided – Owned or Leased – by Railroad. Trailer/Motor Carrier Examples Shown.)

Truck Freight by Rail

Plan II represents one end of the spectrum. Here, a railroad essentially goes into the trucking business, since the unit of shipment becomes a truck-trailer load rather than a carload (which fits in with the desire of many businesses for a smaller unit), and railroad personnel are directly involved with shipper and consignee. It has the advantage of rail line-haul economies in setting its rates.

Engines and Rails Only

The other extreme is Plan IV, widely used by freight forwarders, in which even the job of getting the trailers or containers aboard and providing the flatcar is "farmed out," and the railroad does what it should be best at – hauling cars over the rails, with payment provided whether they're loaded or empty. Between these two plans is a wide choice, of which Plan II ½ has become most popular, within which a railroad may seek its fortune.

International Services

The huge shift of overseas merchandise traffic to container-ships and the concomitant saving of time in transit has led to the establishment of the "land bridge" and "mini" land-bridge (Fig. 15-3); traffic moves on water-carrier tariffs at water rates based on carriage via the Panama Canal; the water carrier pays for the transfers and the railhaul from the money it saves by reducing the turnaround time for its vessels. The containers travel across the United States in "unit trains" on reliable and relatively fast schedules.

While subsequent deregulation (and an enormous increase in domestic COFC traffic) has made the terminology somewhat academic, it was the family of "bridges" illustrated in Fig. 15-3 that presaged the "double-stack" revolution of the late 1980s.

Third-Generation Intermodal Technology

The further increase in fuel costs affecting all modes of transportation in the late 1970s not only increased interest in rail intermodal transportation but, in conjunction with the increase in allowable trailer lengths from 40 to 45 to 48 to 53 ft, caused the reconfiguration of the intermodal car fleet to reduce or eliminate the railcar tare weight and accommodate a variety of longer (and sometimes, heavier) vehicles and containers.

With considerable benefit from railroad, industry, and supplier prototype testing at the Transportation Technology Center to demonstrate the basic stability and trainworthiness of unconventional configurations, a variety of "third generation" equipment is now in service. Fig. 15-4 illustrates examples of seven types which – along with other types in service or test in prototype numbers – were in general service (in quantities of a thousand "platforms" or more each) by 1990.

In addition to the lighter tare weight per box, a most significant advantage of the articulated combinations is a great reduction in train slack – long-travel end-of-car cushioning is not required, while the connectors themselves include an arrangement taking up wear so that the platforms remain snugly connected. As a result, the boxes and their contents enjoy a vastly smoother ride.

The most aerodynamic and fuel-efficient (and oldest, since "RoadRailers" were carrying mail behind passenger trains in the 1950s) of these systems are the bi-modal "carless" trains now running in the Mark V (separable rail bogie) version. The Mark IV (retractable-rail-axle trailers, of lower, over-the-road load capacity because of the

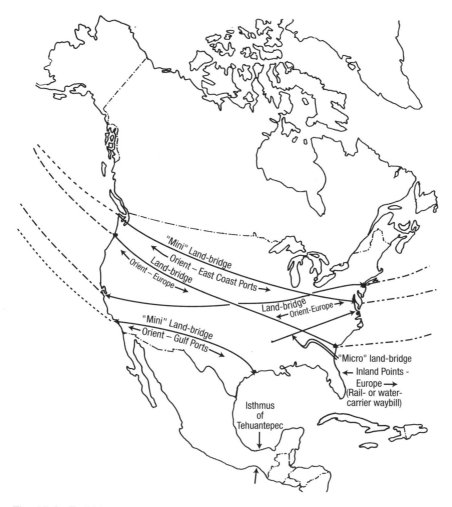

Fig. 15-3. Rail Hauls on All-Water Tariffs

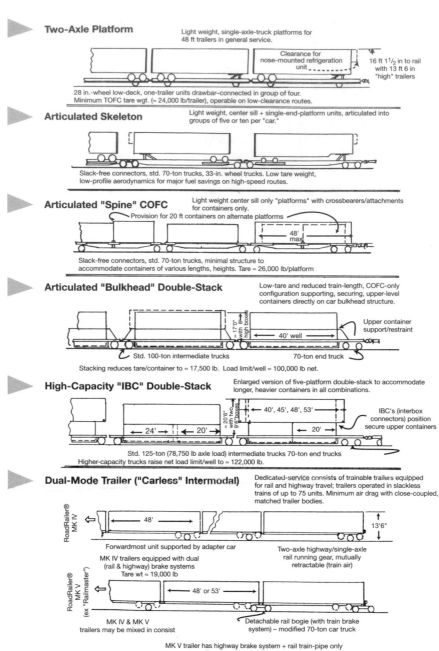

▶ **Two-Axle Platform** Light weight, single-axle-truck platforms for 48 ft trailers in general service.

Clearance for nose-mounted refrigeration unit

16 ft 1¹/₂ in to rail with 13 ft 6 in "high" trailers

28 in.-wheel low-deck, one-trailer units drawbar–connected in group of four. Minimum TOFC tare wgt. (≈ 24,000 lb/trailer), operable on low-clearance routes.

▶ **Articulated Skeleton** Light weight, center sill + single-end-platform units, articulated into groups of five or ten per "car."

Slack-free connectors, std. 70-ton trucks, 33-in. wheel trucks. Low tare weight, low-profile aerodynamics for major fuel savings on high-speed routes.

▶ **Articulated "Spine" COFC** Light weight center sill only "platforms" with crossbearers/attachments for containers only.

Provision for 20 ft containers on alternate platforms

48' max

Slack-free connectors, std. 70-ton trucks, minimal structure to accommodate containers of various lengths, heights. Tare ≈ 26,000 lb/platform

▶ **Articulated "Bulkhead" Double-Stack** Low-tare and reduced train-length, COFC-only configuration supporting, securing, upper-level containers directly on car bulkhead structure.

≈17'0" with 8' high boxes

Upper container support/restraint

40' well

Std. 100-ton intermediate trucks

70-ton end truck

Stacking reduces tare/container to ≈ 17,500 lb. Load limit/well ≈ 100,000 lb net.

▶ **High-Capacity "IBC" Double-Stack** Enlarged version of five-platform double-stack to accommodate longer, heavier containers in all combinations.

≈20'6" with two 9'6" boxes

40', 45', 48', 53'

IBC's (interbox connectors) position secure upper containers

24' 20' 20'

Std. 125-ton (78,750 lb axle load) intermediate trucks 70-ton end trucks
Higher-capacity trucks raise net load limit/well to ≈ 122,000 lb.

▶ **Dual-Mode Trailer ("Carless" Intermodal)** Dedicated-service consists of trainable trailers equipped for rail and highway travel; trailers operated in slackless trains of up to 75 units. Minimum air drag with close-coupled, matched trailer bodies.

RoadRailer® MK IV

48'

13'6"

Forwardmost unit supported by adapter car

MK IV trailers equipped with dual (rail & highway) brake systems Tare wt ≈ 19,000 lb

Two-axle highway/single-axle rail running gear, mutually retractable (train air)

RoadRailer® MK V (ex "Railmaster")

48' or 53'

MK IV & MK V trailers may be mixed in consist

Detachable rail bogie (with train brake system) – modified 70-ton car truck

MK V trailer has highway brake system + rail train-pipe only
Tare wt ≈ 16,000 lb (on highway)
Mark IV/Mark V consists may be hauled on rear of low-slack (e.g. double-stack) trains

Fig. 15-4. "Third-Generation" Intermodal Equipment

weight of the rail wheelset) were phased out by 1993. Although tests demonstrated that RoadRailers could be operated behind low-slack (articulated) consists, all current service is in solid trains operating over an established route network, where they have been most successful in providing premium service for high-rated, time-sensitive traffic. Initially restricted to shorter trains, on the basis of tests and analysis, RoadRailers now have FRA approval for operation in consists of up to 125 trailers.

The Double-Stack "Revolution"

The biggest shift in intermodal transportation, however, resulted from the development of the double-stack container car. Entering land-bridge service in the late 1980s, these trains that could fit within existing passing tracks and yet give as many as 260 forty-foot containers a smooth, fuel-efficient ride across the United States led what had been ocean transportation lines to enter the intermodal business. Since fully balanced traffic could only be achieved with a loaded westbound backhaul, tariffs and service patterns evolved popularizing previously lightly patronized domestic containerized freight traffic.

Railroad and third-party participation in soliciting and handling this water-related COFC traffic (including single-stack connecting services) created the "critical mass" necessary to get purely domestic containerization – much of it in two-way, in larger "boxes" 102 in. wide and 48 or 53 ft long not containership-compatible – off the ground. As a result, much domestic intermodal traffic has shifted from trailers to containers; overall, container loadings have exceeded those of trailers since 1992, reaching 53% of the total by 1994.

The number of "Z vans" (trailers equipped for piggyback service) has declined from a peak of 140,000 in 1984 to about 75,000, 10 years later.

Fig. 15-5 summarizes the shift in size and composition of the intermodal car fleet over a 10-year period, showing not only the shift toward double-stack platforms but also the accelerated growth in the overall capacity of the fleet with the expansion of domestic containerization.

An important addition to the double-stack fleet is the single-platform "stand-alone" car whose trucks can support stacked containers loaded with the dense commodities encountered on some international routes. Also desirable for some services are three-platform cars, better accommodating traffic to smaller markets where the 10-container minimum for a fully loaded five-platform car may not be available on a daily basis.

In comparison to TOFC, domestic COFC traffic represents a generally lower-quality service (time from arrival at the rail terminal to delivery at the consignee's dock will be longer) with the resulting lower rate representing in effect a sharing between railroad and shipper of the line-haul economies of carrying boxes without wheels. Recognition of the importance to industrial localities, and especially seaports, of access to double-stack traffic is illustrated by governmentally assisted projects to help railroads eliminate tunnel and bridge bottlenecks; an example is Pennsylvania's state program to allow unrestricted (stacked 9 ft 6 in. high boxes) entry to the Philadelphia area.

Intermodal Equipment Utilization

Because intermodal railcars are loaded and unloaded quickly, travel in expedited trains, and achieve a high back-haul rate (typically over 90% of car-miles loaded), the fleetwide average of 48 revenue loads per platform per year is more than three times that achieved by freight cars in general.

U.S. intermodal fleet capacity - slots (one slot = space for one 40ft or longer trailer or container)			
Type of equipment	1984	1989	1994
First & second generation 85-89ft. TOFC/COFC Flat (Fig. 15-1)	109,000	79,000	47,000
Third generation TOFC/COFC (Fig. 15-4) Spine or skeleton articulated, 2 axle single or articulated	7,000	8,000	35,000
Double-stack, articulated or stand alone	2,000	30,000	82,000
RoadRailer (Fig. 15-4)	300	2,300	3,600
Total intermodal slots	112,000	116,000	168,000

Fig. 15-5. U.S. intermodal fleet capacity slots

Fig. 15-6. Five-unit articulated 48' well car with 125-ton intermediate trucks, adaptable for double-stacked ISO marine (8' wide) or domestic (8'6") containers.

Fig. 15-7. Mobile side loader ("piggy-packer") capable of loading trailers and containers on single or double-stack rail cars, stacking containers three high on ground.

Special Freight and Package Services

16

The primary business of the railroads in North America is now, as it has always been, the transportation of freight in standard carload lots. Nevertheless, the transportation of LCL (Less than Carload) and express package shipments has always had a relatively higher degree of public visibility because of the sheer number of customers directly concerned and the perceived dependence of big vs. small-business competitiveness upon the relative shipping costs in large vs. small lots. The handling of loads too large or heavy for other overland transport modes also focuses attention on the rail network.

Large and Heavy Loads

Standard clearances and load limits are included by reference as a part of railroad freight tariffs, indicating the size and weight of shipments which can be handled in regular service. Most routes provide at least AAR "Plate B" clearance and 220,000 lbs weight on rail for eight-wheel cars. Many main lines have been modified to be able to handle piggyback and auto-rack traffic without restriction, to the extent that typical limits, beyond which special arrangements are required, are 20 ft above rail, 11 ft 6 in. wide and 125 tons net weight.

High-Wide Load Coordination

Nevertheless, about 100,000 oversize shipments per year on U.S. railroads require special coordination. Railroads maintain special offices for this purpose, to work with shippers in finding routes (sometimes unbelievably roundabout) which will bypass close clearances, bridge load-limitations and other bottlenecks. Railroad limits may actually determine the largest size to which bridge girders, pressure vessels, or generators may be designed and what provisions must be made for piecemeal shipment and on-site assembly. Finally, the operating department of the railroad is involved in determining and observing any special restrictions necessary enroute: low-speed travel by local freight or special train; scheduling to avoid trains on adjacent tracks; inactivating uncoupling levers on multi-car shipments; etc.

Special Equipment

Railroads owning special depressed-center, well-hole or high-capacity flatcars for oversize or overweight loads (AAR Mechanical Designations FD, FW, FM) receive a special payment of $100 to $300 each time one is loaded, as a partial inducement for owning an adequate number of these expensive cars which can't expect steady use. (Fig. 16-1)

For the very largest power-generating machinery, "Schnabel" cars (AAR Mechanical Designation LS) in which the load forms the central part of the car structure (Fig. 16-2) and can extend to the very limits of the clearance diagram have been built. Some include special jacking devices to shift the load a few inches in any direction to clear specific obstacles. Maximum capacity is about 500 tons for a 20-axle car. Since most main-line tracks are spaced on 14-ft centers, the disruption involved in moving an object 20 ft in diameter can only be overcome with the best in advanced planning.

LCL Traffic

With the general availability of over-the-road truck service handling less-than-carload shipments on a regulated common-carrier basis, most railroads have been permitted to discontinue handling LCL traffic, which has traditionally been unprofitable. However, several million tons per year in small freight shipments ride the rails in forwarder- and shipper-association traffic.

Fig. 16-1. Depressed center flat car for oversize or overweight loads. This model is capable of hauling 210 tons.

Forwarders

A *forwarder* accepts LCL and LTL (less than truckload) shipments for transportation at a package rate and puts them together in carload lots for the long haul. The railroad has a carload to haul, the forwarder makes his profit from the difference between the two rates, and the quantities involved allow the dispatch of cars on regular schedules which individual shippers could not support.

Most forwarder traffic is now handled in piggyback service, giving the forwarder reduced terminal and handling costs and making him more competitive with the common-carrier or contract trucker. On the East-West System, the forwarder traffic on his own leased and loaded Trailer Train flatcars (Plan IV) is enough to warrant running Train 151, a first-class schedule, as the first leg of a run-through train to the West Coast. Accepting only TOFC/COFC traffic, 151 is allowed 70 mph and provided enough horsepower to climb the mountain only slightly less vigorously than the passenger runs. Since the completion of a 1988 tunnel-enlargement program to eliminate height/width restriction on the Allegheny Division main line, traffic on the E-W hotshot is primarily COFC (domestic and import/export) riding on double-stack equipment.

Fig. 16-2. Twenty-axle "Schnabel" car of 500 ton load capacity.

Shipper Associations organized on a cooperative, nonprofit basis to perform similar functions to forwarders in obtaining carload rates and larger-scale and more regular traffic flows for their members were specifically exempted from regulation in 1940 when forwarders were brought under the purview of the ICC. With the advent of piggybacking, these organizations, although forbidden from advertising their services commercially as condition of nonregulation, grew rapidly and handled a major portion of LTL shipments. Deregulation (particularly, decisions allowing a company handling its traffic in owned or contract trucks to act essentially as a common carrier in accepting back-haul traffic) essentially negated the advantages of such arrangements.

Shipper agents or consolidators, may be grouped (with forwarders) in a "third party" category as intermediaries between transportation companies and shippers in the management and handling of freight traffic. They handle shipments on land, sea, and air common-carriers at their rates, charging a fee for the services they provide shippers in maintaining regular service patterns and handling the details of the transportation process. The complex transportation alternatives characteristic of expanding international and intermodal traffic – including trade-offs involved in the "just-in-time" inventory-control philosophy of manufacturing – have resulted in expansion and proliferation in both the number and diversity of these organizations.

In the interest of providing a more even flow of traffic the railroad may find it advantageous to establish reduced multi-trailer rates. A piggyback broker can therefore undertake to eke out a profit by consolidating individual trailer loads solicited from shippers whose traffic flow would not otherwise qualify for the bargain rates.

Rail Passenger Services

17

As indicated in Fig. 18-2, less than five percent of U.S. railroad revenue is from passenger services, and in North America throughout railroading history passenger traffic has been a relatively minor segment of the business. Since these services involve direct contact with millions of customers, however, public awareness of the size of the railroad iceberg that doesn't show up above the water is often limited, to the extent that the importance of freight railroading is little appreciated.

Passenger Service

When does a system with two rails and guiding wheels stop fitting the classification of "railroad"? To avoid answering this question directly, Fig. 17-1 lists a spectrum of rail passenger-carrying systems ranging from light rail (space age terminology for yesterday's streetcar) through what is still labeled in ICC records as "steam railroad" passenger-train service, and beyond. Omitted on the left is the San Francisco cable-car system, which probably deserves inclusion since it has the distinction of being the only mass transit system in North America in which (at least until hangers-on were limited to two per running-board slot) the weight of passengers typically exceeds the weight of the vehicle.

Terminology used is generally that used by the U.S. Department of Transportation, with a separation of railroad commutation service into two categories: primary, where the line exists because of the passenger service; and ancillary, where other traffic predominates, at least on a revenue basis. Typical characteristics of the different passenger systems are listed as a means of showing similarities and differences. Several existing systems don't fit any mold in all respects, and technical developments will undoubtedly result in further obscuring the picture. Taken as a whole, the train consist, accommodations, fare, schedule, right-of-way, and performance characteristics lay out the differences between rapid-transit, railroad commuter and inter-city systems.

Fig. 17-1. Rail Passenger Systems

	MASS TRANSIT			COMMUTER		RAILROAD		
	LIGHT RAIL	HEAVY RAIL TRANSIT					INTERCITY	
		URBAN	COMMUTER	PRIMARY	ANCILLARY	CORRIDOR	LONG-HAUL	AUTO FERRY
TYPICAL TRAIN CONSIST	SINGLE OR TWO-CAR ARTICULATED "LIGHT-RAIL VEHICLES"	SELF-PROPELLED MULTIPLE-UNIT PASSENGER CARS	SELF-PROPELLED MULTIPLE-UNIT PASSENGER CARS	SELF-PROPELLED MULTIPLE-UNIT PASSENGER CARS	LOCOMOTIVE-HAULED (PUSH-PULL) OR SELF-PROPELLED PASSENGER CARS	LOCOMOTIVE-HAULED OR SELF-PROPELLED (MULTIPLE-UNIT OR FIXED-CONSIST) PASSENGER & SNACK CARS	LOCOMOTIVE-HAULED BAGGAGE, PASSENGER & NON-REVENUE CARS	LOCOMOTIVE-HAULED AUTOMOBILE-TRANS PORTER, PASSENGER & NON-REVENUE CARS
TYPICAL PASSENGER ACCOMMODATIONS (LIM. SEATING = 54 STANDEE, 125-200 PSGRS./CAR; LOW DENSITY = 40 PSGR./CAR, MEDIUM-DENSITY = 70 PSGR./CAR; SINGLE-DECK COMMUTER = 100/CAR DOUBLE-DECK = 160/CAR)	SINGLE-DECK LIMITED SEATING + STANDEES	SINGLE-DECK, LIMITED SEATING + STANDEES	SINGLE-DECK, FULL SEATING + LIMITED STANDEES	SINGLE OR DOUBLE-DECK + LIMITED STANDEES	SINGLE OR DOUBLE-DECK + LIMITED STANDEES	MEDIUM-DENSITY COACH SNACK- LIMITED 1ST CLASS (LOW DENSITY)	SINGLE OR DOUBLE-DECK LOW-DENSITY COACH, LOUNGE, SLEEPING, DINING	SINGLE-DECK LOW-DENSITY COACH, LOUNGE, SLEEPING, DINING
FARE STRUCTURE, SALE & COLLECTION (TYPICAL)	FLAT-FARE, SINGLE-TRIP FAREBOX OR MACHINE TICKET + RANDOM INSP.	FLAT OR ZONE SINGLE-TRIP FARE MACHINE-ISSUED, TURNSTILE COLLECTION	GRADUATED SINGLE-TRIP FARE MACHINE-ISSUED, FAREGATE COLLECTION	MULT-RIDE, ZONE-FARE AGENT-SOLD FLASH TICKET	MULT-RIDE ZONE FARE, AGENT-SOLD, ON-TRAIN TICKET COLLECTION	SINGLE-TRIP, AGENT-SOLD, UNRESERVED ACCOMMODATIONS, ON-TRAIN COLL.	SINGLE-TRIP, AGENT-SOLD, RESERVED ACCOMMODATIONS, ON-TRAIN COLL.	SINGLE-TRIP RESERVED ACCOMMODATIONS CHECK-IN
SCHEDULES: (TYPICAL) — TRIPS/DAY (EACH WAY, PER LINE)	50-150	100-200	25-150	25-75	1-25	4-40	1/2-4	1
MIN. HEADWAY (RUSH HR, PER TRACK)	5 MIN.	1 1/2 MIN.	3 MIN.	3 MIN.	10 MIN.	15 MIN.	N.A.	N.A.
HOURS OF SERVICE	DAY, EVENING LIM. WEEKEND	DAY, EVENING, WEEKEND	WEEKDAY, EVENING, WEEKEND, LIM. OWL	RUSH-HOUR, LIM. OFF-PEAK, EVENING	RUSH-HOUR WEEKDAY	DAILY, DAY & EVENING	DAILY / OR TRI WEEKLY OVERNIGHT(S)	DAILY (OVERNIGHT)
MILES BETWEEN PASSENGER STOPS (AVERAGE, TYPICAL)	0.2	0.5 (LOCAL) 1.5 (EXPRESS)	1.5	2.5 (LOCAL) UP TO 20 (EXPRESS)	3.0	35	80	900
LENGTH OF ROUTE - MILES (TYPICAL)	10	15	25	30 (LOCAL) 45 (EXPRESS)	50	200 (EXPRESS)	300-2500	900
SPEED/MPH AVERAGE INCL. STOPS	15	15	25	35	35	85-300	50	50
MAXIMUM	50	55	75	79 (ABS) 100 (CAB SIGS.)	79	79 (ABS) 110-125 (CAB SIG/ATC)	79 (ABS) 90 (ATS CAB SIG.)	79
RIGHT OF WAY: PRINCIPAL LOCATIONS, EXCLUSIVITY	SURFACE- STREET OR PRIVATE RIGHT-OF-WAY (WITH GRADE CROSSINGS)	TUNNEL, ELEVATED SURFACE (NO GRADE CROSSINGS)	ELEVATED TUNNEL, SURFACE (NO GRADE CROSSINGS)	SURFACE, TUNNEL (NO GRADE CROSSINGS)	SURFACE (SOME GRADE CROSSINGS)	SURFACE (FEW GRADE CROSSINGS)	SURFACE (MANY GRADE CROSSINGS)	SURFACE (MANY GRADE CROSSINGS)
OTHER NON-PSGR. RAIL	NONE- OR LIM. FREIGHT	NONE	NONE	LIMITED FREIGHT	FREIGHT	FREIGHT	FREIGHT	FREIGHT
NUMBER OF TRACKS	2	2 TO 4	2	2 TO 6	2	2 TO 4	1 TO 2	1 TO 2
SIGNALING/CONTROL	ABS (ON PRIVATE R/W)	ABS / ATC	ABS / ATC	ABS / ATC	ABS	ABS / ATC	CTC / ABS	CTC / ABS
STATION PLATFORMS	LOW	HIGH	HIGH	HIGH	LOW	HIGH & LOW	LOW	LOW
TRAIN CHARACTERISTICS (TYPICAL) PROPULSION / POWER DISTRIBUTION / VOLTAGE (LOW VOLTAGE = 600-750v HIGH = 11-25 KV)	ELECTRIC-OVER HEAD TROLLEY WIRE/LOW VOLTAGE DC	ELECTRIC-THIRD RAIL/LOW VOLTAGE DC	ELECTRIC-THIRD RAIL/LOW VOLTAGE DC	ELECTRIC-OVERHEAD CATENARY/HIGH V. AC; THIRD-RAIL/LOW V. DC	DIESEL-ELECTRIC AND DIESEL-HYDRAULIC	ELECTRIC OVERHEAD CATENARY, HIGH V. AC, GAS TURBINE DIESEL-ELECTRIC	DIESEL-ELECTRIC	DIESEL - ELECTRIC
CARS/TRAIN	1-4	2-12	4-12	2-12	3-18	4-12	4-18	23-45
TRAIN WGT/PASSENGER (LB)	300 (W/STANDEES)	450 (W/ STANDEES)	700	800	1000	2000	5500	8000
ACCELERATION MPH/SEC @ MEDIUM SPEED	4.5	3.5	3.0	3.0	1.0	1.5	0.3	0.2
ACCELERATION CONTROL	OPERATOR	AUTOMATIC	COMPUTER	AUTOMATIC	OPERATOR	OPERATOR	OPERATOR	OPERATOR
BRAKING	DYNAMIC/AIR/MAGNETIC	ELECTRO-PNEU.	DYNAMIC/ELEC-PNEU.	ELECTRO-PNEU.	AUTOMATIC AIR	DYNAMIC/ELEC.-PNEU.	AUTOMATIC AIR	AUTOMATIC AIR

ABS = AUTOMATIC BLOCK SIGNALS
ATC = AUTOMATIC TRAIN CONTROL
CTC = CENTRALIZED TRAFFIC CONTROL

Heavy Rail Transit

"Heavy rail" rapid-transit systems are characterized by an exclusive right-of-way. Although most trackage is usually surface (in cut or on fill), enough must usually be in tunnels to make third rail electric propulsion the choice in the interest of affordable tunnel size; right-of-way and structure costs typically dominate track and vehicle costs. Postwar North American steel rail systems have typically been designed for 70-75 mph speeds with computerized train control in which the operator serves primarily a monitoring and emergency manual-control function. Their traffic pattern approaches that of a commuter railroad.

In common with older (but typically more extensive) 50-55 mph systems upgraded with higher-performance (and air-conditioned) equipment and signaling capable of 90-second rush-hour headways, ultimate line capacity is primarily a matter of the number of doors per train (governing factor is rate at which passengers can get off and on); with trains of eight 75 ft cars, comfortable rush-hour line capacity of 40,000 per hour within the 12-foot width of a single track exceeds that of a hypothetical 20-lane expressway dominated by the typical single-occupant commuter automobile.

Eight of the 14 heavy rail systems in business or under construction by 1990 represent new (since World War II) starts. As a result, nationwide impact of this rapid-transit concept is increasing (even in such automobile-based areas as Southern California), although declines in inner-city population and commercial activity in the larger cities already served by the older systems have held overall ridership at a relatively constant level of 7 million trips per day over the last three decades. Typical heavy rail farebox recovery of operating costs averages somewhat above 50%, although some systems do considerably better. Operating expenses for heavy rail systems in the United States totaled $2.2 billion in 1994.

Light Rail Systems

With 16 new (post-1978) light rail systems in business or under construction by 1995, joining a half-dozen others in cities which never completely lost their "streetcars," light rail has become (judged by ridership, environmental, and farebox cost-coverage ratio considerations) an increasingly attractive and significant alternative to bus (including busway) transit. The new systems are characterized by limited central business district street-running coupled with time-saving overall transit-times made possible (financially and environmentally) by the utilization of existing rail freight corridors reaching growing suburbs. Light rail is the fastest growing segment of rail transit, with passenger-miles increasing 78% between 1978 and 1994. Farebox cost recovery percentages (on average, in the low 30s, but with some much higher) are typically a few points above transit bus levels. Operating costs on U.S. light rail systems totaled $400 million in 1994.

To date, the key to a winning combination of amenities attracting ridership and acceptable operating costs has been the availability of high-capacity articulated cars, capable of running in trains to carry 1,500 to 6,000 passengers per hour at peak periods, of service-proven reliability. Incremental rather than radical performance and technological advances have carried the day.

Railroad Commuter Service

By 1984, the operation (generally including employment of train, maintenance and management personnel) of all railroad commuter services, which had not been self-supporting for many years and had generally been operated by freight railroad companies under some form of cost-of-service contracting by municipal, regional, or state authorities, had been taken over by such organizations. Right-of-way ownership of all primary and some ancillary routes has now also generally been acquired.

After bottoming out in the early 1970s, ridership has tended to increase, to a 30-year high in 1995; passenger-miles increased 22% to a record 8.0 billion between 1987 and 1994. Although only 16 urban areas in the United States and Canada currently have some commuter rail service, traffic amounts to 700,000 round trips per workday. On average, commuter rail fares cover about 50% of operating costs, which totaled $2.2 billion in 1994.

Most of the approximately 4,500 cars in commuter service have been built or rebuilt within the past 25 years, with push-pull locomotive-propelled equipment, requiring no turning at terminals, the choice for diesel ancillary services. Wherever clearances permit, car designs have settled on "gallery" (single-row upper-deck seating with fare-checking capability from the open lower deck) or full double-deck configurations providing 160 to 170 seats per car. All cars in service are air-conditioned.

Inter-City Passenger Service

The National Railroad Passenger Corp. (Amtrak) was created by act of Congress effective May 1, 1971, to operate a nationwide passenger service over a skeleton network of routes designated by the Secretary of Transportation. In return for contributions of rolling stock, facilities, and cash related to the amount of the deficits they had been incurring in operating inter-city passenger service, railroads joining Amtrak were allowed to terminate operation of their existing passenger runs. In 1983, the last of three non-Amtrak inter-city services was taken into the system.

Amtrak Routes and Traffic

Subsequent events, including provisions of the Railroad Revitalization and Regulatory Reform Act of 1976 related to the restructuring of the bankrupt northeastern railroads into the Consolidated Rail Corp. (Conrail), have resulted in Amtrak ownership of about 750 miles of primarily passenger route miles. This includes most of the 456-mile Northeast Corridor line between Washington and

Boston, rehabilitated and upgraded for 125 mph service under the 1978-1985 Northeast Corridor Improvement (NECIP) program.

Under successive federal authorization acts and with the participation of several states under Section 403b of the basic Act (requiring Amtrak operation of trains partially subsidized by the local jurisdictions), the Amtrak network has expanded in extent (despite elimination of routes not meeting patronage standards – 80 and 150 passenger-miles per train-mile for short- and long-haul routes, respectively) and service. By the early 1990s traffic levels reached 21.5 million journeys and 6 billion passenger-miles per year from 450 stations on 25,000 route miles (Fig. 17-2) in the contiguous United States (the state-owned Alaska Railroad operates its own passenger service). Extension of the Los Angeles-New Orleans Sunset Limited schedule to Miami in 1993 gave the United States its first through-train coast-to-coast service in history.

While federal Amtrak appropriations have declined steadily as the proportion of *total* passenger-operation expenses paid by passengers have risen from less than half to 80% in the early 1990s (fares more than cover all "above the rail" train-operating costs), operations remain dependent on establishment of a program supporting continuing capital expenditures (primarily for rolling stock, especially sleeping cars) to expand service in additional profitable markets, reducing unit overhead costs.

Amtrak Equipment

All passenger-train cars and locomotives used in regular service are owned by Amtrak, as are all major maintenance and overhaul shops and most passenger-station facilities. Motive power (diesel, electric and hybrid – diesel also equipped to operate on third rail) in passenger service, all of which has been acquired since the start of Amtrak service, is well into its second generation with the introduction of 140 (4,000/4,250 hp) diesel units of contemporary passenger-locomotive design to supplement and replace 1975-model 3,000 hp F-40PH's. As noted below in connection with high-speed rail, 16 (150 mph) trainsets are to supplement the 55 AEM-7 (7,000 hp) electric locomotives in Northeast Corridor service by 1998.

With the exception of those trains operating through the tunnels restricting access to New York City, all long-haul (overnight) Amtrak trains were re-equipped with 550 double-deck "Superliner I and II" coaches, sleepers, dining, and sightseer-lounge cars by 1996, essentially retiring the "Heritage" fleet of 1948-1969 stainless-steel cars inherited from the pre-Amtrak railroads. These trains have been rebuilt with Head-End Power (HEP) at Amtrak's Beech Grove, Indiana, shop. New "Viewliner" single-deck sleeping cars entered service on the low-clearance Eastern routes in 1996.

Other corridor and day-train services are covered by 635 "Amfleet I" (medium-density) and Amfleet II (low-density) coaches, food-service, and club (first-class)

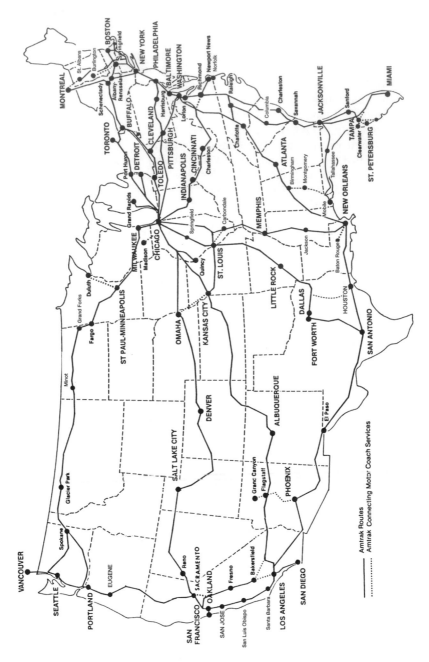

Fig. 17-2. Amtrak (National Rail Passenger Corporation) Routes – 1998

cars supplemented by 100 conventional 1989 "Horizon" cars and additional double-deck medium-density short-haul cars and Talgo trainsets in expanding state-sponsored corridor service in California and the Northwest.

In the interest of service reliability and all-weather maintainability, all locomotives and cars are equipped for HEP (Head-End Power) electric heating and air conditioning; steam-heated Amtrak equipment made its last runs in 1983.

Amtrak Operations

Since the mid-1980s, train crew members (previously employed by the contracting railroads) have become Amtrak employees (retaining some freight-service re-employment rights), as are on-train service, station, and maintenance personnel in full-time passenger-train operations.

Amtrak contracts with the railroads over which its trains operate to cover direct costs for any services provided (Amtrak normally buys and puts aboard fuel and supplies), trackage rights, and a contribution toward overhead. Contracts, which are subject to renegotiation since 25-year stipulations regarding such matters as track quality in the original Amtrak act expired in 1996, may include incentives for on-time performance above a certain standard. On a competitive basis, Amtrak is in turn a contract train operator for some governmental commuter rail agencies.

Other Passenger Services

VIA Rail Canada was established by the Canadian Government as a Crown Corporation to take over the inter-city passenger operations of the Canadian National and Canadian Pacific in an arrangement somewhat similar to Amtrak. Although VIA's network does include some "corridor" short-haul routes in Ontario and Quebec, and total ridership is higher than Amtrak's on a per capita basis, cost recovery over the entire sparsely populated country served, including some lines on which service has been decreed as necessary for otherwise completely isolated communities, has remained far lower; in January 1990, approximately half its trains were eliminated by the government.

Automobile ferry service between the Washington, D.C., area and central Florida was operated, starting in 1971, by the Auto Train Corporation under a specific exemption in the Amtrak authorization act. Equipment deterioration and losses from a similar service on a Kentucky-Florida route resulted in termination of a highly successful service; Amtrak acquired rights to the name and resumed daily Auto Train service (on a mandated fully profitable basis) in 1986.

Tourist railroads, ranging from regional common carriers operating long passenger consists as an adjunct to their freight traffic to volunteer-staffed museums with an abundance of rolling stock and a few hundred feet of track, provide train rides for the public. The principal attraction varies: reaching world-famous or merely

247

pleasant scenic areas, recreating (with wildly varying degrees of "authenticity") rail travel of the recent or more historical past, or perhaps providing a trip-to-nowhere dining experience.

Longevity of the operations also varies – from less than a single season to more than 160 years; majesty of ownership covers the spectrum from struggling, definitely nonprofit local museums to the U.S. National Park Service. (Class I or other railroads with an Amtrak-member heritage may run passenger excursions but are prohibited by the Amtrak act from running scheduled service.)

Train-length and patronage typically varies directly with the size and rarity of the motive power in use as it ascends from industrial switcher through vintage diesel to main-line steam, with trolley operations a popular alternative. With more than 100 lines in the United States and Canada providing at least some scheduled (usually seasonal) trips, some lines attracting as many as 400,000 riders in a season, and safety of operations just as critical a matter as in main-line railroading, tourist railroading cannot be dismissed as a trivial part of the industry.

Mail and Express

With the discontinuance of in-transit mail sorting by the U.S. Postal Service, mail traffic by rail virtually disappeared from public view. However, more than 185,000 trailer loads of U.S. mail are carried each year in piggyback service on expedited freight or, where business is sufficiently concentrated, solid mail and express trains.

Amtrak now carries several tens of millions of dollars worth of mail traffic in head-end cars on its long-distance trains and a reinstituted nightly Northeast Corridor "fast mail" service, as well as operating an expedited package-handling service. In a revival of an experimental service from the 1950s, Amtrak is employing a new generation of RoadRailer to bring mail traffic to its trains to and from additional cities.

High-Speed Rail

Not shown separately in Fig. 17-1 – although one service in North America (the Washington-New York portion of the Northeast Corridor) does fit the definition – is high-speed rail. This term is generally accepted to encompass passenger service operating at a "cruising" speed of 125 mph (200 kmph) or higher between station-pairs where resulting downtown-to-downtown journey times are competitive with air for business travelers. Within this category, rail technology employed varies in maturity from the relatively conventional through the space-age contemporary to the exploratory.

Examples of the former are current versions of the Japanese 1958 "Bullet Train," the British Rail HST-125 ("High-Speed Train – 125 mph," the only diesel-powered entry) or the French TGV ("Tren a Grande Vitesse") Sud-est. Typically, aerody-

248

namically refined, steel-wheel, nontilting fixed-consist trainsets operate over sufficiently curve-free alignments on new and exclusive or highly improved conventional routes to achieve 90 to 110 mph or better start-to-stop times. Unique in the continued presence of significant heavy freight traffic on the same trackage is the 125-mph Washington-New York locomotive-hauled, standard-coach, blunt-ended Metroliner and conventional passenger-train operation.

Under present conditions it appears that, whatever their overall ecological, congestion-relief, or other social benefits, proposals for high-speed systems in corridors on this continent must first demonstrate financial feasibility founded primarily if not wholly on credible private-sector support; a second hurdle is finding a route connecting major population centers yet passing through (or even near) no one's back yard.

Technologically, high-speed rail developments in the 1990s follow three identifiable thrusts:

- *Magnetic levitation,* with or without benefit of high-temperature superconductivity discoveries, undoubtedly rates highest on the glamour scale; trade-offs between systems based on attraction (with an efficiently narrow air-gap between vehicle and track, in turn requiring an extremely precise guideway) and the repulsion-based alternative with its less demanding geometry but formidable power and control challenges are at least as complex as those argued by Edison and Westinghouse when DC and AC electric-power systems were in their infancy. Both can push trains to speeds (beyond the 1989 German test-track "record" approaching 300 mph) where aerodynamic drag–anywhere except in an evacuated tunnel–puts a lid on the practicality of any further acceleration. As of 1996, no "maglev" system is known to be in use or under construction.

- *Steel-wheel* technology based primarily on the practicalities of light axle loads (no freight), sound track, and suspension design, and intensive maintenance in smoothing the track, has continued to dismay its critics. With French TGV Atlantique trains in service at 185 mph, their 1989 cracking of the 300 mph figure in a test cannot be entirely dismissed as a stunt–such flat-out runs in the past have in a matter of a decade or two proven to be precursors of similar service speeds. Given a population pattern allowing a "straight" route to be followed, the hill-climbing ability of such hot trains has kept economical line construction (with relatively few tunnels and major bridges) in the picture. Early on considered incapable of much more than 100 mph, locomotive-propelled (e.g., power-car at each end) rather than fully MU-powered consists are now operating at the high end of the speed spectrum. This technology has been selected as appropriate for the essentially curve-free high-speed-rail system to link the Miami,

Orlando, and Tampa areas for which the state of Florida has provided initial funding.

- *Tilting trains*, tested early on (1937) by three railroads in the United States, maintain physical (and mental) passenger comfort while rounding curves at velocities far higher than the balancing speed for the track superelevation. Tilting the car body keeps the passenger firmly in his or her seat and the coffee in the cup but does not alter the direction or magnitude of the wheel rail forces down below, which must (and can, up to "cant-deficiencies" in the 15 in. range for passenger-train axle loads) remain within the limits of track and car-suspension stability. Despite earlier (1960s-1970s) experiences on both sides of the Atlantic leading to abandonment of the concept after years of development, tilting trains are now routinely allowing usefully faster schedules – at top speeds below as well as above the 125 mph threshold – over existing or less expensively improved curvy routes in several European countries. Cars on 18 trainsets under construction for 150 mph Amtrak corridor service , scheduled in 1999, will tilt to attain three-hour New York-Boston schedules despite numerous curves remaining on an upgraded and electrified line north of New Haven.

The Railroad Organization

18

Railroads come in all shapes and sizes, from less than one to more than 20,000 miles of line and with usually proportional annual revenues. On the smallest of lines, the general manager and a clerk may constitute the entire office force, and a road that's close to ICC Class I status (gross revenues of $255.9 million per year or more) will still have many of its employees taking care of multiple duties that might be handled in disparate parts of the organization on a large railroad. The fact that all use tracks and trains as part of a continental transportation system, however, means that the same things have to be done, and the essentials of the organization are much the same, whatever the size. Names and titles may vary, as well as the ways some of them may be linked together on the organization chart. But a look at the corporate structure of one of the larger systems, one with 20,000 employees and revenues in the 1990 era of about $2.4 billion per year, will show one way in which a railroad corporation can be organized to successfully carry on its business.

Corporate Structure

Railroads are corporations, with a board of directors headed by its chairman, who is sometimes also designated as the chief executive officer, responsible for long-term plans and practices. The railroad president, who also may be designated as the chief operating officer, is directly responsible to the board for running the railroad by making decisions on a shorter-term basis.

Railroad Regulation Effects

While federal regulation of railroad rates was partially eliminated with the passage of the Staggers Act in 1980 and various other long-standing aspects of regulation were eliminated on December 31, 1995, by the Interstate Commerce Commission Termination Act, their effects will continue to show up in railroad organization and operations for some time to come. Under the jurisdiction of the Surface Transportation Board (STB) which inherited remaining ICC functions, railroads remain subject to some constraints beyond those applying to all businesses of similar size, and some aspects of previous restrictions will be discussed in this chapter as a matter of historical background still affecting today's organizations to some degree.

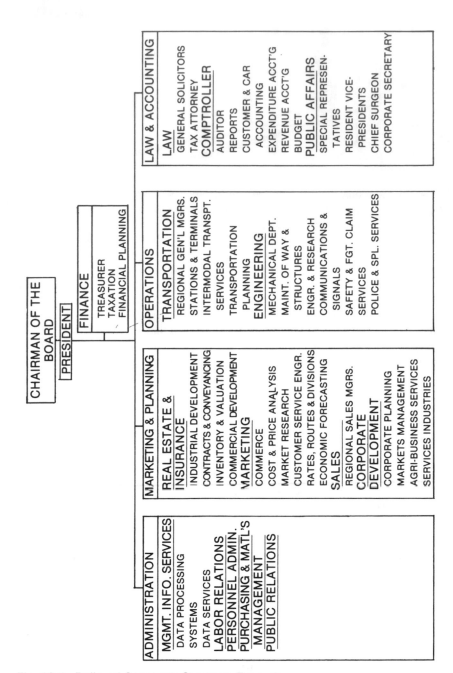

Fig. 18-1. Railroad Corporate Structure Example

Until 1996, for example, under the "Commodities Clause" of the 1906 Elkins Act, it was illegal for a railroad to own mines or factories whose products (other than timber or materials needed for the railroad's own use in producing transportation) would be shipped over its tracks. This law was passed to break up such combinations as coal mining and railroad companies, which were judged to represent unequal competitors for independent producers. A mining or metals company could still own a railroad, but as a common carrier its rates and operations were regulated by the ICC to ensure that it would serve all shippers, particularly its owner's competitors, on an impartial basis.

As a result of this restriction, some railroad corporations have been set up as subsidiaries of railroad holding companies ("East-West Industries," for the East-West Railroad Co.). The holding company could then own and operate other nonrailroad businesses without being subject to such restrictions.

Railroad Accounting and Finance

Fig. 18-1 is the corporate level organization chart for our billion-a-year railroad operating company. Attached directly to the president's office is the finance staff office, including the treasurer who is legally responsible for the corporation's funds, income, and tax liabilities. The financial planning office is there both to keep the company from running out of cash and to manage its investments and borrowings, so the overall cost of meeting its obligations is as low as possible. This includes maintaining as good a financial rating for the railroad's financial paper, and as low an interest rate, as its operating results can support.

One of the theories behind railroad regulation is the determination of a level of rates that will not result in profits beyond a rate of return considered "reasonable." Since the way in which a company's books are kept can have a big effect on its reported profits, the law requires that railroad accounting and financial reports to the ICC follow very specific rules. The financial community which rates and handles railroad securities wants its reports in accordance with "generally accepted accounting principles," which change from time to time and are not always similar to ICC rules. The ICC "Uniform System of Accounts" (U.S.O.A.) which went into effect in 1978 in some ways narrowed the differences, but it has made it difficult or impossible to compare current results with those from prior years in some other accounts important in judging railroad finances.

Railroad Financial Results

Over the years, a few specific terms such as "operating ratio" and "ordinary net income" have become well established in talking about railroad operations. Before going into the rest of the railroad organizational structure, it will be useful to look at just what these terms mean and also get some feel for what are the large and small items in railroad income and outgo.

Fig. 18-2 shows where the railroad operating dollar comes from and where it goes, summing up the 12 Class I U.S. freight railroads as reported to the ICC for 1994. This was the 13th year following the start of partial rate deregulation and in a period of moderate inflation and economic growth. At this time, most of these companies, including the seven which as a result of mergers within the past decade accounted for about 90% of the nation's rail traffic, were relatively profitable. While such industry-wide profit percentages, not directly applicable to any one company, must be considered only generally representative, the distribution of major items of revenue and expense for an individual railroad is not likely to be too far from these percentages.

Leverage

A large portion of railroad expenses, such as interest on long-term borrowed money, office expenses, and real estate taxes, don't vary with the amount of business being done. Therefore, the level of traffic has a great "leverage" on the net profits of the railroad. Fairly small seasonal or business-cycle changes tend to cause much bigger changes in its earnings. Also, operating revenues have been greatly affected by rate increases following years when the rate of inflation has been high. It is necessary to look at longer-term trends to get a good feel for the situation.

Operating Revenues

As Fig. 18-2 shows, the vast bulk of railroad revenues comes from hauling freight. This has always been true for North American railroads, even in the days before the automobile and improved highway.

As a measure of the size of the industry, Class I operating revenues in 1994 amounted to $30.8 billion. In addition, regional and local railroad freight revenues totaled approximately $3.2 billion. Note that all figures in Figs. 18-2 and 18-3 are in percentages of the total operating revenues.

Who Gets the Money?

As the second column of Fig. 18-2 shows, railroading remains a labor-intensive business, although the 35.3% paid for wages and fringe benefits is several percent lower than 10 years previously as productivity (ton-miles per employee hour) has increased somewhat faster than direct per-hour labor costs.

Fuel cost, though still taking almost twice the bit of revenue it did prior to the "oil shocks" of 1974 and 1979, reflects the halving of per gallon costs from their 1981 peak and a 22% reduction in consumption per ton-mile achieved over the same period; in 1981, fuel took 12.5% of revenues. Aside from payroll taxes and fringe benefits, principal percentage *increases* in the past decade (for reasons discussed elsewhere) include awards for injuries and depreciation.

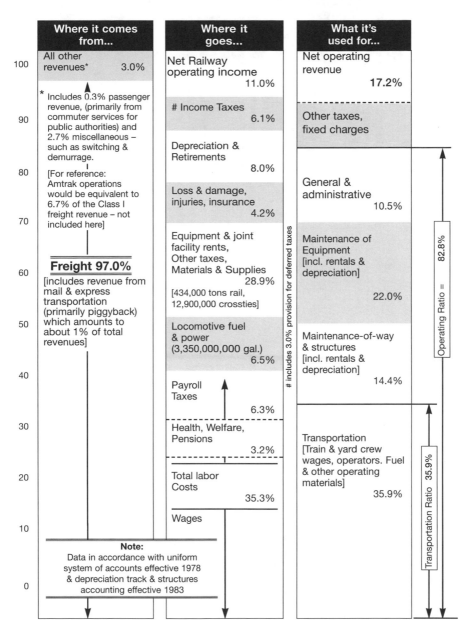

Fig. 18-2. The Railroad Dollar (U.S. Class Freight RR's as reported in 1994 to Interstate Commerce Commission)

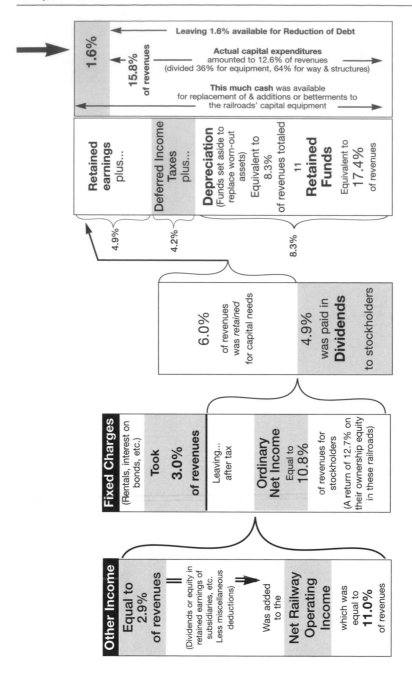

Leaving 1.6% available for Reduction of Debt

1.6%

15.8% of revenues

Actual capital expenditures
amounted to 12.6% of revenues
(divided 36% for equipment, 64% for way & structures)

This much cash was available
for replacement of & additions or betterments to
the railroads' capital equipment

Retained earnings plus...

Deferred Income Taxes plus...

Depreciation
(Funds set aside to replace worn-out assets)
Equivalent to 8.3% of revenues totaled

11

Retained Funds
Equivalent to **17.4%** of revenues

4.9%

4.2%

8.3%

6.0%
of revenues was *retained* for capital needs

4.9%
was paid in **Dividends** to stockholders

Fixed Charges
(Rentals, interest on bonds, etc.)

Took **3.0%** of revenues

Leaving... after tax

Ordinary Net Income
Equal to **10.8%**

of revenues for stockholders
(A return of 12.7% on their ownership equity in these railroads)

Other Income

Equal to **2.9%** of revenues

(Dividends or equity in retained earnings of subsidiaries, etc. Less miscellaneous deductions)

Was added to the

Net Railway Operating Income

which was equal to **11.0%** of revenues

Fig. 18-3. How Net Railway Operating Income Was Used (1994)

Operating Ratio

The third column of Fig. 18-2 shows what the operating revenues were used to accomplish: maintenance, transportation, overhead, etc. A traditional overall measure of a railroad's performance has been the *operating ratio*, defined as the proportion of the revenues received which is required to operate and maintain the railroad. The definition of the *net operating revenue* upon which it is based was changed considerably under the U.S.O.A. rules by including in expenses several additional items, principally taxes (other than income taxes) and net equipment and joint facility rentals. It is therefore meaningless to compare pre-1978 operating ratios directly with current figures – a railroad which was able to bring a good profit down to the "bottom line" of *net ordinary income* in previous years would have to achieve an operating ratio no higher than the low 80s in most cases; under U.S.O.A. rules, an equally healthy railroad may show an operating ratio as much as 10 points higher. Relative differences in operating ratios from railroad to railroad or for the same company from year to year under the same rules tell a good deal about its financial situation, but analysts trying to fully appreciate a road's prospects must also look at some additional factors.

Transportation Ratio

The costs of making up and moving trains over the roadway, excluding maintenance, determine the "transportation ratio," typically somewhat less than 40 percent for a reasonably healthy railroad. Improved equipment and operating practices will tend to bring this ratio down. The extent to which the ratio fluctuates with changes in traffic level may well be more a matter of the railroad's traffic mix than of management efficiency. If most of the line's business is in mineral traffic which can be handled satisfactorily by running proportionally fewer trains of the same length, the ratio may go down with reduced traffic because the latest, most efficient equipment can do the whole job. On the other hand, if most of the traffic is time-sensitive freight handled in trains which must run on schedule, reduced business will rapidly raise the ratio.

Net Railway Operating Income (NROI)

This figure, which has not changed much under U.S.O.A. rules, represents the money available from the operation of a railroad after income taxes, paid or deferred by investment credits and accelerated depreciation under IRS and tax regulations, but before paying the "fixed charge" interest on bonds or other money it has borrowed.

Fig. 18-3 shows how NROI was used in our "sample" year of 1994, when it was a relatively healthy 11.0% of revenues. Adding "Other Income" to it gives the total available to pay interest to the bondholders to whom the railroad owes money and dividends to the stockholders who are its owners.

"Other income" comes primarily from subsidiary companies. Because today's railroad systems have absorbed many earlier companies, some of which remain fiscally separate, this is more than a billion-dollar item industry-wide.

Distribution of Net Income

Taking out the "fixed charges," primarily representing interest on long-term debt paid to bondholders, and adjusting for any "extraordinary" (one-time) charges leaves the *ordinary net income* available for paying the owners. In our sample year about 45% of this was paid the stockholders, as dividends, an amount representing a cash return of about 5.1% on their equity.

Revenue Adequacy

In connection with the Staggers Act partial deregulation of the rail rates, the ICC was to make an annual determination as to the *revenue adequacy* of each railroad – the relationship of its "return on net investment" (ROI) to the *cost of capital*. This cost is roughly equal to the current interest rate or dividend a company would have to promise to raise debt or equity capital to equip itself to handle additional business. In concept, this is similar to the "rate of return" regulatory authorities allow a public utility holding an exclusive franchise to earn on its approved "rate base" investment.

Under rate regulation, if a railroad were found to be "revenue adequate," it would lose its "zone of rate freedom"– freedom to raise rates by 4% more than changes in the *railroad cost-recovery index* (RCRI)) without their being subject to ICC review or shipper protest. The RCRI is a weighted-average "cost-of-living" index based on the prices of the items – wages, fuel, crossties, equipment, etc.-making up railroad expenses. The ROI used for this purpose involved several accounting adjustments in both net income and investment base, and so was not exactly comparable to the 1994 fiscal ratios above.

While post-Staggers railroad earnings have been far above those in most of the previous years, industry-average ROI on this ICC basis (9.4% in 1994 on a net investment base of $54 billion) has not approached "revenue-adequate" cost-of-capital (12.2% in 1994) levels. Since boxcar and intermodal ("piggyback") traffic has been completely deregulated, most other traffic moves under contracts rather than tariffs, and competitive pressures have continued to restrain rail rates (revenue-per-ton-mile averages have declined relative to the cost index for every year since deregulation), the effect on the few roads which have attained revenue adequacy has been essentially nil.

However, the RCRI index and related Rail Cost Adjustment Factor (RCAF) which takes into account the effect of improvements in the productivity of rail transportation continue to be used as factors in the terms of the long-term freight-rate contracts under which much of today's traffic moves.

Retained Funds vs. Capital Expenditures

Another measure of the health of the industry is its actual ability to generate the cash it takes to maintain, replace, expand, and modernize a "plant" that can attract and handle the traffic. As the last two columns in Fig. 18-3 show, in this relatively good year, the earnings, deferred taxes (an item largely counterbalanced by reserves for deferred taxes in the operating-expense accounts), and depreciation reserves which add up to the sum of *retained funds* available for capital replenishment was slightly more than the expenditures made for roadway and equipment capital expenses. The balance was available for such purposes as improving future net earnings by reducing debt.

During the pre-Staggers years of the 1970s the freight railroads as a whole were able to acquire sufficient equipment to handle the traffic only by borrowing money (selling more equipment trust certificates than were paid off) and paying high rental rates for privately owned cars; capital expenditures were more than double retained funds, but maintenance was deferred (roadway capital expenditures were only about one-third of those for equipment) and track conditions deteriorated.

However, in most of the years since the early 1980s, retained funds have been sufficient to exceed a greatly increased level of capital expenditures. At the cost to car and locomotive builders of a disastrous decline in orders, improved car and locomotive utilization permitted applying the bulk of these funds to restoring the condition of a slimmed-down track network to a state generally conceded to be free from *deferred maintenance* at the end of the decade.

In recent years, retained funding (augmented by massive private investment in leased rolling stock) has generally supported a level of capital spending better balanced between equipment and roadway needs but sometimes strained in meeting the needs of increased traffic.

Deferred Maintenance

The nature of railroad track is such that it can go for quite some period of time without major repairs or much apparent deterioration. Thus, should management want to present a favorable-looking operating ratio, it can make major cuts in the maintenance-of-way account. In periods of reduced traffic, of course, the track is receiving less wear, and some reduction in maintenance expense would not result in a net decline in track condition. Beyond this point the track is accumulating "deferred maintenance." To look for this, rail and crosstie replacement figures may be studied and compared to past years.

To some extent, the same is true for maintenance of equipment, though this will usually show up in the "bad order ratio," the percentage of cars and locomotives in unserviceable condition. A conscientious management, of course, wants to have a good estimate of any deferred maintenance it may be incurring, but changes in technology make this somewhat difficult at best; a good estimate of the life of improved rail or of a new type of crosstie may not be available until a dozen years after installations in quantity may have begun. Since, in the days of rate regulation, the ICC sometimes required that all proceeds from general rate increases it permitted be used to reduce deferred maintenance, whether and to what extent it existed was often a topic of great importance to the railroad's financial planners.

Equipment Depreciation

When parts of the track or some cars are repaired, the cost is a business expense which reduces net income for the year, and therefore, no income taxes are involved. In theory, a car wears out at the rate for which "depreciation" is allowed by the ICC and could be replaced at the end of its life for the original cost. The money which had been set aside (tax-free) in the depreciation account during the car's lifetime would purchase another. The railroad would be right back where it started, with a new car and no money in the depreciation account.

But what's a repaired car and what's a new car? A car that is in need of major repairs may be rebuilt into something bigger, better, and suitable for some entirely different lading that has become important in the railroad's traffic mix during the car's lifetime. If it is determined to be a repair and replacement-in-kind job, it is done with tax-free money. If it is a retirement of one car and purchase of a new one, the increase in value is made with "retained income" money (on which income tax has been paid) or by borrowing money to be paid back over a period of years, with interest. Since the income tax rate for large corporations can be as much as 50% or more, a good part of the net income of the railroad can rest on these rules and decisions. The car body may be virtually replaced at one time and the trucks and couplers at another, resulting in a car that is nominally 50 or more years old but which actually contains no parts that are anywhere near that ancient.

Equipment Trusts

The relatively unattractive rate of return in past years and the resulting difficulty in borrowing money at advantageous rates has meant that major improvements in the railroad physical plant, such as the new multi-million dollar "electronic" classification yards, had to be paid for out of retained earnings from current operations. Since general-purpose rolling stock can be "repossessed" and re-sold if necessary, financing has been more readily available to help pay for cars and locomotives. In one common, long-used arrangement, called the "Philadelphia Plan," equipment trust notes covering about 80 percent of the cost of specific equipment are issued by a financial institution, with the railroad making a down payment of 20 percent. The notes are paid off in installments by the railroad, with the bank retaining title to the rolling stock until the last notes are retired, usually in 15 years.

Equipment Leases

Investment tax credits and provisions for accelerating depreciation (in effect deferring income taxes) intended to encourage industrial investment in productive facilities have at various times had a major effect on investment decisions. As a result of the legalization of contract freight rates, railroads and shippers may share the benefits (which will exist only if it *and the traffic for which it is suited* last long enough) of more expensive but cheaper-to-haul equipment. Since railroads at some times may not have had enough earnings to take full advantage of the tax savings resulting from ownership and so many other circumstances affect the relative risks and benefits of ownership, a variety of leasing schemes exist within two principal categories:

- Capital leases are those in which the terms are such that the lessee (renter) is so committed to the use of the equipment over an extended period that the lease is required to appear on its balance sheet; the lessee is entitled to any associated tax benefits under these conditions.

- Operating leases are those in which the lessor (owner) retains sufficient responsibility for the continued use of the equipment to be entitled to associated tax and depreciation benefits.

Track: Depreciation vs. Addition/Betterment Accounting

Until 1982 railroad accounting for track and structures was required to be on a basis in which only "additions and betterments" could be capitalized. If 90 lb rail was replaced with 132 lb steel, for example, $^{42}/_{32}$ of the cost of the rail could be capitalized and its cost charged off as depreciation over a period supposed to be related to its useful life. The rest of the steel and the entire cost of installing it was an expense and so would reduce net income immediately, even though the benefits of the resulting improved track conditions would endure for a number of years.

As a result, there was a great incentive to hold down income taxes by plowing money into the track during periods of good traffic and correspondingly maintaining bottom-line profit figures during low-traffic periods by sharply cutting track programs, even though it has long been known that such peak-and-valley track maintenance represents a much less efficient use of manpower and materials. In 1983, such roadway maintenance was essentially capitalized by shifting it to a "ratable depreciation" basis tending to iron out the humps. Earlier-year reported capital expenditures and net earnings are therefore not comparable with current figures.

Tunnels and Embankments

The cost of boring a tunnel or building an embankment to run trains efficiently through the mountains has been a tough question for the tax accountants and lawyers – do such things depreciate? Since it's literally nothing, the hole through the hill will never "wear out." But it must be expected that with the passage of time, it may become less useful as traffic patterns and the relative power, weight, and cost of trains change. The hole will be as good as ever, but in the wrong place or, perhaps, not quite big enough. Rulings in the late 1970s allowing such depreciation under certain circumstances were of considerable one-shot benefit to some railroads.

Deferred Taxes

Several tax decisions in recent years on such subjects as tunnel and grading cost depreciation and temporary or regular changes in the tax laws intended to encourage industrial investment in production facilities and produce jobs have had the effect of allowing companies to set aside money for depreciation at a faster-than-normal rate and thus pay less income tax during the early years of the life of the facilities. Since you can only depreciate anything once, depreciation in later years will be less, and the taxes then will be higher. Initially, however, money representing deferred taxes is available (Fig. 18-3) to help meet the railroad's capital requirements. U.S.O.A. requirements include provisions to bring this aspect of railroad financial reporting in line with generally accepted accounting principles.

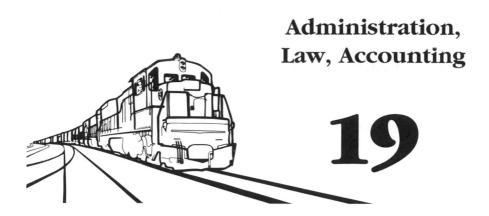

Administration, Law, Accounting

19

The many corporate functions not directly involved in attracting and handling traffic or operating and maintaining the railroad may be arranged in as many different ways as there are railroads. In the example of Fig. 18-1, they are grouped into two major departments called *Administration* and *Law and Finance*, each headed by an executive or senior vice president. Many of the matters under the various titles within these areas are reasonably self-explanatory and what would be expected in any organization of this size, with appropriate adjustments for railroad's singular characteristics. Some offices are found only on a railroad and are worth some discussion.

Management Information Services (MIS)

Digital computers which can talk to each other over long-distance fiber or microwave links have been as important to the railroads as to any other industry. So many different parts of the railroad organization (operations, sales, accounting, purchasing and materials management, personnel) use the computers that it is now usual to have a special group responsible for developing, maintaining, and operating an integrated central system and the computer programs used to receive, process, and display the data for all. If the railroad does not have its own computer facility, leased or owned, it will still need people who can handle the company's input/output data exchange with the UMLER and TRAIN II systems of the AAR Car Service Division.

Labor Relations

While the railroad industry is not a closed shop, its operations in almost all aspects are governed by contracts with a relatively large number of separate unions, often referred to as "The Brotherhoods," representing both railroad-only occupations (such as train and yard service or car maintenance) and general trades. While the railroad managements are usually represented in industry-wide bargaining by the National Railway Labor Conference Organization, local agreements govern actual operations on each railroad.

Personnel Administration

The personnel department of a railroad, similar to that found in general industry, makes sure that the company has complied with all applicable laws, regulations, and interpretations of the EEO, IRS, NLRB and not a few other agencies plus their counterparts in the various states where the railroad has employees. In addition, railroad operations are subject to the Federal Hours of Service Law which provides extremely severe penalties for allowing any employee concerned with train operation from being on duty more than 12 hours at a stretch.

Training program coordination is of increasing importance with the continual rise in the complexity of technology, both railroad and nonrailroad, which employees must be able to handle. Most railroaders will continue to learn the critical aspects of their work on the job, but many skills are being developed through more formal training programs and facilities.

Purchasing and Materials Management

"Purchasing and Stores," as it is known on many roads, is often set up as a separate department, though on the smaller railroads it may be located within the operating department. It is responsible for spending almost one-quarter of all the railroad's revenue.

Inventory carrying costs are now so high and the volume and variety of materials and supplies used so great that a railroad's net income can practically be consumed if the purchasing organization consistently buys items too far in advance of need or in quantity not closely related to need.

Running out of critical items can be even more serious, and buying competitively and in quantity can also lead to major savings, so the purchasing organization has the clear-cut job of handling its affairs so that its "customers" throughout the railroad have confidence in its responsiveness and reliability. Otherwise, every operating group will squirrel away material in a thousand scattered hideaways, and the road may be buying items it already has in surplus. Most purchasing and materials management departments are computerized to some degree, but the storekeeper out in the field is still very much a key person.

Public Relations

Beyond its specific assignments of handling the railroad's advertising, generating press releases, and publishing whatever newsletter or employee's magazine management authorizes, "PR" has the job of keeping the company's image as positive as possible throughout its territory. PR is truly everybody's business, and an undamaged shipment delivered on time every time counts more than a catchy slogan. There is no way the public relations staff can offset the effects of a sloppy railroad with disgruntled employees. What it can do is help keep the record straight with timely, correct, well-phrased information about the capabilities and accomplishments of a good railroad and help the president or the chairman of the board make each employee a plus rather than a minus in establishing the railroad's identity in all the many communities through which it passes.

Law and Public Affairs

As public utilities regulated by federal, state, and local authorities, railroads are in need of legal counsel to a degree beyond that typical of most businesses of the same size. The impact of changes in laws and court rulings on the railroad is such that many lines, including our example, find it worthwhile to have officers of high rank located at key points in the various areas served whose main duties are concerned with such "public affairs" matters.

Accounting

The various money matters handled by the office of the comptroller or accountant on a railroad include those such as billing the customer and paying the company's bills, plus the extra complexities of auditing inputs from dozens or hundreds of agents, conductors, or collectors and keeping track of the charges and revenues resulting from the wanderings of all those freight cars. There are also certain ICC rules, dating from the days when preventing illegal rebates to favored shippers was its principal concern, prohibiting handling freight charge on a credit basis; these must be observed.

Traffic

The direct interface with the railroad's customers is the Traffic Department, the agents who quote rates, receive and receipt shipments, make out shipping papers, notify consignees their goods are in, and (on occasion) try to find out why the goods haven't arrived. Using the more modern and general terminology for such functions, our example railroad has a Marketing and Planning Department, which includes two functions (corporate development and real estate) often located in the law or administration areas of the corporate structure.

Corporate Development

On a small railroad, the chairman of the board or the president may be the only person specifically planning ahead in terms of the direction the company should follow in enhancing its future. It helps to have everyone in the organization working today to make tomorrow better, but studying the company's choices is a top management function. In this structure, since the main opportunities are in developing new transportation needs which the railroad can profitably meet, a corporate planning staff is located in the marketing/planning area.

Real Estate and Insurance

All railroads own at least one long, narrow piece of real estate, the right-of-way. Additionally, most companies have adjacent land which they own which is zoned for industrial or commercial use and can be used to help induce important shippers and receivers of freight to locate where the railroad can readily serve them. Thus, real estate management, contracts, insurance, and related functions find a logical home in the department charged with developing the market for freight service.

The *industrial development* organization's success in convincing companies planning new or expanded plants that the best location is at some available site along the railroad (or accessible to its piggyback service) will have a lot to do with what the company's income looks like years from now. A good "plant hunter" makes it his business to know more about plant sites, zoning laws, water supply, labor availability, tax rates, and possible new-business concessions than anyone else in the area, as well as respecting the confidential nature of such inquiries.

The *insurance* organization of the railroad is concerned with providing appropriate protection against major loss. In general, a railroad's property is so spread out or relatively indestructible that all but the most major catastrophes are more economically handled by relying upon self-insurance rather than by taking out insurance. The insurance manager's job is to study these trade-offs. On a smaller line, particularly with respect to public liability, the answer may be considerably different.

Markets Management and Development

In this organization, the development of particular types of business, including some that may not exist at present (for example, the hauling of compacted trash collected in a city to a distant disposal site) is promoted by offices attached directly to the chief of marketing and planning.

In railroad tradition, this line continues to foster the development of agriculture and forestry practices suitable for its territory through its agribusiness agents; many important products which are quite literally "growth industries" can be traced back to improved species, fertilizers, and crop-management schemes pioneered by such experts.

The *services industries* office works on a long-term basis to develop auxiliary services, such as warehousing, which the railroad can provide as add-ons to its basic transportation to: increase its overall profitability; attract more business; or create a function that makes money itself.

Marketing – Longer-Range Sales

In accordance with most present-day terminology, the longer-range aspects of getting the freight onto the trains are the responsibility of the "marketing" organization. The job of making up a package of rates and service, often including innovations in loading, unloading, or railroading technology, which will capture, increase, or retain traffic has several essential parts.

Cost and Price Analysis will consider the price the railroad must charge to be better off handling the traffic than not; it must cover the out-of-pocket costs and make some contribution toward the overhead costs of the railroad. It will also calculate how much the transportation is worth to the customer, taking into account his costs and alternatives, such as decentralizing his plants so that less transportation is required, or shipping via the competition.

Market Research generates information on the amount of prospective traffic. In general, goods aren't produced just because a wonderfully low freight rate may become available but rather because somebody has a use for the item, though a favorable transportation situation may make a new producing area become competitive.

Customer Service Engineering develops concepts for hardware which will cut costs, reduce damage, or otherwise significantly improve the total process of getting the goods from where they are to where they're needed.

Rates, Routes, and Divisions considers: the various routes over which the traffic can be moved; the rates which can be established legally, considering their relationships to others in effect; and the division of the revenue between the carriers involved.

All of this must be done in collaboration with the operating department, of course, before the *Commerce* organization can put together a marketing program that goes after the business. A major change in the rate structure may keep the law and public affairs people busy for a long time overcoming tariff suspensions, rate appeals, and other roadblocks. Aggressive, imaginative, and precise work in marketing is the key to railroad prosperity, though, so there is nothing else to do but keep after the matter.

Economic Forecasting

To handle the business, the railroad still has to have the cars, locomotives, and track capacity. If new or different traffic is forecast, there may be lead time of anywhere from six months to two years or more for ordering new equipment. As much as anything, the general level of business activity at this future date will determine whether or not the railroad should commit its capital funds to be in a position to make money later. The railroad thus finds it advisable to have an economist on its staff to provide as informed a basis as possible for making the necessary preparation.

Sales – The NOW of Marketing

The direct contact with the customer occurs mostly through the sales organization. Headed up by regional sales manager, agency sales offices are located in all the major shipping and receiving localities on the railroad. The outposts of the system

267

are the *off-line agencies* – in 25 cities in 12 states in the case of the E-W – soliciting and making arrangements for interline traffic. Since over 75 percent of all railroad freight shipments travel over more than one line, such agencies are maintained by most roads, and several have agencies in foreign countries as far off as Japan.

Much of the push for marketing actions originates from the sales organization, which also has the job of making sure that customers are made aware of what a new rate, schedule, or service can mean in terms of their traffic.

Since familiarity with the customer's particular product, processes, and needs is often the key to effective sales and marketing, individual sales agents will specialize in one or more commodity groups. On some railroads, the entire traffic organization is set up on this basis, with its major groupings by coal, merchandise, forest products, grain, or other traffic elements. Railroad expenses charged to "traffic" as a whole amount to less than two percent of revenues, but it's a vital function if there is to be enough for the operating department to haul to keep the railroad in the black.

Operations

20

About 85 of every 100 railroaders work in the Operations Department. Fig. 20-1 is a typical organization chart for this department of a large railroad, condensed by leaving out many important staff and support positions attached to officials at various levels and by listing only examples of the many employee classifications at the working level throughout the department. On a smaller railroad – say one with 300 to 2,000 miles of track, grossing up to $100 million a year and with perhaps 3,000 employees – some consolidation of positions and simplification might occur.

Operations is headed up by a vice-president or senior vice-president, to whom report the vice-president (or general manager) in charge of transportation and the vice-president of engineering (or chief engineering officer) in charge of the maintenance-of-way and mechanical (motive power and car) organizations. Two other organizations are usually supervised directly by the head of the Operations Department; since the safety and freight claims group and the railroad security force are concerned with both train operations and maintenance and facilities, they logically report to the person in charge of all the railroad's facilities and their use.

Safety and Freight Claims

These two elements are often placed in one organization because technology, training, and discipline to minimize personal injury and equipment damage also contribute toward reducing damaged shipments. Pilferage and vandalism, increasingly serious causes of freight claims, come under the jurisdiction of the railroad police force which also comes directly under the chief of operations.

Railroad Safety and Accident Reporting

Over a period of time, railroad travel remains the safest mode, but the hazard potential of train and railroad maintenance operations must be respected. Since 1910, railroads have been required to report, under oath, all collisions, derailments, and accidents resulting in a personal casualty or in damage to equipment or track exceeding a specified dollar amount. Fig. 20-2 summarizes frequency, casualty, and dollar-damage statistics for all types of accidents and incidents connected in any

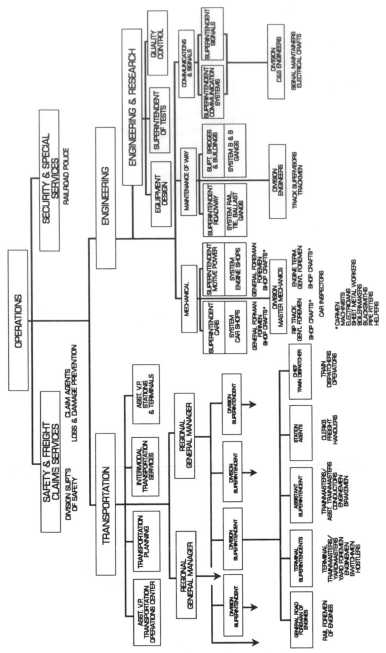

Fig. 20-1. Condensed Organization Chart – Operating Department

way with railroad operations as reported by the FRA for 1994. Casualty totals for a few of the most prevalent classes of reportable incidents have been categorized by the class of person involved. While a single accident can cause a major bump in the annual total in such rare occurrences as passenger deaths, trends in more frequent events such as injuries in boarding trains are stable enough to permit assessing trends in evaluating the relative need for and effectiveness of safety programs addressing specific problems.

Train Accidents/Incidents

Major changes in railroad accident and casualty reporting took place in 1975 and in 1979, primarily to bring the reporting of injuries into agreement with that for other industries, data for which are collected by the Occupational Safety and Health Administration (OSHA). This makes comparisons between current figures and those for prior periods difficult or impossible; in general, with all injuries requiring medical attention counted as casualties, rather than those involving lost work days, the total number of incidents *appeared* to have trebled. Illnesses considered related to conditions in the workplace were also added to the statistics. As a means of assessing progress since the unification of reporting standards, Fig. 20-2 includes a summary of OSHA injury/illness data for railroad, other transportation modes and industries, and all private employment for the years 1979, 1988, and 1994.

Nomenclature has also changed significantly: the current distinction between train wrecks – involving significant damage to railroad rolling stock and track – and such casualty-producing eventualities as unanticipated severe slack run-ins or highway grade crossing accidents not resulting in a derailment is between *train accidents* and *train incidents*. The threshold dollar damage, starting in 1981, is adjusted annually to reflect inflation and thus maintain some degree of comparability over longer periods of time. For 1994, it was $6,200.

Train accident reportable damage is limited to that which includes railroad property – equipment and track – and thus is only a portion of the total cost, which, of course, includes loss and damage to lading, liability claims, disruption of operations, and cost of clearing wrecks. Despite inflation which raised roadway and equipment costs by 70% over this period, the 1994 dollar total of $180 million was *43% lower* than that 15 years earlier, although ton-mileage has increased by a third – a remarkable safety achievement, though accident costs remain a burden warranting continual efforts to root out or cut down accident causes and consequences. Within an overall decrease over this period of 72% in the number of accidents, improved condition of the roadway – from capital investments made possible by improved financial performance – was the greatest single factor, cutting the number of track-caused derailments from almost 4,000 in 1979 to fewer than 900 in 1994.

Train incidents not involving major damage to railroad equipment account for about 90 percent of all fatalities associated with railroad operations. More than half

Cause / Type	Operating Practices	Equipment Failure	Track Defects	Other	Total No. Train Accidents	Total Damage to RR Property
Collisions	195	9	13	23	230	$30M
Derailments	462	256	857	250	1,825	$125M
Other	254	28	7	80	369	$16M
Highway grade xing	–	–	–	165	165	$10M
Total number train accidents	901	293	877	518	2,589	↓
Total damage to R.R. property	$44M	$32M	$56M	$48M	→	$181M

Source: R.R. Accident-Incident report, FRA - 1994

Employee Injury/Illness Rates			
Employee job/industry category	Reportable injuries/ illnesses per 100 employees		
Railroad:	1979	1988	1996
Executives	0.9	0.4	0.4
Professional, clerical, general	2.4	1.9	1.7
Maint. way & structures	20.4	9.8	8.3
Maint. equipment & stores	15.6	8.6	7.3
Transportation - nontrain	4.8	3.8	3.6
Train & engineer service	13.3	7.9	6.8
Railroad, Total	12.0	6.8	5.8
Trucking, warehousing	15.7	13.8	13.8
Water transportation	13.9	12.1	10.4
Transportation by air	13.4	12.8	13.8
Construction	16.0	14.4	12.2
All manufacturing	12.8	13.1	12.1
All private-sector employment	9.2	8.3	8.5

Source: OSHA - 1979, 1988, 1996

Fig. 20-2. Annual Accident Summary – All U.S. Railroads

Casualties

	Employees on duty		Passengers		Non-tresspassers		Tresspassers		Total	
	K	I	K	I	K	I	K	I	K	I
Train Accidents (Damage to RR Equipment/Track above threshold - $6,200 in 1994)										
Collisions	8	83	–	18	–	–	–	–	8	116
Derailments	–	46	2	48	–	14	–	–	2	120
Other	–	15	–	4	2	4	—	–	2	24
Higway grade crossing	1	62	–	82	17	44	15	20	33	198
Total, Accidents	9	196	2	152	19	62	15	20	45	460
Train Incidents (Damage less than threshold - equipment in motion)										
Getting on/off trains	–	255	3	35	–	7	7	31	10	328
Flying/falling objects	–	77	–	11	–	–	–	–	–	90
Operating locomotives	1	389	–	–	–	–	–	–	–	392
Struck/run over	3	38	–	–	35	33	481	307	520	382
Coupling incidents	4	148	–	–	–	–	–	–	4	148
Highway grade crossing	–	73	–	2	440	1,350	138	287	578	1714
All others	9	652	–	59	1	14	29	65	37	790
Total, train incidents	17	1,632	3	107	476	1,404	652	690	1,149	3,857
Nontrain incidents (Including rolling stock when not in motion)										
Maint. way & structures	1	2,981	–	–	–	–	–	1	1	3,037
Maint./serv. equipment	–	2,372	–	–	–	1	–	–	–	2,409
Stumbling/fallling	–	1,356	–	73	–	312	2	12	–	1,948
Getting on/off equipment	–	648	–	113	–	5	–	1	–	778
Operating switches	–	641	–	–	–	–	–	–	–	642
All others	4	3,254	–	52	10	149	13	42	–	3681
Total, nontrain	5	11,252	–	238	10	467	15	56	32	12,495
Total Casualties	31	13,080	5	497	508	2,165	682	764	1,226	16,812

Source: R.R. Accident-Incident report, FRA - 1994

Fig. 20-2. Annual Accident Summary – All U.S. Railroads *(cont.)*

of all deaths occur from highway grade crossing accidents while an additional 35 percent involve trespassers on railroad property. Installations of gates, flashers, and other safety improvements at grade crossings, along with the joint railroad/public authority educational program "Operation Lifesaver" in states where it has been established, have succeeded in reducing the fatalities (including "trespassers" who drove through or around lowered gates) only from 760 to 580 over the 1979-1994 period.

Nontrain Incidents

The innumerable combinations of function, location, occupation, equipment, and time associated with personal-injury accidents are reported and cross-indexed by the FRA with a detail probably exceeded only by the compilation of statistics for professional sports. Fig. 20-2 includes separate figures for some of the larger single causes of train and nontrain incidents. Probably primarily because of the general elimination of cabooses, injuries getting on and off moving trains have decreased by 90%, and this is no longer the single largest source of train-incident employee injuries.

Under a recent reporting rules change, casualties from getting on or off, striking, or otherwise being injured in connection with operating or maintaining railroad rolling stock are classified as train incidents *only if the equipment is moving at the time*; otherwise they show up in the "nontrain incident" category. Nontrain incidents, which account for more than 85% of all employee injuries, are essentially similar to those resulting from the hazards to which workers in any heavy industry are exposed.

Injury/illness rates per 100 employees as reported by OSHA are presented in Fig. 20-2 as a measure of safety progress; *fatality* rates for other industries are not available on a comparable basis, and in the railroad case are too small to be meaningful in terms of the different employment categories. While the hardness, mass, and inertia of rolling wheels, track equipment, and machine tools remain unforgiving of any careless move and it's still more hazardous to be out on the line or in the shop than in the office, railroad injury rates – down by almost half in this 15 year period – have improved much more than in other transportation modes and are now lower than for the average of all private employment.

Freight Claims

After a long period in the 1.2% to 1.6% range, the ratio of loss and damage (L & D) claims to freight revenue has decreased to 0.3% - 0.4% levels in the 1990s. The resulting annual translation from cost to net of as much as $200 million represents a significant boost in railroad profitability. Individual railroads and the Freight Claim and Damage Prevention Division of the AAR endeavor to pinpoint the places where prevention efforts, including new packaging and load-securing car designs and intensified training efforts on the part of railroad and shipper personnel, will pay off. On any particular commodity, cooperative work on the part of equipment suppliers, railroad damage prevention and operating people, and the industry involved have been able to reduce L & D, whether the principal problem is primarily impact, environmental control, handling, vandalism, pilferage, or some peculiar combination not immediately apparent. An example of a major factor in L & D reduction –at a price – is the fully enclosed multi-level car, which has almost completely superseded its open- or side-panel predecessor in safeguarding new automobiles and trucks in transit.

An across-the-board factor in L & D performance has been the major reduction in train accidents noted above, a factor previously responsible for about 25% of all payments.

FELA

Despite the major decrease in casualties, railroad payments for employee injuries more than doubled between 1981 and 1988, to the point that they consumed over 2.5% of gross revenues in the latter year. This is because the industry (including Amtrak and the commuter rail agencies) remains under the Federal Employees Liability Act, passed in 1908, long before any state workmen's compensation laws (which now cover workers in all other industries, including interstate highway and air transportation) were in effect.

Unlike the no-fault workmen's compensation laws, tort-based FELA requires that compensation for death or injury be obtained via individual litigation establishing the employer's fault and allowing, if the employee's suit is successful, an eventual lump-sum award for compensatory and punitive damages (including contingency legal fees) of unlimited amount.

Transportation

21

Somewhat over half of the railroad's employees are in the transportation segment of the operation organization, which, to put it as simply as possible, runs the trains. To keep the operation manageable, a railroad of more than a few hundred miles will be organized into a number of segments, traditionally known as divisions. Since the traditional day's work for road train crews was 100 miles or 10 hours in freight service or 150 miles in passenger service, a railroad's main line was likely to have its division point yards at about these intervals, unless there was some reason (an established city or a marked change in the terrain, as in going from prairie to mountain country) to dictate otherwise. With faster trains, better communications, and less short-haul business, most railroads have combined these segments into longer divisions, which may include 500 miles of line or more. Within these divisions, lines will be divided into subdivisions or districts for operating purposes. Larger railroads – those with thousands of miles of line or more may group their divisions into regions or areas. On the other hand, if a railroad has several main lines coming together in one city, it may set up all its tracks and yards in the area as a terminal division, with only a few miles of line but hundreds of miles of track to manage.

Transportation Headquarters Organization

The Transportation Headquarters Organization will be staffed to take care of those system-wide functions which cannot logically be handled on a regional or division basis, such as through and interline train scheduling and system freight car distribution. In the example of Fig. 20-1, the Vice-President-Transportation has four staff offices. The Assistant-Vice-President-Transportation is in charge of a "control center" located in the railroad's operating headquarters city from which, with the aid of several status displays, CTC panels, data read-outs, and other modern pieces of management information gear, the trains of the system are controlled. With information as detailed as the temperature of each journal bearing on every train passing any one of more than 50 wayside hot box detectors located at intervals on all the railroad's main lines, and a microwave/radio system which can communicate with each train, the minute-by-minute operation of the system is literally controlled from one point. This makes it possible to consider, almost instantly, what any person, office, locomotive, car, or piece of track on the system can do to correct any problem that threatens to disturb the scheduled operation or to provide quick response to any opportunity for improved service.

Transportation Planning looks ahead to work out the future schedules and operating practices that will most efficiently produce the system's basic product. Additionally, a special office has been established to coordinate intermodal (piggyback) service. Both of these offices are heavily involved in run-through services with connecting railroads. The Assistant-Vice-President-Stations and Terminals is a troubleshooter, bringing a system-wide approach to improved ways of running these expensive parts of the railroad.

Similar positions at the transportation headquarters level are often set up to manage other operating areas of special importance to a particular railroad: passenger-train service, unit-train service, merchandise transportation, and so on.

The Division

In our example, the railroad is set up on what is sometimes known as the "departmental" form of organization. The officers of the mechanical, maintenance-of-way, and communications and signal organizations at the division level – the division master mechanic, division engineer, and division C & S engineer – report to their respective organization heads at the system or regional headquarters. Some railroads are set up on the "divisional" basis, with these officers reporting to the division superintendent while carrying out the functions of their departments. In practice, of course, all the officers of the division must work closely together, and there is little essential difference in the way the work of the railroad gets done.

Division Transportation Functions

The division head, the superintendent, has five main transportation functions to supervise, reflected in those reporting to him:

Trainmasters, usually reporting to the assistant superintendent and responsible for specific districts within the division, determine (within the limits established by the system schedules) how the traffic is arranged in specific trains, scheduling and supervising the train crews to move them over the line.

Terminal Trainmasters, usually reporting to a terminal superintendent in the case of major terminals, supervise yardmasters, yard crews, switch tenders, and hostlers in making up trains, getting locomotives to them, switching cars to local industries, and moving road trains into and out of the terminal within yard limits.

Station Agents are responsible for the local agencies and their facilities at which business with customers is transacted, and for the supervision of the clerks, freight handlers, porters, and others on the railroad's property.

Chief Train Dispatchers are responsible for authorizing and directing all movements of trains over the railroad, through dispatchers transmitting instructions to train crews, via operators at stations, offices and interlocking towers, or via the signal system or radio within CTC and DTC/TWS territory, respectively.

Road Foremen of Engines supervise the operation of locomotives in moving the traffic of the division, instructing and qualifying enginemen, and representing the mechanical department of the railroad in seeing that motive power is used efficiently.

Who's in Charge Here?

Perhaps the single most important fact affecting the railroad organization, particularly in the transportation department, is that *most of its employees must carry out their work away from their supervisor;* yet the railroad is a system whose parts must all work together in precise timing. This high level of individual responsibility has made railroading a proud profession, and it has also meant that the limits of individual initiative in carrying out duties must be established by written rules. The operations of a railroad are goverened by a current Book of Rules which may vary from railroad to railroad. In practice, rules are bound to conflict with each other and also to fall short of covering many situations. To keep reliance on rules alone from tying the railroad in knots, the operating department (the only one that runs trains) establishes a series of documents, in levels of increasing authority in case of conflict, with authority to deviate delegated to the level of supervisor issuing the document. For train operation, a typical arrangement is illustrated in Fig. 21-1. Many railroad's employees are responsible to different chains of command for various parts of their duties. The station agent is the person on the scene for the traffic or sales organization in his dealings with the customers, but usually reports to the division superintendent. To clarify the situation on the road, trainmen and most others report to the trainmaster. Operators, who actually give train orders to the conductor and engineer, follow rules such as Rule 839. A typical Rule 839 states:

> Operators report to the trainmaster and receive instructions from the chief train dispatcher. In matters pertaining to agency work they receive instructions from the agent.

Conductors

The conductor is in charge of the train, but the engineer runs it! Conductor's responsibilities are specified by rules such as, Rule 886:

> The general direction and government of a train is vested in the conductor and all other persons employed on the train must obey his instructions except when such instructions imperil the safety of train or persons, or involve violations of rules...Should there be any doubt as to authority or safety of proceeding, from any cause, he must consult with the engineer and be equally responsible with him for the safety and proper handling of the train...

279

Engineers

Engineers report to and receive instructions from the trainmaster. Their responsibilities with respect to the machine they are running and in train operation are spelled out in Rules 1000 and 1001:

> They must comply with instructions of the road foreman of engines (known as the "transportation engineer" on some roads). In mechanical matters, they must comply with instruction of proper officers and supervisors of that department. They are under the direction of the conductor of the train with respect to its operation and must comply with his instructions, except when such instructions imperil the safety of train or themselves or involve violations of rules.

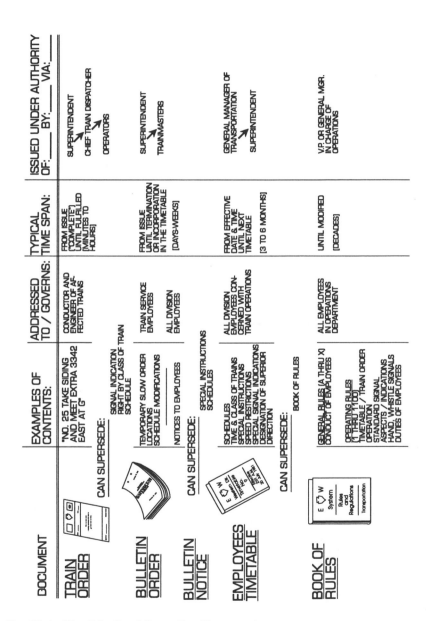

Fig. 21-1. The Priority of Operating Documents

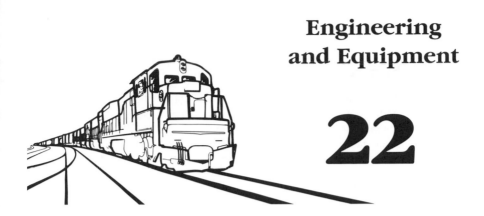

Engineering and Equipment

22

In our example, the Vice-President-Engineering has charge of organizations responsible for building and maintaining both the railroad's cars and locomotive and its track, roadway, and structures. On many lines, these organizations (usually known as mechanical and engineering, respectively) report directly to the official in charge of operations. In either case, their task is to provide the rolling stock and right-of-way which transportation uses to haul the traffic.

In the organization shown in Fig. 20-1, the Vice-President-Engineering has three staff groups responsible, system-wide, for: engineering design of equipment to meet the railroad's requirements; planning and conducting tests of track and rolling stock in the field and in the railroad's research laboratory; and methods for quality control of materials, and items used by the railroad.

Maintenance-of-Way (M/W) (Engineering)

The M/W organization responsibility is actually broader than indicated by its title, since it's in charge of both maintaining and building tracks, bridges, buildings, and other structures.

When railroad construction began, there were only two types of engineering, military and civil, so the title "chief engineer" on the railroad continues to refer to the man in charge of its roadway and structures, while his counterpart in charge of the mechanical department is usually known as the "chief mechanical officer."

The M/W organization shown is typical of that which has evolved with the high degree of mechanization of most track work in recent years. Most rail laying, tie replacement, and track surfacing operations are done by large gangs equipped with highly specialized equipment enabling one or, at the most, a few of them to take care of the entire system. These gangs, and the system M/W engineering and planning office (not shown) come under the Superintendent of Roadway, who also has a single shop maintaining all the track maintenance equipment for the system. A similar organization takes care of system bridge and building work.

Division Engineers

The M/W organization located at each division point is headed by the division engineer, with his staff to handle design and minor construction projects on the division. Track supervisors, or foremen, and their gangs, assigned segments of track, handle all maintenance not accomplished by the system gangs, and have the field responsibility for the quality and safety of the railroad's most basic item, its track.

Communications and Signals

Communication and signaling system responsibilities are usually combined organizationally, since both are primarily electronic and electrical. In our example, each area has a superintendent at the system level, sharing a common organization out in the field at the division level where signals, microwave terminals and relay stations, hump-yard car retarders, grade crossing gates and hot box detectors are installed, maintained, and modified. Signalmen are responsible for the entire job of installation of these items, including a variety of both light and heavy work.

Mechanical Department (Motive Power and Cars)

Like the M/W organization, the mechanical department is responsible not only for the maintenance and servicing of the items under its care but also for selecting or designing and obtaining them. While diesel locomotives are basically designed by their manufacturers rather than by the railroad, there is still a strong "do-it-yourself" tradition and capability. The superintendent of cars and the superintendent of motive power typically have strong design and industrial engineering staffs to develop specifications for equipment and procedures for its servicing and maintenance (not shown on the chart).

In recent years the cost-saving from certain mechanized maintenance operations has tended to result in more centralized repair facilities, such as automated wheel shops capable of turning out all the freight car wheelsets needed on an entire railroad system or locomotive heavy repair shops rebuilding all the engines of one manufacturer for the system on a production-line basis. These system shops come directly under the system superintendent's organization, though they may not all be located at the same terminal.

The heavy cranes and other equipment necessary to lift and position cars and locomotives for heavy repair work can do the same thing in a manufacturing operation. Therefore, some railroads, of all sizes, make use of their shops for car building programs (often using "kits" supplied by car builders) and major locomotive rebuilding and upgrading (modernizing) work. The organization for these shops, with general foremen and foremen of the various trades required, along with planning and quality control elements, is not unlike that in a production-line manufacturing business.

Division Master Mechanics

Heading up mechanical department organizations at the divisional level are the master mechanics. Each division will have several points at which the mechanical department will operate: maintenance, service, and inspection facilities; "rip tracks" for running repairs to cars; heavy repair car shops; engine terminals, varying in capability from simple fueling and sanding to major repairs; and interchange points where cars received from connections are inspected.

The employees performing the maintenance and inspections tasks in these facilities include: carmen (specialists in a variety of inspection and maintenance operations peculiar to railroad cars); machinists and electricians concerned primarily with locomotive maintenance and check-out; members of the metal-working trades (sheet metal workers, boiler-makers, blacksmiths and pipefitters) who can repair, rework, or rebuild car, locomotive and shop structural and accessory parts; along with store-keepers, equipment operators, and helpers to make up a team matching the job, which must be expected, particularly in isolated areas, to include the unexpected.

Task Forces

It is clear from the inter-related nature of the responsibilities of the organizational units discussed in these four chapters that the degree of success of the railroad in selling and producing transportation depends not only on how well organized, staffed, equipped, and trained the individual segments are but even more on how effectively they work together. This shows up particularly if a railroad – whose operations are by nature day-by-day, repetitive, and likely to get into a comfortable rut – is to enter a transportation market in which it has been inactive.

Suppose that a railroad has found that, under existing conditions, traffic bringing fairly large quantities of grain from various small elevators on its lines to a huge processing mill is highly unprofitable; utilization of the expensive covered hopper cars used is poor because of erratic loading at the elevators uncoordinated with less than daily train service on the branch lines and slow unloading at the mill. Since raising rates on this traffic under the existing operating conditions will make them uncompetitive with trucking, while the covered hoppers, of which there are frequent shortages, can earn impressive profits in long-haul service, the railroad has been planning to simply leave this market, jeopardizing some branchlines, elevators, and the economic health of affected communities.

However, if rapid-turnaround train movements operating within the area without intermediate crew changes, coordinated with multi-car elevator loading and speeded-up unloading, achieved with minor improvements to dedicated cars by matching modified facilities and switching at the mill, car utilization may improve to the extent that the traffic becomes profitable to the railroad at rates sharing the benefits among all parties involved.

It is clear that almost every part of the organization, from motive power to law, will be involved. In such cases, a special organization is needed, whether it be called a "creativity team," a task force, or some other term. A good measure of the strength of the railroad's management is its ability to get it all together, on a temporary or continuing basis, and produce the results which can only come from the coordinated efforts of people with experience and responsibility working as a team.

Glossary of Terms

A

AAR or A.A.R. (Association of American Railroads) An industry association whose responsibilities include safety standards (including design standards and approval), maintenance, operations, service and repair standards car service rules research, etc.

AAR Manual Of Standards And Recommended Practices (MSRP) Publication containing the technical specifications and quality assurance requirements for interchange freight cars and components. Considered mandatory when specifically referenced in AAR Interchange Rules.

ABS (Automatic Block Signals) On a specific section or length of track, an arrangement of automatic signals governing each block.

ACI Automatic Car Identification System used to provide for automated identification of cars in a train by owner, number and equipment classification, etc. when read by a wayside scanner. *See AEI*

AREA (American Railway Engineering Association) Professional organization whose membership is comprised of Railroad maintenance-of-way officials. The AREA develops and establishes material specifications and track construction standards. *See AREMA.*

AREMA (American Railway Engineering and Maintenance-of-Way Association) Organization formed in 1998 encompassing the AREA, Roadmasters and Bridge and Building Associations and the AAR Communications & Signals Division in establishing and maintaining standards and recommended practices across the board.

Adhesion A measure of the ability of locomotive driving wheels to generate tractive force, usually expressed as a percent of the total weight on the drivers.

AEI (Automatic Equipment Identification) An automatic car scanning system to assist railroads in tracking and tracing cars. The system requires a transponder mounted on diagonally opposite corners of each railcar or other equipment to respond to radio-frequency interrogation.

Air Brake The general term used to describe the braking system used on most railways operating in North America.

Alternating Current An electric current that serves its direction at regular intervals.

Alternator A device that generates alternating current electricity, or, an electrical machine on a locomotive unit and driven by the diesel engine. When rotated, the alternator generates alternating electrical current subsequently adapted for use by the traction motors.

Ammeter An instrument for measuring electric current in a circuit.

Amperage A unit of measure of electrical current.

Angle Cock Manually operated valve at ends of car or locomotive opening or closing air brake train line.

Anti-Creeper *See Rail Anchor.*

APB (Absolute Permissive Block). On a specific section or length of track, an arrangement of signals and circuits automatically providing absolute protection from control point to control point against opposing train movements while permitting following movements under block signal protection.

Approach Locking A time sensitive electrical locking system to prevent the movement of track switches in a given route after a train is committed to that route, while at the same time protecting that route from opposing or conflicting movements.

Armature The rotating part of a direct current motor or generator. It consists of a laminated iron cylinder or core keyed to a shaft, in the slots of which are wound the armature coils of insulated copper wire or bars. In alternating current machinery the armature is frequently the stationary element.

Articulated Cars Two or more car bodies permanently coupled by slackless connections over shared trucks.

Automatic Brake The air brake system used on a train. The automatic brake is controlled by a pressurized air pipe or brake pipe which runs the length of the train. A reduction or drop in the pressure in this train line, called a brake pipe reduction (BPR), causes air brakes to apply on each car.

Automatic Coupler *See Coupler.*

Automatic Train Control System (ATC) 1) A track-side system working in conjunction with equipment installed on the locomotive, so arranged that its operation will automatically result in the application of the air brakes to stop or control a train's speed at designated restrictions, should the engineman not respond. 2) When operating under a speed restriction, an application of the brakes when the speed of the train exceeds the predetermined rate and which will continue until the speed is reduced to that rate. ATC usually works in conjunction with cab signals.

Automatic Train Operation (ATO) A system by which speed and other control signals from the wayside are automatically received and translated into train response, with appropriate ATC supervision to assure operating safety.

Automatic Train Stop System (ATS) A track side system working in conjunction with equipment installed on the locomotive, so arranged that its operation will result in the automatic application of the air brakes should the engineman not acknowledge a restrictive signal within 20 seconds of passing the signal. If the restrictive signal is acknowledged, ATS will be suppressed.

Automatic Interlocking *See Interlocking Automatic.*

Axle The steel shaft on which the car wheels are mounted. The axle holds the wheels to gauge and transmits the load from the journal bearing to the wheels.

B

"B" End of Car The end on which the hand brake is located. If the car has two hand brakes, the "B" end is the end toward which the body-mounted brake cylinder piston moves in the application of brakes or the end on which the retaining valve is located (if such a valve is used). If none of the above definitions are applicable, the car owner shall arbitrarily designate the "B" end.

"B" Unit A diesel unit without a cab and without complete operating controls. "B" units are usually equipped with hostler controls for independent operation at terminals and engine houses.

Balance Speed A speed at which the tractive effort of the locomotive exactly balances or equals the sum of all the train, grade and curve drag forces. At balance speed, there is neither acceleration nor deceleration.

Ballast Car A car for carrying and distributing ballast for repair and construction work, usually of either the flat, gondola, or hopper type.

Ballast Material selected for placement on the roadbed for the purpose of holding the track in line and surface.

Ballast Undercutter Cleaner A production machine that removes the ballast from the track, cleans it, and returns it back to the track in one continuous operation.

Ballast Regulator A track-mounted machine for moving ballast to provide the desired cross-section, usually including brooms to clear ballast from the ties.

Bessemer Process A steelmaking process whereby liquid pig iron is converted to steel by forcing air at atmospheric temperature through the metallic bath in a converter in which no extraneous fuel is burned, resulting in the oxidation or reduction of the carbon, manganese and silicon to the extent desired and their removal in the form of slag.

Bill of Lading A carrier's contract and receipt for goods specifying that the carrier has received certain goods which it agrees to transport from one place to another, and to deliver to a designated person or assignee for such compensation and upon such conditions are specified therein.

Block Signal A fixed signal at the entrance of a block to govern trains and engines entering and using that block. (Standard Code)

Block 1) A length of track of defined limits, the use of which by trains is governed by block signals.
2) A group of cars, assembled in the process of classification for movement to a specified common destination.

Body Center Plate A circular cast or forged steel plate on body bolster at the car center line, the function of which is to mate with the truck center plate and transmit the body bolster load to the truck.

Body Side Bearing Flat steel bearing pads fastened to the body bolster, a standard distance outboard from the center pin hole, the function of which is to support the car or the mating truck side bearing when variations in track cross level or other train dynamics cause the car to rock transversely on the center plates.

Bolster See *Container Bolster, Truck Bolster.*

Bolster Anchor Rods One at each end of the bolster of passenger car trucks, the ends of which are mounted in rubber, one on an arm integral with the truck frame and the other on the end of the bolster so as to guide the lateral and vertical movement of the bolster and position that it is always free from contact with the truck transoms.

Bolster Gibs Small projections at each end of a truck bolster that engage the side frame column guides and provide vertical guidance for the bolster and lateral restraint to the side frames when assembled as a truck.

Bolster Pad In a tank car, a plate welded directly to the exterior of the tank at each body bolster location to which the remaining body bolster structure is attached.

Bolster Springing The secondary suspension element in a car truck, supporting the truck bolster, on which the weight of the car rests, on the truck frame or swing hangers.

Boxcar A closed car having a floor, sides, ends and a roof with doors in the sides, or sides and ends. Used for general service and especially for lading which must be protected from the weather, subsequent damage.

Brake Beam The immediate supporting structure for the two brake heads and two brake shoes acting upon any given pair of wheels. In freight service the virtually universal type is of truss construction consisting primarily of tension and compression members fastened at the ends and separated at the middle by a strut or fulcrum to which the truck brake lever is attached. Brake beams are said to be inside hung or outside hung, according to whether they are in the space between the axles or outside the axles.

Brake Pipe A term properly used, applied to describe the continuous line of brake pipe extending from the locomotive to the last car in a train, with all cars and air hoses coupled. It acts as a supply pipe for the reservoirs and also is usually the means by which the car brakes are controlled by the engineman. When a train is made up and all brake pipes on the cars are joined, the entire pipe line comprises what is commonly called the train line. The term is often used to refer to the brake pipe on a single car.

Brake Pipe Reduction (BPR) A reduction in air pressure in the train brake pipe. This pressure reduction causes air to flow from the air reservoir on each car to the brake cylinder, thus causing the brake to apply and produce a retarding force on the train.

Branch Line A secondary line of a railway, as distinguished from the main line sometimes defined as a line carrying from 1.0 to 5.0 million gross tons per year.

Bridge Plate A hinged device affixed to a TOFC flatcar at the BR and AL corners used to span the gap between coupled cars to enable circus loading of trailers. Flatcars with 15" end of car cushioning require auxiliary bridge plates at the BL and AR corners to provide the additional spanning length necessary when coupled to standard draft gear cars.

Buff A term used to describe compressive coupler forces. The opposite of draft.

C

Cab Car A passenger-train car equipped with train-line connected controls such that it can serve as the lead unit in a train being pushed by a locomotive at the rear of the consist.

Cab Signal A signal located in engineman's compartment or cab, indicating a condition affecting the movement of a train or engine and used in conjunction with interlocking signals and in conjunction with or in lieu of block signals.

Caboose A car usually placed at the rear of a train which provides an office and quarters for the conductor and/or trainmen while in transit, and for carrying the various supplies, tools, etc., used in freight train operations. From the caboose, the crew is also able to observe the condition of the train and initiate measures to stop the train if unfavorable conditions arise. Sometimes called "Cabin Car," "Way Car," or "Van."

Cant (of a Rail). A rail's inward inclination effected by using inclined surface tie plates, expressed as a height-to-width ratio: e.g. 1:20.

Capacity As applied to a freight car, the nominal load in pounds or gallons which the car is designed to carry. These figures, formerly stenciled on the car, are identified as "CAPY." Car capacity figures are recorded in UMLER. Capacity is not to be confused with load limit, which is the maximum weight that can be loaded in a given car. *See UMLER.*

Car Body The main or principal part in or on which the load is placed.

Car Days An expression referring to the number of days a car owned by one railroad is on the line of another railroad.

Car Float A flat-bottomed craft without power and equipped with tracks upon which cars are run from the land by means of a float bridge, to be transported across water.

Car Mile An operating term defined as one car, moved over one mile of track.

Car Retarder A braking device built into a railway track to reduce the speed of cars being switched over a hump. Power activated shoes press against the lower portions of the wheels and slow the car to a safe coupling speed.

Car Service A term applicable to the general services of railroads with respect to car supply, distribution and handling; involving such matters as demurrage, interchange, per diem charges and settlements, private car line mileage statements and allowances.

Car Service Rules Rules established by agreement between railroads governing interchange of cars. *See Interchange Rules.*

Catenary On electric railroads, the term describing the overhead conductor that is contacted by the pantograph or trolley, and its support structure that supplies electricity to propel railroad trains.

Center Pin The large steel pin which passes through the center of both body and truck center plates and assists in keeping the two plates in proper alignment as the car is being placed on its trucks. In passenger train cars, also locks truck to car.

Center Plate *See Body Center Plate and Truck Center Plate.*

Center Sill The center longitudinal structural member of a car underframe, which forms the backbone of the underframe and transmits most of the buffing shocks from one end of the car to the other.

Centrifugal Force The force which seems to push a rotating object or its parts outward from a pivotal point.

Circus Loading A term used to describe an older method of loading highway trailers on TOFC (piggyback) flatcars, whereby a tractor backs the trailer up a ramp placed at one end of a cut of cars, and along the decks of the cars to the point of securement. Circus loading requires bridge plates at each end of all cars to enable the trailer and tractor to pass from car to car. See Side Loading, Overhead Loading.

Class I Railroad A railroad whose operating revenues are more than an annually designated amount – in 1998 $255 million.

Class II Railroad A railroad whose operating revenues are between $20.4 million and the Class I threshold.

291

Clearance Diagram An outline or cross section drawing representing the maximum limiting dimensions to which rail equipment can be built. Specific limiting dimensions have been established and are shown on standard clearance diagrams known as "plates."

COFC An acronym for "Container On Flat Car." A type of rail-freight service involving the movement of closed containers on special flat cars equipped for rapid and positive securement of the containers using special pedestals or bolsters.

Cog Railroad A tourist railroad climbing steep grades (e.g. 25+%) with the aid of a locomotive cog wheel engaging a rack rail.

Coil Spring A spring made by winding round wire or rods in a helical pattern around a circular core, used extensively in rail car suspension systems.

Coke Rack A slatted frame or box, applied above the sides and ends of gondola or hopper cars, to increase the cubic capacity for the purpose of carrying coke or other freight, the bulk of which is large relative to its weight.

Commodity A general term used to describe the contents of a car. Other terms such as "lading," or "product" mean the same thing and are often used interchangeably.

Common Carrier One who holds himself out to the general public to transport property and passengers in intrastate, interstate or in foreign commerce, for compensation. Common carriers must operate from one point to another over routes or in territory prescribed by the Surface Transportation Board (U.S. interstate) and by a Public Service or Public Utilities Commission (intrastate).

Consist (noun) The coupled vehicles making up a railroad train.

Container Bolster A container securement device generally used on raised center sill COFC cars. Container bolsters are arranged to mount transversely on a flatcar, and support the container at each end.

Continuous Action Tamper (CAT) A production machine equipped with a small internal tamper unit that starts and stops while the rest of the machine moves constantly.

Continuous Welded Rail (CWR) Rails welded together in lengths of 400 or more feet.

Coupler A device located at both ends of all cars and locomotives in a standard location to provide a means for connecting a locomotive units together, for coupling to cars, and for coupling cars together to make up a train. The standard AAR coupler uses a pivoting knuckle and an internal mechanism that automatically locks when the knuckle is pushed closed, either manually or by a mating coupler. A manual operation is necessary to uncouple two cars whose couplers are locked together. See E Coupler, and Shelf Coupler Interchange Rule.

Coupler Shank That part of a coupler behind the head and containing either a slot or a pinhole at the rear portion for connection to the yoke and draft system.

Coupler Yoke A cast steel component of the draft system that functions as the connecting link between the coupler and the draft gear.

Covered Gondola A gondola car which has been equipped with some form of removable cover which can be placed over the lading to protect it from weather exposure in transit.

Covered Hopper Car A hopper car with a permanent roof, roof hatches and bottom openings for unloading. Used for carrying cement, grain or other bulk commodities requiring protection from weather.

Creep *See Rail Creep.*

Cross Bar A bar with locking devices at each end that fit and lock to belt rails in DF ("Damage Free") boxcars to provide longitudinal restraint for lading.

Cross Level The distance one rail is above or below the intended level of the other – not to be confused with superelevation on curves.

Crossover Platform A drop step located on the engine front and rear permitting movement of personnel between units.

Cross Tie Intermediate transverse structural members of a freight car underframe extending from the center sill to the side sill.

Crossing In trackwork, an arrangement of four frogs allowing one line to cross another.

CTC (Centralized Traffic Control) A term applied to a system of railroad operation by means of which the movement of trains over routes and through blocks on a designated section of track or tracks is directed by signals controlled from a designated central point. Also called TCS (Traffic Control System).

Curve (of a Railroad Line) In the United States, it is customary to express track curvature as the number of degrees of central angle subtended by a chord of 100 feet. The degree of curvature is equal to 5,750 divided by the radius in feet.

Cushion Underframe A term generally used to describe a freight car designed so that a hydraulically cushioned inner sill, free to slide with respect to a rigid outer sill, isolates the car body from a major portion of the end impact loads experienced in switching. Not to be confused with end-of-car cushioning devices, which are independent long-travel units installed in the draft gear pockets behind each coupler.

Cushioning A term referring to the energy-absorbing capabilities of a car underframe or draft system. Although standard draft gears do have energy-absorbing capabilities, the term "cushioning" or "hydraulic cushioning" is generally understood to mean systems with a minimum travel of ten inches.

D

Dampener Any material or device used to reduce vibration by absorbing energy.

Dead Head An operating term used to describe off-duty travel of a train crew member from some point back to his or her home terminal. Sometimes the term is used to identify any railroad employee traveling on a pass.

Deferred Maintenance The accrued expenses chargeable to current operations for the estimated cost of repairs which cannot be made during the year due to priorities for materials and supplies or shortage of labor.

Depreciated Value The reproduction value of a freight car adjusted for depreciation up to the date of damage.

Depressed Center Flatcar A flatcar having that portion of the deck between the trucks lower or closer to the rail to accommodate loads with excessive vertical dimensions.

DF A term used to describe an interior lading restraint system for boxcars, using transverse bars (cross bars) engaging special belt rails mounted to the car sides. The initials DF stand for "damage free." See Cross Bar.

Diesel-Electric Locomotive A locomotive in which power developed by one or more diesel engines is converted to electrical energy and delivered to the traction motors for propulsion.

Ditch The part of the right-of-way that is lower than the ballast section which drains the water from the track into a stream or drainage facility.

Division On some railroads, the part of a railroad generally under the control of a Division Superintendent.

Division of Revenue The share of revenue enjoyed by one carrier in an interline movement.

Double-Slip Switch A combination of a shallow-angle crossing and two other tracks, located within the limits of the crossing, each connecting a right-hand switch from one crossing track and a left-hand switch from the other, to provide routes between the crossing tracks without additional frogs.

Draft A term used to describe forces resulting in tension in the coupler shank. The term "draft" means the opposite of the term "buff."

Draft Gear A term used to describe the energy-absorbing component of the draft system. The draft gear is installed in a yoke which is connected to the coupler shank and is fitted with follower blocks which contact the draft lugs on the car center sill. So-called "standard" draft gear use rubber and/or friction components to provide energy absorption, while "hydraulic" draft gear use a closed hydraulic system consisting of small ports and a piston to achieve a greater energy-absorbing capability. Hydraulic draft gear assemblies are generally called "cushioning units." See Cushioning.

Draft System The arrangement on a car for transmitting coupler forces to the center sill. On standard draft gear cars, the draft system includes the coupler, yoke, draft gear, follower, draft key, draft lugs and draft sill. On cushioned cars, either hydraulic end-of-car cushion units and their attachments replace the draft gear and yoke at each end; or a hydraulically controlled sliding center sill is installed as an integral part of the car underframe supplementing the draft gears.

Dragging Equipment Detector (DED) A sensor between and along side the rails to detect dragging equipment.

Draw Head The head of an automatic coupler.

Drawbar Pull A tensile coupler force. Locomotive pulling power is sometimes expressed in terms of "pounds of drawbar pull."

Drawbridge Another term to describe a movable bridge.

Dump Car A car from which the load is discharged either through doors or by tipping the carbody.

Dynamic Track Stabilizer A track machine that consolidates ballast by subjecting the track to high vibratory forces. A compactor applies forces through the rails themselves, simulating the stabilizing effects of accumulated train traffic and thus reducing or eliminating post-trackwork slow orders.

294

Dynamometer A device for determining the power of an engine.

Dynamometer Car A car equipped with apparatus for measuring and recording drawbar pull, horsepower, brake pipe pressure, and other data connected with locomotive performance and train haul conditions.

E

"E" Coupler A standard AAR automatic coupler. Type "E" couplers are cast in several grades of steel, and have several shank configurations to meet varying service requirements.

Electronically-Controlled Freight Brake Braking system using the communication capability of digital electronics over a two-wire trainline to provide instantaneous control and monitoring of all air braking functions throughout trains of any length, initially applied in special service pending standardization in the late 1990's.

Electro-Pneumatic Combination of electrical and compressed air devices and equipment used in controlling and operating such devices as power track switches and car retarders.

Electro-Pneumatic Brake A braking system used multiple-unit (MU) electric passenger trains. Brakes are applied and released on each car through the action of electro-pneumatic valves energized by current taken from contacts on the engineman's brake valve and continuous train wires. Brakes can be applied instantaneously and simultaneously, eliminating undesirable slack action and providing more positive control of train speed.

Elliptic Spring A spring whose shape resembles an ellipse. Made of two sets of parallel steel plates called "leaves," of constantly decreasing length. Because of the damping provided by friction between the leaves, such springs have been widely used for bolster springs for passenger cars.

Empty-and-Load Brake A freight car air brake incorporating gear to increase braking power automatically when the car is loaded

Empty Weight See *Light Weight.*

E.M.U See *Multiple-Unit Cars*

End-of-Car Cushioning Device A unit installed at the ends of a car that develops energy-absorbing capacity through a hydraulic piston arrangement supplemented by springs to assure positive repositioning of the unit. These devices replace the standard draft gear, and provide up to 15 inches of travel.

End-of-Train Device Device that monitors air brake system and train integrity on trains being operated without a caboose. Includes flashing marker light (night) and rear-of-train emergency brake application capability.

Energy The ability to do work. See *Work.*

Equalizer In six-wheel and some four-wheel truck arrangements, a system of bars, rods, levers and springs that serves to equalize the loads on the axles and provide improved riding qualities for the truck.

Extra Train A train not represented on and authorized to move by the timetable.

F

Fail Safe A term used to designate a design principle of any system the objective of which is to eliminate the hazardous effects of a failure of the system by having the failure result in nonhazardous consequences.

False Proceed (Railway Signal Indication) A clear or green signal displayed because of a system failure when a more restrictive indication should be displayed. Sometimes called "False Clear."

Fare Box Recovery Ratio Measure of the proportion of operating expenses covered by passenger fares; found by dividing fare box revenue by total operating expenses for each mode and/or systemwide.

FAST An acronym for The Facility for Accelerated Service Testing located at the Transportation Technical Center near Pueblo, Colorado.

Field Weld A weld joining two rails together after rails are installed in track.

Flange Any projecting surface or area, generally small with respect to the main component of which it is a part, included to serve some special purpose.

Flange of a Wheel The vertical projection along the inner rim of a wheel that serves, in conjunction with the flange of the mating wheel, to keep the wheel set on the track, and provides the lateral guidance system for the mounted pair.

Flatcar A freight car having a flat floor or deck laid on the underframe, with no sides, ends or roof, designed for handling commodities not requiring protection from weather.

Flat Switching Switching movements in a yard where cars are moved by a locomotive on relatively level tracks as opposed to over a hump.

Float Bridge A structure with an adjustable apron to connect tracks on land with those on a car float, thus permitting cars to be transferred between the land and the car float at varying water levels.

Foreign Car Any car not belonging to the particular railway on which it is running.

FRA (Federal Railroad Administration) An agency of the U.S. Department of Transportation with jurisdiction over matters of railroad safety and research.

Frog A track structure used at the intersection of two running rails to provide support for wheels and passageways for their flanges, thus permitting wheels on either rail to cross the other.

Frog Number The length in units along the frog point at which it is one unit wide – a measure of the sharpness of its angle.

G

Gallery Car A passenger car normally employed in commuter service which contains a main seating level and an upper deck level with an open aisleway through the center which gives a "gallery" appearance to the car interior.

Gate Sometimes used to describe the bottom door assembly that serves as a discharge opening on covered hopper cars, usually called the "discharge gate."

296

Gauge Line (1) The spot on the side of the railhead ⅝ inch below the rail tread, where track gauge is established. Gauge lines other than ⅝ inch are found on light rail transit. (2) The side of the railhead of a third rail where the third rail gauge is measured.

Gibs The vertical ridges on each end of a truck bolster which engage the column guide surfaces of the side frame when the truck is assembled.

Girder Rail A special rail cross-section for use on light-rail trackage in paved streets incorporating an integral flangeway on the gauge side of the railhead.

Gondola Car A freight car with low sides and ends, a solid floor, and no roof. It is used mainly for transportation of coal, iron and steel products and other lading not requiring protection from the weather. Special types of gondola cars are built with high sides (for coal), removable covers, load-scouring devices, drop-ends (for long loads) etc., for specialized service.

Grade The rise or fall in elevation of railroad track. A rise of 1 foot in elevation in 100' of track is a 1% ascending grade. Similarly, a decrease of 0.75' or 9' in elevation in 100' of track is a 0.75% descending grade.

Grade Crossing An intersection of a highway with a railroad at the same level. Also, an intersection of two or more railroad tracks at the same elevation.

Grade Resistance The resistance to motion of a train on a gradient due to the pull of gravity. Grade resistance is always 20 pounds for each ton of train weight for each percent of grade. Thus, a train on a 0.75 per cent grade (.75 feet or nine inches change in elevation per 100 feet of length of track) would have 15 pounds grade resistance for each ton of train weight. If the track rises, the grade drag is positive; if the track decreases in elevation, the grade drag is negative.

Grain Door A temporary arrangement for sealing the openings around boxcar sliding doors so that the car may be used for bulk handling of grain. One common type consists of heavy reinforced paper nailed to strips of wood which are fastened to the door posts on either side of the car door opening.

Gravity Switch Move A switching maneuver whereby gravity causes a stationary car to roll when the handbrake is released rather than being propelled by an engine.

Guard Rail 1) A short, heavily braced rail opposite a frog to prevent wheels from striking the frog point or taking the wrong route. 2) Auxiliary rails between the running rails on bridges, in tunnels or near other obstacles or hazards to keep derailed cars from leaving the road bed before exiting the danger area.

H

Hand Brake 1) A device mounted on railway cars and locomotives to provide a means for applying brakes manually without air pressure. Common types include vertical wheel, horizontal wheel and lever type, so named because of the configuration or orientation of their operating handles. 2) The brake apparatus used to manually apply or release the brakes on a car or locomotive.

Hazardous Material 1) When used with respect to lading in transportation vehicles, a term identifying the lading as subject to specific safety requirements set forth by the Department of Transportation and/or the Interstate Commerce Commission. Examples of hazardous materials are explosives, poisons, flammable liquids, corrosive substances, and oxidizing or radioactive materials. 2) A substance or material which is capable of posing an unreasonable risk to health, safety, and the environment.

Heavy Rail Transit An electric railway constructed on an exclusive right-of-way to transport passengers in an urban environment. Operations generally consist of trains with several passenger cars coupled together operating on a subway, elevated, or grade-separated surface right of way, usually with power via third rail.

Heavy Repairs As reported to the Association of American Railroads, repairs to revenue freight cars requiring over 20 man-hours.

Held for Orders Cars in repair facilities waiting on authorization to proceed with repairs.

Helper Locomotive A locomotive usually placed towards the rear of a train, to assist in the movement of the train over heavy grades. Helper locomotives can be either manned, or remotely controlled from the lead unit in the train.

High Side Gondola Car A gondola car, with sides and ends over 36 inches high, for carrying coal or minerals.

High Speed Rail Passenger rail transportation system in densely-traveled corridor over exclusive right-of-way at speeds of 125 mph (200 Kmph) or greater.

High & Wide A term referring to outside dimensions of a car or open top load that exceed the normal clearances on the route to be traveled.

Horsepower A unit of power equivalent to 33,000 foot-pounds per minute or 746 watts.

Horsepower Limited Speed The maximum speed obtainable from the horsepower developed by the locomotive.

Hot Box Railroad slang for a dangerously overheated journal bearing.

Hot Box Detector A heat sensitive device installed along railroad mainline track at strategic locations for measuring the relative temperatures of passing journal bearings. Bearing temperatures may be transmitted to wayside stations and monitored by personnel who can act to stop a train if an overheated journal is discovered. Most detectors report any bearing temperatures above a threshold value by radio directly to the train crew for appropriate action.

Hump Yard A railroad classification yard in which the classification of cars is accomplished by pushing them over a summit, known as a "hump," beyond which they run by gravity into their assigned track.

I-J

I.C.C. Abbreviation for Interstate Commerce Commission, superseded by the Surface Transportation Board in 1996.

Idler Car Usually a flatcar used in the transportation of a long article or shipment, which extends beyond the limits of the car carrying the shipment; the "idler" being a car on which the shipment or article does not rest, but overhangs. Also, a car used to move cars into or out of trackage (e.g., car float) where locomotive may not go.

IDT Initials that stand for "In-Date-Test," periodic test of the air brake equipment on every car to assure its continued proper operation. The month, day and year of the most recent IDT must be stenciled on every car.

Independent Brake The air brake control valve on a locomotive unit that controls the brakes on that locomotive (or multiple unit consist) independently from the train brakes.

Insulated Rail Joint A joint in which electrical insulation is provided between adjoining rails.

Interchange The transfer of cars from one road to another at a common junction point.

Interchange Rules Rules established and maintained by committees made up of representatives of railroad and car owners. If offered in interchange, a car complying with all interchange requirements must be accepted by an operating railroad, to another at a common junction point.

Interlocking At a point where one or more routes meet or cross, an arrangement of signals and signal appliances (e.g. power switch machines) so interconnected that their movements must succeed each other in proper sequence, train movements over all routes being controlled by signal indication.

Interlocking, Automatic An arrangement of signals, with or without other signal appliances, which functions automatically upon the approach of a train, as distinguished from those functions are controlled manually.

Intermodal Traffic Transportation of goods in containers or trailers involving more than one mode – rail, water, highway.

Invert The inverted arch in the lower portion of the cross-section of a tunnel supporting the track, walls and roof.

Joint The junction of members or the edges of members that are to be joined or have been joined.

Journal Bearing The general term used to describe the load bearing arrangement at the ends of each axle of a railcar truck. So called plain journal bearings are blocks of metal, usually brass or bronze, shaped to fit the curved surface of the axle journal, and resting directly upon it with lubrication provided by oil supplied by spring-loaded wick-fed lubricator pads beneath the axle in the journal box. Journal roller bearings are sealed assemblies of rollers, races, cups and cones pressed onto axle journals and generally lubricated with grease. Vertical loads are transferred from the journal bearing to the truck side frame through the journal bearing wedge (in plain bearing designs), or through the roller bearing adapter in roller bearing trucks.

Journal Box The metal housing on a plain bearing truck which encloses the journal of a car axle, the journal bearing and wedge, and which holds the oil and lubricating device.

K-L

Kilowatt Hour A unit of energy measured equal to the continuous flow of one kilowatt (1000 watts) for one hour.

Knuckle (1) The pivoting casting that fits into the head of a coupler to engage a mating coupler. (2) The pivoting hook-like casting that fits into the head of a coupler and rotates about a vertical pin to either the open position (to engage a mating coupler) or to the closed position (when fully engaged). Coupler knuckles must conform to a standard dimensional contour specified by the Association of American Railroads.

LCL (Less-Than-Carload) A term applicable to a quantity of freight which is less than the amount necessary to constitute a carload.

Light Engine A locomotive or locomotive consist running as a train without cars.

Light Rail An urban/suburban passenger system employing manned vehicles ("LRV's" – usually articulated) operating singly or in short trains over routes including some in-street running on overhead catenary or trolley wire power.

Light Weight Empty or tare weight of a railroad car, new or as determined by reweighing after any repairs, stenciled on car in conjunction with the load limit abbreviated LT.WT.

Line Haul The movement over the tracks of a carrier from one city to another, not including switching service.

Link and Pin Coupler An old type of connection between cars employing a single link attached to each drawhead by a vertical pin manually inserted when coupling.

Local Service The service rendered by a train which stops to deliver and receive freight by setting out and picking up cars at intermediate points along its route.

Locomotive Unit A single carbody with power and transmission equipment, but not necessarily with controls.

LRV Abbreviation for "Light Rail Vehicle."

L/V Ratio The L/V ratio is defined as the ratio of the lateral force to the vertical force of a car or locomotive wheel on a rail. An important factor affecting the tendency of the wheel to overturn or climb the rail it is often a point of discussion in evaluating the cause of a train derailment.

M-N-O

Magnetic Field A term applied to the space occupied by electric or magnetic lines of force.

Mainlines The primary tracks of a railroad, those carrying more than 5 million gross tone per year.

Main Track A track extending through yards and between stations over which trains are operated by time table, track warrant, train order or signal indication.

300

Manifest A document giving the description of a single shipment or the contents of a car.

Mechanical Designation An alphabetic code two- to four-letter assigned by the Association of American Railroads to every freight car to designate its general design characteristics and its intended purpose. E.g., XF = food-service boxcar.

Mechanical Refrigerator A term applied to refrigerator cars equipped with a self-contained power plant and mechanical refrigeration equipment including a compressor, condenser, evaporator, and fans for distribution of cold air around the lading.

Motive Power A term relating to the self-propelling equipment of a railroad, usually taken to mean locomotives.

MPH Abbreviation for "Miles Per Hour."

Multiple Unit Operation Practice of coupling two or more locomotives or electric passenger cars together with provision made to control the traction motors on all units from a single controller. Sometimes referred to as "MU-ing."

Multiple-Unit Train Two or more electrically-operated passenger cars coupled with provision made to control the operation of the cars from a single controller. Sometimes referred to as "EMU".

Normally Aspirated (Internal Combustion Engine) An engine that uses are at atmospheric pressure for combustion.

Open-Top Car Any of a group of cars with or without sides and ends, and with no roof, all being intended for transportation of commodities not requiring protection from the weather, such as steel products, coal or rough forest products. Flat, gondola and hopper cars are all classed as open top cars.

Operating Ratio The ratio of operating costs to gross revenue.

Ore Car An open top gondola or hopper car designed specifically to carry iron or some other metallic ore. Because of the high density of most ores, cars for this service are built with relatively low cubic capacities, and some are equipped with empty-and-load brake equipment.

OSHA Occupational Safety and Health Administration.

Overhead Loading A method of loading highway trailers or containers on intermodal cars by the use of an overhead (usually a gantry type) crane.

P

Pantograph A device for collecting current from an over headed conductor (catenary) and consisting of a jointed frame operated by springs or compressed air, and having a suitable collector at the top.

Per Diem The amount or rate paid by one carrier to another or to a private car owner for each calendar day (or each hour) it uses a car belonging to the other.

Piggyback A term referring to the practice of transporting highway trailers on railroad flatcars. See TOFC.

Piggyback Cars Flatcars designed and equipped for the transportation of highway trailers.

Pilot A qualified employee assigned to a train or other on-track equipment when the engineer, conductor or driver is not qualified on the physical characteristics or rules of the portion of the railroad over which movement is to be made.

Pickup A term descriptive of a car or cars added to a train enroute between dispatching and receiving yards: or added at dispatching yard to train operating over two or more divisions on a continuous wheel report.

Plain Journal Bearings *See Journal Bearing.*

Plate B, C, E, F and H An AAR clearance diagram for unlimited interchange. *See Clearance Diagram.*

Platform An intermodal freight car unit capable of carrying 40 ft. container or trailer – term used to clarify situation since platforms permanently connected (by articulation or drawbars) are given a single car number. Also called a "slot."

Plug Door 1) A type of side door used on insulated box and refrigerator cars that fits flush with the interior car side when closed. Plug doors provide a better seal and are, therefore, more desirable than the common sliding door for insulated car applications. 2) A freight car door designed to fit into the door opening rather than sliding across it.

Power Work done by a force divided by the time required to do the work. A high power locomotive can do a relatively large amount of work in a short amount of time.

Preventative Maintenance Inspection to discover if something needs repairing before it fails and performing the necessary work in order to stop or slow that failure.

Push-Pull Train Operation Passenger service, typically over commuter or medium-haul routes, with locomotive-powered consists train-line connected for control from either end which shuttle between terminal stations without being turned.

Puzzle Switch *See Double Slip Switch.*

R

Rack Rail A notched rail mounted between the running rails that engages the gears of a locomotive so equipped, for traction ascending and braking descending on a cog railroad.

Rail As used in car construction, any horizontal member of a car superstructure. The term is usually used in combination with some additional identifying word such as "belt rail" or "hand rail." As used in track, a rolled steel shape, commonly a T-section, designed to be laid end to end in two parallel lines on crossties or other suitable support to form the supporting guideway constituting a railroad.

Rail Anchor A device attached to the base of a rail bearing against a crosstie to prevent the rail from moving longitudinally under traffic.

Rail Creep The occasional lengthwise movement of rails in track. Rail creep is caused by the movement of trains or temperature changes. It is common practice to stop the effect of creeping by the use of rail anchors or resilient fasteners.

Rail, Head-Hardened A rail with only the railhead heat treated to a higher hardness for reduced wear, longer life on curves.

Rail Section The shape of the end of a rail cut at right angles to its length. The rail mills identify the different shapes and types of rails by code numbers, as for example, 131-28 for the 131 RE rail section.

Rail Tread The top portion of the railhead where rail/wheel tread contact occurs. Also called Running Surface.

Rail Web The vertical member of a rail connecting head and base to form a beam.

Rapid Transit Heavy-rail systems for urban/suburban passenger service not directly connected to the lines of commuter or freight railroads.

Raised-Wheel Seat Axle Current design of axle in which wheels are pressed onto enlarged, parallel section of axle eliminating failures caused by stress concentration at the wheel-axle interface.

Rate Bureau The tariff setting and publication agency for all carriers within a certain freight classification territory in the era prior to deregulation.

Rate of Return The ratio of net operating income (also called "net railway operating income" in railway accounting) to the value of the property in common carrier use, including allowance for working capital.

Real Estate Land, including all the natural resources and permanent buildings on it.

Receiving Yard A rail yard used for receiving trains from over-the-road movements in preparation for classification.

Regenerative Braking The retardation system on electric cars or locomotives which can return power developed by traction motors acting as generators to the third rail or catenary for use by other units.

Remote Control A term denoting the control of any apparatus from a location apart from the location of the apparatus.

Repair 1) Reconstruction of a car, or a part or parts of a car to its original design. 2) Physical work performed upon a railcar in order to restore original structure because of damage, decay, injury, deterioration or partial destruction. See also Preventative Maintenance.

Resilient Fastener Any of a variety of proprietary designs of rail fastener other than cut spikes that provide a more positive connection between the rail and tie or a track support slab.

Reverser The handle on a locomotive control stand that selects the direction in which the locomotive will move by reversing the traction motor field connections.

Right of Way 1) The strip of land on which a railroad truck is built. 2) Sometimes, the real property of a railroad other than its rolling stock.

Rip Track A small car repair facility, often simply a single track in a classification yard or terminal. In larger yards, the rip track may be quite extensive with several tracks and shop buildings. Larger car repair facilities are generally known as "car shops." The name "rip track" is derived from the initials RIP which stands for "repair, inspect and paint."

Roadbed That part of the roadway upon which the track is supported.

Rock-and-Roll A slang term for the excessive lateral rocking of cars, usually at low speeds and associated with jointed rail. The speed range through which this cyclic phenomenon occurs is determined by such factors as the wheel base, height of the center of gravity of each individual car, and the spring dampening associated with each vehicle's suspension system.

Roller Bearing The general term applied to journal bearings that employ hardened steel rollers to reduce rotational friction. Roller bearings are sealed assemblies that are mechanically pressed onto an axle, and transfer the wheel loads to the truck side frames through a device known as a roller bearing adapter that fits between the bearing outer ring and the side frame pedestal.

Rolling Stock General term for all locomotives and cars.

Rotary-Dump Car Open-top car equipped with rotary coupler at one end allowing load to be dumped by overturning without need for uncoupling.

Rotating End-Cap Roller Bearing Modern type of journal roller bearing in which the outer grease seal is between the car/ridge-type bearing assembly and a cap attached to the axle.

Running Rail The rails which rolling stock and on-track equipment runs directly on as opposed to guardrail, rack rail or third rail.

Running Surface *See Rail Tread.*

S

Schnabel Car A specially designed car used for transportation of extremely large and heavy machinery. The car is constructed with two separate units, capable of empty movement as a single car when bolted together. The load is placed between the two carrying units, and rigidly fastened to them, thus becoming literally part of the carbody.

Shatter Cracks A rail defect in the form of minute cracks in the interior of rail heads, seldom closer than $\frac{1}{2}$ in. from the surface, and visible only after deep etching or at high magnification. They are caused by rapid (air) cooling, and may be prevented from forming by control cooling the rail.

Shelf Coupler A special coupler, required on some cars designed for transporting hazardous commodities, having top and bottom "shelves" cast integral with the head to prevent vertical disengagement of mating couplers in the event of an excessive impact as in a derailment. Shelf couplers are fully compatible with other standard A.A.R. couplers.

Short Line Railroad A railroad company which may originate or terminate freight traffic on its track, participates in division of revenue and is usually less than 100 miles in length.

Side Bearing A load bearing component arranged to absorb vertical loads arising from the rocking motion of the car. There are various types of side bearings ranging from simple flat pads to complex devices which maintain constant contact between the truck bolster and carbody. *See Body Side Bearing.*

Side Frame In the conventional three-piece truck, the heavy cast steel side member which is designed to transmit vertical loads from the wheels through either journal boxes or pedestals to the truck bolster springs.

Side Loading A method of loading or unloading containers or highway trailers on or off flat cars by physically lifting the unit over the side of the car with heavy duty mobile loading equipment.

Signal Indication The information conveyed by the aspect of a signal relative to speed and conditions on the track ahead.

Skate A metal skid or chock (wedge) placed on rail to stop the movement of rolling stock.

Slack Unrestrained free movement between the cars in a train.

Sliding Sill A term used to describe a type of hydraulic cushioning for freight car underframes. In sliding sill designs, a single hydraulic unit is installed at the center of the car and acts to control longitudinal forces received at either end of an auxiliary center sill, which is free to travel longitudinally within a fixed center sill. See *Cushion Underframes*.

Slug A cabless locomotive which has traction motors, but no means of supplying power to them by itself. Power is provided by power cables from an adjacent unit. Slugs are used where low speeds and high tractive effort are needed, such as in hump yards.

Snubbers Hydraulic or friction damping devices used in suspension systems of cars to improve lateral stability. Some snubbers are designed to replace one spring in the truck spring group, some are incorporated as part of the truck side frame or bolster design, and others require special installation. Supplemental hydraulic snubbing is used most often on cars with high centers of gravity such as 100-ton coal hoppers or gondolas and tri-level automobile rack cars.

Solid-State Inverter A sophisticated, computer-driven device used to generate, modify, or alter electrical waveforms and frequencies, an essential component used to generate and regulate alternating-current for the AC induction traction motors of modern locomotives.

Spike Killing The damage and reduction of the holding power of a tie resulting from repetitive removal and installation of spikes in changing or transposing rail.

Spiral When used with respect to track: a form of easement curve in which the change of degree of curve is uniform throughout its length in going from tangent to curve.

Spring A general term referring to a large group of mechanical devices making use of the elastic properties of materials to cushion loads or control motion. See *Coil Spring, Elliptic Spring, and Truck Springs*.

Spring Group Any combination of standardized coil springs used in each truck side frame, and selected to match car capacities and obtain desired vertical suspension characteristics. Cars are often stenciled to show the number of specific springs of various designations, e.g., 5 D5 outer 3 D5 inner, that make up the spring group standard to the car.

Staggers Rail Act of 1980 An act of Congress which fundamentally altered the regulatory environment of the railroad industry by reducing regulations including the elimination of antitrust immunity in certain areas of activity.

Stake Pocket A "U"-shaped collar attached to the side or end sill of a flat car to receive the lower end of a stake used for securing open top loads.

Standard Gauge The standard distance between rails of North American railroads, or 1735 mm, being 4' 8½" measured between the inside faces of the rail heads ⅝" below the rail head

Static Load The load or weight on the roadbed applied by track material or standing rolling stock.

Subballast Any material which is spread on the finished subgrade of the roadbed below the top-ballast to provide better drainage, prevent upheaval by frost, and better distribute the load over the roadbed.

Subgrade The finished surface of the roadbed below the ballast and track.

Superelevation The vertical distance the outer rail is raised above the inner rail on curves to resist the centrifugal force of moving trains.

Swing Hanger Bars or links, attached at their upper ends to the frame of a swing motion truck, and carrying the spring plank at their lower ends. Also called "bolster hanger."

Swing-Nose Frogs A frog in a turnout with a movable frog point connected to a switch machine to match the switch position.

Switch A track structure with movable rails to divert rolling stock from one track to another in a turnout. By eliminating the gap across which wheels must pass, the swing nose eliminates impact and also allows the use of frogs longer than No. 24. (e.g., No. 32, allowing 80 mph operation through the diverging route of a turnout.)

Switch and Lock Movement A device, the complete operation of which performs the three functions of unlocking, operating, and locking a switch, movable point frog, or derail.

System Car A car owned by the subscriber railroad.

System Repair A repair performed by owner of the car.

T

Tariff (freight) A schedule containing matter relative to transportation movements, rates, rules and regulations.

Tariff Circulars (I.C.C.) Circulars issued by the Interstate Commerce Commission or its successor containing rules and regulations to be observed by the carriers in the publication, construction and filing of tariffs and other schedules.

Tee Rail The typical rail shape used in track construction. The tee rail consists of a head, web and base, and is so called because of the inverted "T" shape it assumes.

Third-Rail A current distribution system for electric railroads consisting of an insulated rail laid parallel to one of the running rails and arranged to provide a continuous supply of power to electric locomotives.

Tie The portion of track structure generally placed perpendicular to the rail to hold track gauge, distribute the weight of the rails and rolling stock, and hold the track in surface and alignment. The majority of ties are made from wood. Other materials used in the manufacture of ties include concrete and steel. Also called Crosstie.

Tie Down Any device for securing a load to the deck of a car. Chain tie downs with ratchets are probably the most common type and are used to secure wheeled vehicles and lumber products on flat cars.

Tie Plate A steel plate interposed between a rail or other track structure and a tie.

Toe (of a Frog) End of a frog nearest the switch.

TOFC An acronym for "trailer on flatcar" intermodal service or equipment.

Track An assembly of fixed location extending over distances to guide rolling stock and accept the imposed dynamic and static loads. See *Track Structure*.

Track Circuit An electrical circuit of which the rails of the track form a part. (I.C.C)

Track Gauge (Measurement) Measured at right angles, the distance between running rails of a track at the gauge lines.

Track Geometry Car A passenger or self-propelled car equipped with necessary instrumentation to provide quantitative track evaluations.

Track Modulus A quantitative measure of the vertical deflection of track under wheel loads (pounds per inch per inch of length) used to assess the suitability of track structure and subgrade for heavy axle-loading traffic.

Track Maintenance The process of repairing a track defect or track condition.

Track Structure A term relating to the various components that comprise a track, such as tie plates, fasteners, ties, rail anchors, guardrails, etc. See *Track*.

Trackage Rights The privilege of using the tracks of another railroad, for which the owed railroad is duly compensated.

Traffic Control Systems A block signal system under which train movements are authorized by block signals whose indications supersede the superiority of trains for both opposing and following movements on the same track. See *CTC*.

Train For dispatching purposes, an engine or more than one engine coupled, with or without cars, displaying markers. (e.g., headlight and rear-end device).

Train Consist The composition of the complete train excluding the locomotive. The cars in a train.

Train Line A term properly applied to describe the continuous line of brake pipe extending from the locomotives to the last car in a train, with all cars and air hoses coupled. The term is often used to refer to the brake pipe on a single car.

Train Resistance A force which resists or opposes movement of a train. Resistance to motion along the track, attributed to bearings, wind and air resistance, flange contact with rail , grade, etc.

Transpose Rail To swap the rails of a track to extend their service life.

Trimmer A signal located near the summit in a hump yard, which gives indication concerning movement from the classification tracks toward the summit.

Truck Bolster The main transverse member of a truck assembly that transmits car body loads to the side frames through the suspension system. The ends of the bolster fit loosely into the wide openings in the side frames and are retained by the gibs, which contact the side frame column guides. Truck bolster contact with the car body is through the truck center plate, which mates with the body center plate and through the side bearings.

Truck Center Plate The circular area at the center of a truck bolster, designed to accept the protruding body center plate and provide the principal bearing surface, often fitted with a horizontal wear plate and a vertical wear ring to improve wearing characteristic and extend bolster life.

Truck Center Spacing On a single car, the distance between the truck center pins as measured along the center sill from the center line of one body bolster to the center line of the other.

Truck Hunting A lateral instability of a truck, generally occurring at high speed, and characterized by one or both wheelsets shifting from side to side with the flanges striking the rail. The resulting motion of the car causes excessive wear in car and truck components, and creates potentially unsafe operating conditions. For freight vehicles, the phenomenon occurs primarily with empty or lightly loaded cars with worn wheelsets.

Truck Side Bearing A plate, block, roller or elastic unit fastened to the top surface of a truck bolster on both sides of the center plate, and functioning in conjunction with the body side bearing to support the load of a moving car when variations in track cross level cause the car body to rock transversely on the center plates.

Truck Springs A general term used to describe any of the several types of springs used in the suspension of trucks to provide a degree of vertical cushioning to the car and its load.

Turbocharger A centrifugal blower driven by an exhaust gas turbine used to supercharge an engine.

Turn-Around Time The time required to complete the cycle of loading, movement, unloading and placement for reloading of a freight car.

Turnout An arrangement of a switch and a frog with closure rails by means of which rolling stock may be diverted from one track to another. Engineering term for "track switch."

U-V

UMLER Acronym for Universal Machine Language Equipment Register. A continuously updated computerized file maintained by the Association of American Railroads. UMLER contains specific details on internal and external dimensions capacity and other information affecting the loading and use of freight cars as of UMLER includes data on intermodal (piggyback) trailers and locomotives shown in The Official Railway Equipment Register.

Unit A locomotive unit. *See Locomotive Unit.*

Unit(s) A car, multi-unit car, articulated car, or multi-level superstructure which is identified by a unique reporting mark and number.

Unit Train A train transporting a single commodity from one source (shipper) to one destination (consignee) in accordance with an applicable tariff.

Variable Cost A cost that varies in relation to the level of operational activity.

Voltage A unit of electromotive force which causes electrical current to flow in a conductor. One volt will cause an electrical current of one ampere to flow through a resistance of one ohm.

W-X-Y-Z

Waybill The primary written documentation of every freight shipment that forms the basis for railroad freight revenue accounts.

Well Car A flatcar with a depression or opening in the center to allow the load to extend below the normal floor level when it could not otherwise come within the overhead clearance limits.

Wheel The specially designed cast or forged steel cylindrical element that rolls on the rail, carries the weight and provides guidance for rail vehicles. Railway wheels are semi-permanently mounted in pairs on steel axles, and are designed with flanges and a tapered tread to provide for operations on track of a specific gage. The wheel also serves as a brake drum on cars with on-tread brakes.

Wheel Flange The tapered projection extending completely around the inner rim of a railway wheel, the function of which, in conjunction with the flange of a mate wheel, is to keep the wheel set on the track by limiting lateral movement of the assembly against the inside surface of either rail.

Wheel Plate The part of a railway wheel between the hub and the rim.

Wheel Report A listing of the cars in a train as it leaves a yard, made from waybills, on which the conductor posts set-offs and pickups.

Wheel Set The term used to describe a pair of wheels mounted on an axle.

Wheel Slip An operating condition where in there is driving wheel rotation on its axis with motion of the wheel at the point of contact with the rail. Wheel rotation speed during wheel slip is greater than it is during rolling, to the extent that tractive force is significantly reduced.

Wheel Tread The slightly tapered or sometimes cylindrical circumferential surface of a railway wheel that bears on the rail and serves as a brake drum on cars with conventional truck brake rigging.

Wide Gauge Track defect caused by failure of tie/rail fastening system to withstand lateral wheel forces, leading to derailment when wheel drops off railhead.

Woodchip Hopper Open-top hopper or gondola car of high cubic capacity used to transport woodchips.

Work The force exerted on an object multiplied by the distance the object moved. The work a locomotive does is the tractive effort of the locomotive multiplied by the distance the train moves as a result of the tractive effort.

Yard A system of tracks defined by limits within which movements may be made without schedule, train order of other authority for the purpose of classification, etc.

Yard Engine An engine assigned to yard service and working wholly within yard limits.

Yard Plant Compressed air supply facility allowing charging of train air line and conduct of terminal air brake tests before arrival of road locomotive.

Yoke The component in a railroad car draft system that transmits longitudinal coupler forces to the draft gear. *See Coupler Yoke.*

Suggested Readings

Accounting and Finance

Railway Accounting Rules. Mandatory and Recommendatory Interline Accounting Rules and Forms and Rules of Order. Accounting Division, Association of American Railroads Annual.

Economics and History

American Railroads, 2nd Ed. by John F. Stover. University of Chicago Press, 1998. 302 pages. (Hard/paper editions) LC No. 97-449. ISBN: 0-226-77658-1.

Domestic Transportation, 6 Vols., by Sampson et al. 6th Ed. Houghton Mifflin, 1990.

The Economics of Transportation, by D. Philip Locklin. 7th Edition. Richard D. Irwin, 1972. 925 pages. LC No. 76-187057.

Enterprise Denied: Origins of the Decline of American Railroads, 1897-1917, by Albro Martin. Columbia University Press, 1971. 402 pages. LC No. 71-159673.

Modern Transportation Economics, by Hugh S. Norton. 2nd Edition. Charles E. Merrill, 1970. 463 pages.

Railroad Land Grants. by Frank N. Wilner. Association of American Railroads, 1984.

Railroad Mergers; History Analysis Insight. by Frank N. Wilner. Simmons-Boardman Books, Inc., 1809 Capitol Avenue, Omaha, NE 68102, 1997 474 pages

Rails Across America, Ed. by William L. Withuhn. Smithmark Publishing Co., 1994, 192 pages.

Railway Pricing and Commercial Freedom: The Canadian Experience, by T.D. Heaver and James C. Nelson. The Centre for Transportation Studies, The University of British Columbia. 1977.

Transportation: Economics and Public Policy, by Dudley F. Pegrum. 3rd Edition. Richard D. Irwin, 1973. 612 pages. LC No. 72-90533.

Transportation Law, by John Guandolo. 4th Edition. Wm. C. Brown, 1983. 1054 pages.

Transportation Subsidies- Nature and Extent, edited by Karl M. Ruppenthal. University of British Columbia, 1974. 125 pages. LC No. 73-93911.

Engineering and Maintenance

Car and Locomotive Cyclopedia – 1997. Simmons-Boardman Books, 1809 Capitol Avenue, Omaha, NE 68102. 1136 pages.

Fundamentals of Transportation Engineering, by Robert G. Hennes and Martin I. Ekse. McGraw-Hill, 1955. 520 pages.

An Introduction to Transportation Engineering, by William W. Hay. John Wiley, 652 pages, 1977.

Locomotive Engineering Guide to Fuel Conservation. by Paul Rhine. Simmons-Boardman

Books, Inc., 1809 Capitol Avenue, Omaha, NE 68102. 1996. 76 pages. ISBN: 0-911382-17-8.

Track Cyclopedia – 1985. 10ᵗʰ Edition. Simmons-Boardman Books, 1809 Capitol Avenue, Omaha, NE 68102. 459 pages.

Transportation Engineering – Planning and Design, by Radnor J. Paquette, Norman Ashford, and Paul Wright. Ronald Press, 1972. 760 pages. LC No. 79-190209.

Railroad Engineering, by William W. Hay Wiley. 2ⁿᵈ edition, 1982. 758 pages. ISBN: 0-471-36400-2.

Geography

Geography of Transportation, by Edward J. Taaffe and Howard L. Gauthier, Jr. Prentice-Hall, 1973. 226 pages. LC No. 72-8995.

A Geography of Transportation and Business Logistics, by J. Edwin Becht. Wm. C. Brown, 1970. 118 pages. LC No. 70-11884.

Guide to Industrial Site Selection, by M. J. Newbourne and Colin Barrett. The Traffic Service Corp., 1971. 37 pages.

Labor Relations

Collective Bargaining and Technological Change in American Transportation, by Harold M. Levinson, Charles M. Rehmus, Joseph P. Goldberg and Mark L. Cahn. The Transportation Center at Northwestern University, 1971. 723 pages. LC No. 71-154981.

Labor in the Transportation Industries, by Robert Lieb. Praeger, 1974. 125 pages.

Technological Change and Labor in the Railroad Industry, by Fred Cottrell. D.C. Heath, 1970. 160 pages. LC No. 71-114364.

The Hoghead – Industrial Ethnology of the Locomotive Engineer, by Frederick C. Gamst. Holt, Rinehart and Winston, 1980. 142 pages. LC No. 80-12232.

Railroad Retirement – Past, Present and Future, by Frank N. Wilner, Association of American Railroads, 1989.

The Railway Labor Act & the Dilemma of Labor Relations, by Frank N. Wilner. Simmons-Boardman Books, Inc., 1809 Capitol Avenue, Omaha, NE 68102. 1990. ISBN: 0-911382-12-7.

Logistics, Traffic or Distribution Management

Business Logistics – Physical Distribution and Materials Management, by J. L. Heskett, Robert, M. Ivie, and Nicholas A. Glaskowsky. 2ⁿᵈ Edition. Ronald Press, 1973. 789 pages. LC No. 73-78570.

Cargo Containers: Their Stowage, Handling and Movement, by Herman D. Tabak. Cornell Maritime Press, 1970. 386 pages. LC No. 78-100658.

Container Services of the Atlantic, by John R. Immer. 2ⁿᵈ Edition. Work Saving International, 1970. 396 pages. LC No. 69-20211.

Distribution and Transportation Handbook, by Harry J. Bruce. Cahners Books, 1971. 393 pages. LC No. 76-132669.

The Essentials of Distribution Management, edited by Herschel Cutler. Distribution Economics Educators, 1971. 311 pages. Accompanying workbook, Freight Classification, Rates and Tariffs.

Logistics Management, by Grant M. Davis and Stephen W. Brown. D. C. Heath, 1974 441 pages.

Management of Transportation Carriers, by Grant M. Davis, Martin T. Farris and Jack J. Holder. Praeger, 1975. 289 pages.

Management of Physical Distribution and Transportation, by Charles A. Taff. R. D. Irwin. 7th Edition, 1984. 545 pages.

Model Legal Forms for Shippers, by Stanley Hoffman. Transport Law Research, Inc., 1970. 508 pages. Available from Traffic Service Corp. LC No. 73-114997.

Modern Transportation: Selected Readings, by Martin T. Farris and Paul T. McElhiney. 2nd Edition. Houghton Mifflin, 1973. 466 pages. LC No. 72-6891.

Physical Distribution Case Studies, by Jack W. Farrell. Cahners Books, 1973. 489 pages. LC No. 72-91987.

Practical Handbook of Industrial Traffic Management, by Richard C. Colton and Edmund S. Ward. 5th Edition revised by Charles H. Wager. The Traffic Service Corp., 1973. 640 pages. LC No. 72-95464.

The Railroad, What It Is, What It Does – The Introduction to Railroading.4th Edition. CD-Rom Version. Simmons-Boardman Books, Inc., 1809 Capitol Avenue, Omaha, NE 68102. 1996. ISBN: 0922383186.

Railroad Management, by D. Daryl Wyckoff. D.C. Heath, 1976.

Readings in Physical Distribution, edited by Hale C. Bartlett. 3rd Edition. The Interstate Printers and Publishers, 1972. 576 pages. LC No. 72-075080.

Traffic Management, by Kenneth U. Flood. 3rd Edition. Wm. C. Brown, 1974. 505 pages.

Transportation and Traffic Management, by E. Albert Owens. College of Advanced Traffic, 1972-1973. 4 volumes.
>   Volume 1 –13th Edition (1972)   Volume 3 – 9th Edition (1977)
>   Volume 2 –11th Edition (1976)   Volume 4 – 11th Edition (1976)

Rates and Regulation

Criteria for Transport Pricing, edited by James R. Nelson. The American University, 1973. 320 pages. Available from Cornell Maritime Press. LC No. 73-4373.

Economic Considerations in the Administration of The Interstate Commerce Act, by Marvin L. Fair. The American University, 1972. 182 pages. Available from Cornell Maritime Press.

Freight Transportation: A Study of Federal Intermodal Ownership Policy, by Robert C. Lieb. Praeger Publishers, 1972. 225 pages. LC No. 79-168341.

A Glossary of Traffic Terms and Abbreviations. 8ᵗʰ Edition. The Traffic Service Corp., 1972. 37 pages.

Miller's Law of Freight Loss and Damage Claims, by Richard R. Sigmon. 4ᵗʰ Edition. Wm. C. Brown, 1974. 425 pages.

Railroad Revitalization and Regulatory Reform, edited by Paul W. MacAvoy and John W. Snow. American Enterprise Institute for Public Policy Research. 246 pages. 1977.

Railroads and The Marketplace, by Frank N. Wilner. Association of American Railroads, 1987.

Cases and Materials on Regulated Industries, by William K. Jones. Foundation Press, 1976. 1278 pages. 2ⁿᵈ Edition.

Tariff Guide No. 9, by E. Albert Owens. The Traffic Service Corp., 1973. 20 pages.

Transport Competition and Public Policy in Canada, by H. L. Purdy, University of British Columbia, 1972. 327 pages, LC No. 72-81827.

The Railroad Dictionary of Car and Locomotive Terms. Simmons-Boardman Publishing Corporation, 1980. 168 pages.

Transportation Regulation, by Marvin L. Fair and John Guandolo. 7ᵗʰ Edition. Wm. C. Brown, 1972. 608 pages.

Statistics

Moody's Transportation Manual, Published annually by Moody's Investors Service.

Transport Statistics in the United States. Published annually by the Bureau of Accounts, U.S. Interstate Commerce Commission. U.S. Government Printing Office.

Urban Transit

Beyond the Automobile: Reshaping the Transportation Environment, by Tabor R. Stone. Prentice-Hall, Inc., 1971. 148 pages. LC No. 72-140266.

Supplementary References

The Future of American Transportation, edited by Ernest W. Williams, Jr. Prentice-Hall, Inc., 1971. 211 pages. LC No. 72-160529.

The Practice of (Transport) Law, by Colin Barrett. The Traffic Service Corp., 1971. 51 pages.

Research in Transportation: Legal/Legislative and Economic Sources and Procedures, by Kenneth U. Flood. Gale Research, 1970. 126 pages. LC No. 72-118792.

Transportation: Management, Economics, Policy, by John L. Hazard. Cornell Maritime Press, 1977. 608 pages.

Transportation: Principles and Perspectives, by Stanley J. Hille and Richard F. Poist. Interstate Printers and Publishers, 1974. 561 pages. LC No. 73-93578.

Transportation Research Forum Proceedings, published annually by The Transportation Research Forum.

Periodicals

Canadian Guide. Published monthly by International Railway Publishing Company. Limited. A complete shippers' guide and gazetteer for Canada. Canadian railway timetables are included.

Canadian Transportation and Distribution Management. Published monthly by Southam Business Publications, Ltd. Carries articles, statistics, and news stories on Canadian railway, highway, air and marine transportation.

International Railway Journal. Published monthly by Simmons-Boardman Publishing Corporation. Subscription rates on request (Circulation Dept., 1809 Capitol Avenue, Omaha, NE 68102. Phone: 1-800-895-4389) Reports the latest developments and practices the world over. Articles are in English with resumes in French, German and Spanish.

The Official Intermodal Equipment Register. Published quarterly by KIII Press, 424 W. 33rd St., N.Y., NY 10001. Contains information on dimensions and capacities tariff for containers, trailers and chassis in intermodal use by U.S. and foreign companies. Lists ramp locations and port facilities and names of officials concerned with reports and payments.

The Official Railway Equipment Register. Published quarterly by KIII Press, 424 W. 33rd St. N.Y., NY 10001. Contains information on dimensions and capacities tariff for freight cars operated by railroads and private car companies of North America. Includes interchange points for railroads and home points for private car owners, with instructions regarding payments, movements and repairs. (LC A19-162).

The Official Railway Guide, Freight Service Edition. Published bi-monthly by KIII Press, 424 W. 33rd St. N.Y., NY 10001. Contains names and addresses of railroads operating freight service in North America. Includes rail freight schedules, mileages, connections and other facilities of North American railroads, as well as systems maps and personnel listings. Station index for 50,000 points, with line and schedule cross references.

The Official Railway Guide, Passenger Travel Edition. Published monthly except February and August, by KIII Press, 424 W. 33rd St. N.Y., NY 10001. Complete Amtrak and other timetables for U.S., Canada and Mexico, with fares, equipment, ticket offices and station index cross references. Also, connecting bus and ferry, short-haul and commuter service tables.

The Pocket List of Railroad Officials. Published quarterly by KIII Press, 424 W. 33rd St. N.Y., NY 10001. Contains the names, titles, addresses and phone numbers of 20,000 officials of railroads, truck affiliates, transit systems and associated industry and governmental bodies. Covers railroads in North, Central and South America, Australia, the Philippines and Japan. Carries advertising of 400 supply companies, whose products and sales representatives are listed. (LC 7-41-41367).

Railway Age. Published monthly by Simmons-Boardman Publishing Corporation. Subscription rates on request. (Circulation Dept., 1809 Capitol Avenue, Omaha, NE 68102. Phone: 1-800-895-4389). Circulates extensively among railway officers and others interested in railway affairs. Discusses current railway problems, progress and developments, and carries general news and statistics of the railway industry. (LC CA8-

3111; CA19-395).

Railway Gazette International. Published monthly by IPC Transport Press Limited. A journal of management, engineering and operation containing railroad news from all over the world. Frequently includes electric and diesel traction supplements.

Railway Line Clearances. Published annually, with interim change circulars, by National Railway Publication Company. Presents weight limitations and vertical and horizontal clearances for more than 250 railroads of North America.

Railway Track and Structures. Published monthly by Simmons-Boardman Publishing Corporation. Subscription rates on request. (Circulation Dept., 1809 Capitol Avenue, Omaha, NE 68102. Phone: 1-800-895-4389). Published for railway employees who build and maintain tracks, bridges, buildings and other parts of the railway plant. (LC 14-435; 54-31791).

The Short Line. Published bi-monthly by G. M. McDonald, editor and publisher. A journal of short line and industrial railroading. Covers news, operations, and motive power rosters and acquisitions. Every other issue features a location survey for a particular state or metropolitan area.

Traffic World. Published weekly by the Traffic Service Corporation. Publishes news concerning U. S. Interstate Commerce Commission decisions and hearings, legislation affecting rates and railway service, rate revisions and other transportation developments of special interest to shippers and industrial, commercial and railway traffic officers. (LC 42-22198).

Trains. Published monthly by Kalmbach Publishing Co., P.O. Box 1612, Waukesha, WI 53187. Railroad industry news and history.

Our thanks to the Association of American Railroads for the assistance provided in compiling this list.

Index

W, X, Y, Z